# THE CHITTAGONG HILL TRACTS

*Roaja Twekam, a Khumi chief of the Chittagong hills, photographed by T.H. Lewin (about 1867).*

# The Chittagong Hill Tracts

## Living in a Borderland

Willem van Schendel
Wolfgang Mey
Aditya Kumar Dewan

The University Press Limited

**The University Press Limited**
Red Crescent Building
114 Motijheel Commercial Area
G.P.O. Box 2611
Dhaka 1000
Bangladesh

Fax: (88 02) 9565443
E-mail: upl@bttb.net
Website: www.uplbooks.com

First Published, 2001



Photographs
*Front cover: Claus-Dieter Brauns, 1960s*
*Back cover: Recter, 1965*

Cover designed by *Ashraful Hassan Arif*

ISBN 984 05 1553 5

Published by Mohiuddin Ahmed, The University Press Limited, Dhaka. This book has been set in Times New Roman by Color Horizon and produced by Abarton, Malibagh, Dhaka. Printed at Alam Printing & Packages, Fakirapool, Dhaka.

# Contents

# *Maps*

# *Acknowledgements*

The photographs in this book come from over fifty collections. Most of these are private collections. Without the gracious permission of the owners to use their material, we would not have been able to put together this book. We are most grateful to the following individuals (in alphabetical order) for sharing their material with us and allowing us to reproduce a selection in this book:

Astrid Anderson (Sweden)
Kathleen Arton (U.K)
George C. Band (U.K.)
Peter Barblan (Switzerland)
Harry G. Belitz (Germany)
Willem Bientjes (Canada)
Donald J. Bottoms & Jennifer Maslen (U.K.)
Dr Hugh Brammer (U.K.)
Claus-Dieter Brauns (Germany)
Arindam Chakma (Bangladesh)
Dipak & Gautam Chakma (India)
Prof Niru Kumar Chakma (Bangladesh)
Saradendu Sekhar Chakma (Bangladesh)
Mong Sathowai Choudhury & Mee Shwe Hpru (Bangladesh)
Dr Aditya Kumar Dewan (Canada)
Devashish Dewan (Canada)
Sailendra Narayan Dewan (Bangladesh)
Dr Michael Flowers (U.K.)
Geraldine Hobson (U.K.)
Eric & David Hosking (U.K.)
Boris Kegel-Konietzko (Germany)
Krishna Khisa/Karbari (India)
Srota Ranjan Khisa (India)
Pankajini Larma (India)
J.C. Laurence (Canada)
Dr C.C. Lindsey (Canada)
Prof Lorenz G. Löffler (Switzerland)
Gerhard Lübker (Germany)
Rani A Nue Ching Marma & Maung Ngwe Prue (Bangladesh)
Maung Kyo Maung & Ching Kwai Hpru (Bangladesh)
Hans Meier (Switzerland)
Dr Almut Mey (Germany)
Dr Wolfgang Mey (Germany)
Dr Peter Penz (Canada)
Dick H. Recter (Netherlands)
Rajkumari Chandra Roy (Switzerland)
Raja Devasish Roy (Bangladesh)
Rajkumari Unika Devi & Rajib Roy (Bangladesh)
Raja Tridiv Roy (Pakistan)
Dr F. Keith Sandercock (Canada)
Dr Jürgen Seyfried (Germany)
Erwin Sigl (Germany)
Edna & Rev Keith Skirrow (U.K.)
Lily Smith & Christopher Smith (U.K.)
Tressa L. Sopher (U.S.A.)
Donald H. Stevens (U.K.)
A.P. & Tripti Talukdar (Bangladesh)
Dr Alan R. Taylor (U.K.)
Dr H.W. van Tellingen (Netherlands)
Dr Håkan Wahlquist (Sweden)
W.J. Welsh (Canada)
Rev E. Leslie Wenger (U.K.)
Dr Brian Whitty (U.K.)

Many other individuals and institutions have helped us in various ways in collecting the material for this book, giving permission for publication, or providing information. We would like to thank (in alphabetical order):

A. Mong Akhyai (Bangladesh)
Dr Shahidul Alam (Bangladesh)
Anthropological Survey of India (India)
Bangla Academy (Bangladesh)
Rev W.W. Bottoms (U.K.)
Hans-Rudi Brawand (Australia)
British Library (U.K.)
Dr Lionel J. Carter (U.K.)
Amiya Chakma (Bangladesh)
Sonaton Chakma (Bangladesh)
Suniti Chakma (France)
Congregation of Holy Cross (Bangladesh)
Elizabeth Christie (U.K.)
Dr Ramendu S. Dewan (U.K.)
Shahana Dewan of the Tribal Cultural Institute, Rangamati (Bangladesh)
Mary Deighton (U.K.)
Kathleen Emery (U.K.)
Erasmus University (Netherlands)
Dr Roman Fischer (Switzerland)
Institut für Völkerkunde und Afrikanistik der Ludwig-Maximilians Universität München (Germany)
Prof Amarendra Lal Khisa (Bangladesh)
Dr Bipash Khisa (Bangladesh)
R.R. Langham-Carter (South Africa)
Rev Neil B. McVicar (U.K.)
Prof John Mercer (U.S.A.)
Susan J. Mills & Rev R.G.S. Harvey of the Baptist Missionary Society (U.K.)
Museum für Völkerkunde Berlin (Germany)
Dr George S. Nagle (Canada)
National Geographic Society (U.S.A.)
Dr Cornelis Op 't Land (Netherlands)
Prof Md Mahbubar Rahman (Bangladesh)
Brigitte Saal (Germany)
School of Oriental and African Studies (Library, Special Collections) (U.K.)
David Stockley (U.K.)
Ann Taylor (U.K.)
Prof Baas Terwiel (Germany)
Prasanta Tripura (Bangladesh)
Tate Gallery Publishing Ltd. (U.K.)
University of Amsterdam (Netherlands)
University of London Library (U.K.)
John Whitehead (U.K.)
Theon Wilkinson of the British Association for Cemeteries in South Asia (BACSA) (U.K.)
Prof Erik-Jan Zürcher (Netherlands)

We would also like to express our appreciation to several contributors who preferred to remain anonymous.

# INTRODUCTION

What is an 'üa'? Few people in Asia or elsewhere would have a clue. In fact, very few would even have heard about the language to which this word belongs. It is the Mru language, one of several languages spoken in the Chittagong hills, a region which forms a bridge between Burma, India and Bangladesh. An *üa* is a hill field, a plot of slash-and-burn cultivation, and therefore of central importance to survival in the hills.[1]

This book is about the *Chittagong Hill Tracts*. It is an introduction on the basis of photographs of what life there was like from the 1860s to the 1970s. An out-of-the-way, unusual and little known district of Bangladesh, the Chittagong Hill Tracts form part of one of Asia's most ignored regions: the mountainous belt where Southeast Asia meets South Asia. For decades this extensive region (comprising the borderlands of Western Burma, Northeast India and Southeast Bangladesh) has attracted little attention, partly because it has been closed to outsiders. And although news of regional wars, ecological change, migration and drugs occasionally reaches international audiences, such news has rarely been placed in a wider social or historical context. The region remains hidden behind a curtain of ignorance.

This book intends to lift that curtain to some extent. Using photographs and focusing on the section of the region which falls within Bangladesh, it also hopes to provide new insights into the recent history of Bangladesh. So far Bangladesh has not been blessed with books which look seriously at its photographic record and present it to a general readership.[2] In this respect, the country has been much less fortunate than all its neighbours. This book also seeks to demonstrate how useful photographs can be in constructing historical accounts.

Southeastern Bangladesh consists of two distinct geographical parts: a long narrow plain along the Bay of Bengal and a mountainous zone to the east. Today most of the larger mountainous region is under the jurisdiction of Burma and India; the sizeable portion in Bangladesh has for over a century been known as the 'Chittagong Hill Tracts.' It is Bangladesh's only mountain or hill area; as one travels east the foothills soon give way to higher peaks of up to 900 meters.

The boundary between plain and hills is much more than just a geographical divide. It also marks an old and deeply-felt cultural division. The plain, inhabited by Bengalis, can be seen as the easternmost extension of the South Asian cultural realm, and the hills, inhabited by various non-Bengali groups, as the western cultural frontier of Southeast Asia.[3] The largest of these groups are the Chakma, Marma, Tripura, Mru and Taungchengya (see **Table 1**).

Historically, the Chittagong Hill Tracts' ecological, cultural, linguistic and economic links with the mountains to the east and south have been more significant than those with the Bangladesh lowlands. Partly for this reason, within Bangladesh the region is often seen as marginal, remote and irrelevant. It tends to be overlooked whenever generalisations are made about Bangladesh.

The Chittagong hills were never much in the public eye until they suddenly sprang into national and international view in the early 1980s. The reason was clear: something 'newsworthy' was happening. An armed conflict had broken out in the 1970s between a regional political party and the Bangladesh armed forces. The conflict resulted in serious human rights abuses, the militarisation of the entire region and a national political problem of the first order.[4]

But those who were interested in learning more about the background of this conflict found that very little reliable information was available. This book fills in some of this background. It is not concerned with the armed conflict itself. Its aim is to show the necessity of looking at current events historically; it is an exploration of themes in the history of the Chittagong hills through photographs. It also explores the various ways in which history has been constructed and how the hills and their inhabitants have been perceived.

## History and Photography

Although many people think of history as the dead past, history is never *over*. We humans are historical animals: our thoughts, actions and dreams for the future are shot through with a sense of history and numerous notions about the past. In many ways we identify ourselves by situating ourselves in specific historical contexts. Our identity is embedded in multiple stories about history: our personal history links up with that of our family, community, region and nation.

These stories change as our circumstances and hopes for the future change. Histories are constantly rewritten, and what seemed forgotten and dead yesterday may suddenly spring to life in today's version of history. At any given time, then, we are confronted with several accounts of history, often contradictory ones, and we may feel obliged to align our actions and thoughts with one rather than another. The study of history is not an exercise in antiquarianism; it is a vital tool for understanding our present predicament, for making political choices and for charting an acceptable future.

Studying history can be done in many ways, and all of them produce a partial and coloured result. In Asia, as elsewhere, history writing has leaned heavily on written sources, and the inherent biases have been towards the views of those who manned the state, the literate classes, and the press.

Historians of Asia have always subjected their material to critical scrutiny in order to limit these biases. Some of them have even tried to 'read between the lines,' to ferret out hidden meanings and discourses. This search for other views of history can be helped by using non-written sources. Not trained to deal with these, many historians view non-written sources with suspicion. Nevertheless, these can and should be subjected to critical scrutiny, just as in the case of written sources.

Non-written sources of information on Asian history come in many shapes and voices. They may engage any of the researcher's senses, or indeed any combination of them. In interpreting the historical contents of music, songs, stories and other 'oral' sources, the researcher's ears become a primary research tool, whereas pictorial art, sculpture and photography may provide clues to his or her eyes. In the case of drama, dance, food, or fabrics several senses are brought into play at the same time. Non-written sources allow the historian to use a wider range of sensory information about the past but they also require the historian to develop new ways of assessing the quality of the information which they provide.

## The Photograph in South Asian History Writing

This book is based largely on a single type of non-written source, photographs. Described as a 'strange, confined space' (Price, 1994), the photograph and the description (caption, title, text) that sometimes go with it have deeply influenced our understanding of the modern world. The use of photographs by historians of South Asia is nothing new - in many historical studies photographs are included to support the written text. Such photographs allow the reader to connect mental images generated by texts with visual ones. Usually, they are used as an adjunct and clearly subordinate to the text, and not subjected to explicit source criticism.

There is also a range of recent books on historical photography in South Asia. Most of these focus on the splendour of South Asian photography and some attempt a rigorous criticism of photographs as sources of historical information.[5] These books tend to concentrate on the work of colonial professional photographers, located in urban centres, and the themes which appealed to them and their mainly upper-class clientele. These books contain a wealth of information on political and social relations, on aesthetic conventions, and on audiences and depositories of photographic output.

They also do no more than scratch the surface. As photography took root in South Asia and photographic equipment became cheaper, photography came within reach of larger groups of people, reached more peripheral regions of the subcontinent, and found new themes. In this book, we explore this development. We focus on the photographic record of one little-known rural district in Bangladesh. Such a narrow geographical focus is uncommon. In publications of historical photography the unit of interest, and the criterion of selection, has usually been the oeuvre of an individual artist or studio, the conventions of 'colonial' photography, the construction of the 'Other,' or the lifestyle of the ruling classes. These studies commonly impose a 'national' or even larger framework: photographs showing localities and events in different parts of the subcontinent are presented as instances of 'Indian photography,' or as representing 'Orientalist' constructions of colonial societies.

Our starting point has taken us in a different direction. Although many of the photographs in this book could fit easily into the usual frameworks, our interest is less in the development of photography, or the subjectivity of the photographer, than in how photographs can contribute to our understanding of history. To this end we have looked at different bodies of photography and the historical stories and visions that they suggest. In the process, we have grouped photographs to bring out themes which we—three authors with different backgrounds and outlooks—consider important. We are quite conscious of the arbitrary and personal nature of this process of imposing patterns of meaning. This is true not only regarding the selected themes but also regarding our geographical scope. As an administrative unit the Chittagong Hill Tracts were a colonial creation; to employ this unit to frame photographs has implications for the meanings we attach to them. The archive of images now at our disposal would have allowed the composition of several other books. Our purpose has been to focus on themes which we consider important in view of current debates concerning the struggle in the Chittagong hills, besides a concern with how best to conceptualise the history of Bangladesh.

## Decentring Nationalist History

Most of the stories and visions suggested by photographs of the Chittagong hills are little known in the rest of Bangladesh, let alone the outside world. They have not been incorporated into mainstream histories of Bangladesh and do not fit in easily with the nationalist narratives which have so dominated history writing in the British, Pakistan and Bangladesh periods. There are now essentially two varieties of nationalist history writing in Bangladesh. The first deals with the '*Struggle for Bengali Nationhood*.' It creates, celebrates and naturalises an ethnic category, the Bengali, and traces its tortuous rise to power and self-esteem. The second is the '*Emancipation of the Muslim*,' which does the same for a religious category. Today, the big debates in Bangladesh swirl around these two narratives and how they impinge on individual and group identities, the state, and the destiny of Bangladesh society. The intensity of these debates has made it easy to ignore, marginalise and suppress other accounts of the history of Bangladesh. And this is where the stories suggested by the material in this book become of wider than local interest: they show us that the history of the people living in Bangladesh can be imagined differently. Today emancipatory narratives of the nation are being questioned, not only in Bangladesh but all over the world; it is high time for us to explore the multitude of alternative histories that these narratives have covered up.

This book can be seen as part of the much larger collective project of decentring nationalist history-writing by highlighting identities which are hidden by this approach. It is particularly important, for example, to (re)inscribe gender and class into histories of Bangladesh. The decentring power of the stories in this book is slightly different. It derives from the fact that the Chittagong Hill Tracts, though certainly part of Bangladesh, stood outside either of the principal categories of nationalist historiography because the area was overwhelmingly non-Bengali and non-Muslim. Stories such as the ones suggested by the photographs in this book unsettle and disrupt any attempt to equate the history of Bangladesh with either the history of Bengalis or the history of Islam in Bengal. And this has been the reason why nationalist historians of Bangladesh have ignored and suppressed such accounts.

The political results have been very serious indeed. Historians of Bangladesh have been deeply implicated in both nationalist myth-making and an almost complete silence about those who were not included in the nation but did find themselves living in the territory of Bangladesh. Historians and other intellectuals have by and large remained silent when the civic rights of these groups, including the inhabitants of the Chittagong Hill Tracts, were shoved aside time and again in the name of development or national security. Until quite recently we seemed hardly bothered by the devastating social effects of the Kaptai reservoir, the exploitation of the forest reserves, the transmigration of lowland agriculturists, militarisation, repeated grave human rights abuses, or the casting out of refugees. We have not given convincing historical analyses of the armed conflict which emerged in the Chittagong hills in the early 1970s and soon grew into one of South Asia's most bitter internal wars, and neither have we utilised these events for a serious re-examination of nationalist historiography. In other words, the peoples of the Chittagong Hill Tracts have been largely excluded from the 'nation,' with dire results. This book argues that other visions, so far marginalised in the historiography, must enrich our historical understanding of Bangladesh.

## The Photographs in this Book

Photography started in the Chittagong hills shortly after they were occupied by the

British and annexed to their colony of British India in 1860. Photographically speaking, however, the Chittagong Hill Tracts remained highly peripheral till the 1960s. The colonial photographic record is patchy. None of the famous professional photographers of British India were active here, there were few resident Europeans, and the local ruling class was extremely small. The local 'camera density' must have been infinitesimal. Moreover, the district attracted few anthropologists, archaeologists, or tourists. Not surprisingly, photography never developed into an art form here and hardly any photographs of the Chittagong Hill Tracts can be found in the great depositories of colonial photography.[6] The majority of the photographs in this book are snapshots; they were taken by amateur photographers and come from numerous family albums and private collections scattered around the globe. Many were intended for private use only and few of them have been published before. Most were intended as records of personal experiences, social events, adventures, or loved individuals.[7]

As these photographs generally had no commercial value and were not kept in museums, archives or research institutes, many of them suffered considerable damage. The older photographs also suffered from technical shortcomings which shortened their life-span. Moreover, climatic, social and political conditions in the Chittagong hills led to the destruction of many photographs (and almost all negatives) which were kept there. But what the surviving photographs may lack in technical sophistication, artistic vision, or proper preservation is richly compensated by the wealth of new information which they provide to the historian. In this book, we have made a small selection and grouped the photographs in thematic chapters. Wherever possible, we have supported the images with quotations from written accounts, many of them previously unpublished private reminiscences which came our way in the process of collecting the photographs.

The result is a book which, we expect, will surprise many readers. We hope some of you will take it as a challenge, a starting point for forays of your own into the largely uncharted field of popular photography as a source of social memory. If one small, largely rural region in an out-of-the-way corner of Asia can yield such rich material, the possibilities may be endless.

Finally, we know that our coverage is not exhaustive. We are aware of the existence of several collections of photographs, mainly from the 1950s and 1960s, which we could not locate or which were not available to us for a variety of reasons. It is probable that there are more collections that have not come to our notice. Therefore, we urge readers to provide us with more information on photographs and other material regarding the Chittagong Hill Tracts. We are working towards a research collection of visual images of the Chittagong Hill Tracts which will in due course become publicly available.[8]

**TABLE 1**

*Population of the Chittagong Hill Tracts*[1]

| Group[2, 3] | Main religion | 1956 | 1981 |
|---|---|---|---|
| Chakma | Buddhism | 140,000 | 230,000 |
| Taungchengya | Buddhism | 15,000 | 20,000 |
| Marma | Buddhism | 80,000 | 120,000 |
| Sak | Buddhism | 2,000 | 1,500 |
| Khyeng | Community religion | 1,000 | 1,500 |
| Tripura | Hinduism | 30,000 | 40,000 |
| Riang/Brong | Hinduism | 7,000 | 10,000 |
| Mru | Community religion | 17,000 | 20,000 |
| Khumi | Community religion | 2,500 | 1,000 |
| Bawm | Christianity | 3,500 | 8,000 |
| Pangkhua | Christianity | 1,500 | 2,000 |
| Lushai/Mizo | Christianity | 500 | 1,000 |
| | | 300,000 | 455,000 |
| Bengali | Islam | 30,000 | 290,000 |
| Total | | 330,000 | 745,000 |

[1] Population figures are all based on estimates in the available literature whose reliability cannot be established. Here we reproduce the figures given by Brauns and Löffler (1990, 37).

[2] There is considerable disagreement about the boundaries of various groups. For example, Tripura and Riang are sometimes considered as one group. There is also confusion about the proper naming of various groups, partly because these have adopted new names over time and partly because of unclarity about proper designations and spelling of names. For example, the terms Riang, Brong, Mrung and Uchay have been used for the seventh group mentioned in this list. The umbrella term *Jumma* has been in use since the 1970s to refer to all inhabitants of the Chittagong Hill Tracts, excluding Bengalis.

Information about different ethnic groups in the Chittagong Hill Tracts varies markedly. For some, detailed anthropological monographs are available, notably for the Khyeng (Bernot and Bernot, 1958), Bawm (Spielmann, 1966), Marma (Bernot, 1967a), Sak (Bernot, 1967b) and Mru (Brauns and Löffler, 1990). Others, e.g. the Tripura or the Khumi, have never been the focus of detailed social science inquiry. Even for the Chakma, the largest group in the region, nothing even close to Bernot's landmark study on the Marma is available.

[3] The pattern of human settlement throughout the Chittagong hills showed much territorial intermingling. Some groups dominated in certain parts of the Chittagong Hill Tracts (e.g. the Chakma in the centre, and Marma in the tract between the Karnaphuli and Sangu rivers) and others were concentrated in specific areas (e.g. Tripura in the north, Mru in the south). There was also a distinction between groups living in hill valleys and groups living on the ridges of the hills. Nevertheless, in many places local settlement patterns were highly complex. For example, seven different groups could be found living in close proximity in an area of about 15 by 10 km around the township of Ruma on the Sangu river in the southern Chittagong hills. Following the calculation of Brauns and Löffler (1990), their distribution in 1960 is presented schematically below.

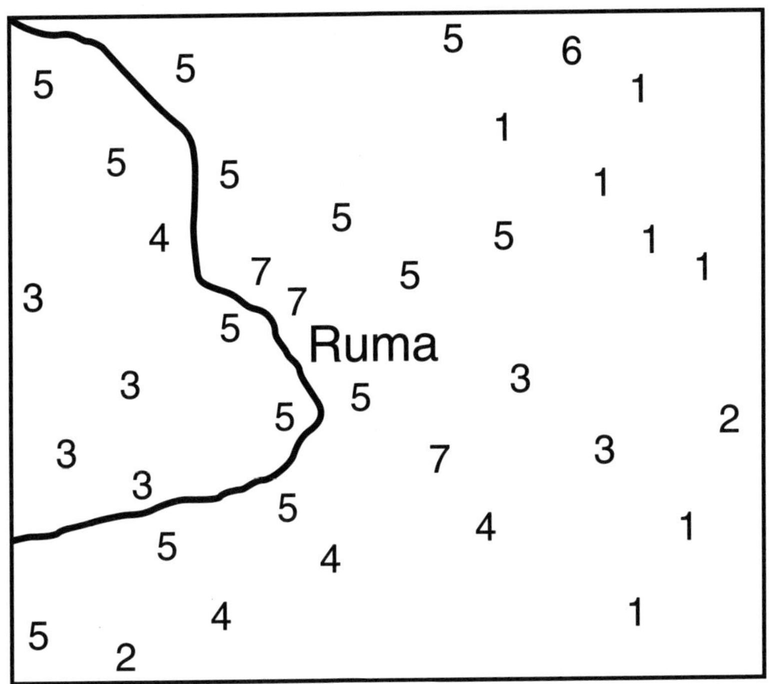


| | |
|---|---|
| 1 | Bawm |
| 2 | Riang/Brong |
| 3 | Mru |
| 4 | Khumi |
| 5 | Marma |
| 6 | Taungchengya |
| 7 | Bengali |

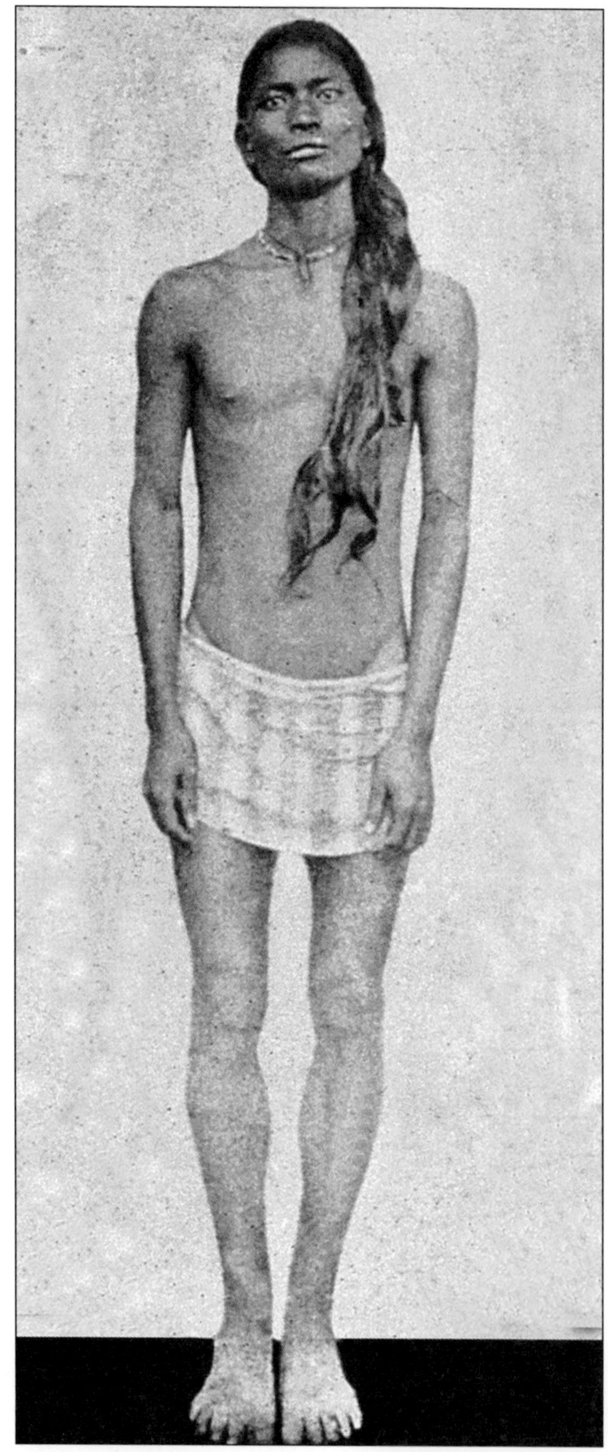

***Plate 1**: 'Lushai' (Riebeck, 1885)*

## *Chapter 1*

# PHOTOGRAPHIC OBSESSIONS

The technology of photography developed within European cultural contexts. In its early phases photography was a new means for Europeans to explore themselves and others. The spread of photographic techniques around the world went hand in hand with the spread of images reflecting European cultural conventions and representations. And although European dominance declined over time, many of the early ways of representing reality through photographs proved to be long-lived.

When looking at a particular body of photographs, as in this book, it may be helpful to know something about these conventions. Photography did not arrive in the Chittagong Hill Tracts as a neutral technology to be used freely by any takers. At first it was a European technology, not only because it was already saturated with European ideas about representation, but also because it was available only to Europeans. When in the course of the twentieth century the first hill people took up the camera, they had to come to terms with a well-established tradition of visually imagining the Chittagong Hill Tracts. We outline this tradition very briefly in terms of five 'obsessions.'

## 1.1 Obsessions

### *Dancing Girls, Fakirs and Snake-Charmers*

The peoples of South and Southeast Asia and their rich cultures had offered Europeans a vast playground for the production of visual images long before the arrival of photography. Through paintings and engravings, South Asia had been imagined as a world of dancing girls and maharajas, fakirs and snake-charmers, romantic scenery and pig-sticking. In the 1850s commercial photo studios opened their doors in the big cities, wealthy travellers began to take along cameras, and anthropologists and archaeologists added photography to their toolkits. Photography reproduced established styles and genres and also added new ones, e.g. 'great events' and 'tribes and peoples.' It fed a romantic interest in The East and at the same time supported the notion of the beneficial influence of colonial rule. This link between romantic images and support for the established order was long-lasting. We recognise it when we look at photographs made in the Chittagong hills much later. The 'dancing tribal belle' of today's tourist leaflets is the imaginary descendent of the 'nautch girl' of the 1850s.

### *Origins of Mankind*

Photography developed in a period in which Europeans were much concerned with the origins of the human species. European thinkers and scientists were looking for the birthplace of mankind and they considered South Asia a likely candidate, although not always for the same reasons. The antiquity of Indian philosophy made German philosophers suspect that behind the Brahmanic teachings lurked still older wisdom which might lead them to the origins of human thought. British anthropologists felt that it might be possible to identify the cradle of human evolution by studying the multitude of South Asia's 'races'; this led to

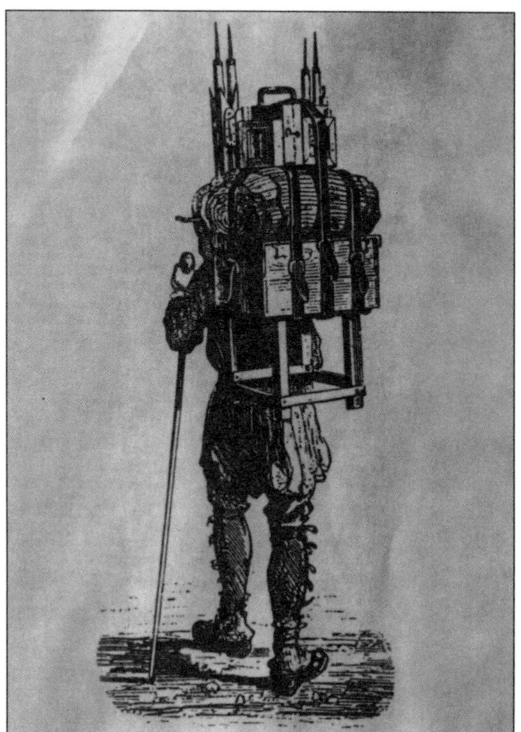

**Plate 2**. *Comparatively portable outfits such as this one made it possible to create photographic images in the Chittagong hills in the 1860s and 1870s. (Focal Encyclopedia, 1956)*

**Plate 3**. *By the 1880s and 1890s, the folding roll-film camera became popular. (Focal Encyclopedia, 1956)*

an increasing interest in physical anthropology. It soon became clear, however, that the existing pictorial material on 'primitive peoples' was inadequate for their purposes: drawings invariably reproduced these people with Europeanised features and postures. It was thought that photography could produce really objective representations which would be of use to researchers.

In this way, photographs of 'racial types' became a new genre. Large collections were shown at international exhibitions in Paris (1855) and London (1862), together with living representatives of these 'races.' The success of these exhibitions led to more ambitious plans. The Asiatic Society of Bengal supported Dr Joseph Fayrer's idea to organise a conference and exhibition of representatives of all races of the Old World. These 'living specimens' would be exhibited in booths, neatly classified according to race and tribe. The public could study them, talk with them, and even make plaster casts. It was thought that this was the only way really to understand scientifically the pertinent historical, linguistic and anatomical facts and develop an adequate theory of human evolution. Practical problems prevented the project from being realised but what started as its catalogue developed into Edward Tuite Dalton's *Descriptive Ethnology of Bengal* (1872), a book with lithographs based mainly on photographs by Benjamin Simpson. Two of these photographs have been reproduced in the following pages. Another influential publication of those years was the eight-volume *The People of India* (1868-1875), edited by John Forbes Watson and John William Kaye. This work owed its appearance 'to the photographic enthusiasms of Lord and Lady Canning, who wished to build up a collection of photographs to remind them of India in later life' (Falconer, 1990, 274-275). The project received official support and amateur photographers in the civil service and the military toured South Asia to contribute to it **(plate 2)**. The book was published under the imprint of the India Museum in London. It benefited from an increased administrative interest in the peoples of India resulting from the Indian Revolt of 1857.

> 'Implicit in the use of photography to study the races of India was the assumption that the gathering of such data would serve a pragmatic function in the administration of the congeries of racial and religious groupings that came under British rule' (Falconer, 1990, 275).

A photographic survey of the Chittagong Hill Tracts was ordered as part of this project. It began well enough but soon failed because the camera would not work and it could not be replaced. Just one picture from the Chittagong Hill Tracts was included; it is reproduced in our chapter 'Creating a Colonial Aristocracy.'

In other words, there was a connection between the need to record human variability for scientific inquiry and the administrative use to which such data could be put. It is important to be aware of such a connection when looking at the photographs in this book. For example, the way in which 'tribal groups' from the Chittagong Hill Tracts were presented at the Folk Festival and Exhibition in 1969 not only owed much to colonial exhibitions, but also reaffirmed the connection between 'racial' representation and political control.

### *Objectivity*

'Scientific photography' commanded enormous respect during the closing decades of the nineteenth century. It promised an objective registration of reality; it was seen as a new universal language that anyone could readily understand. Therefore it was superior to, and more authentic than, earlier representations. In physical anthropology, the 'correct photograph' displayed people standing to attention, ready to be scrutinised. When Emil Riebeck travelled in the Chittagong Hill Tracts (1882), he made sure that his photographs lived up to this model (**plates 1** and **4**).

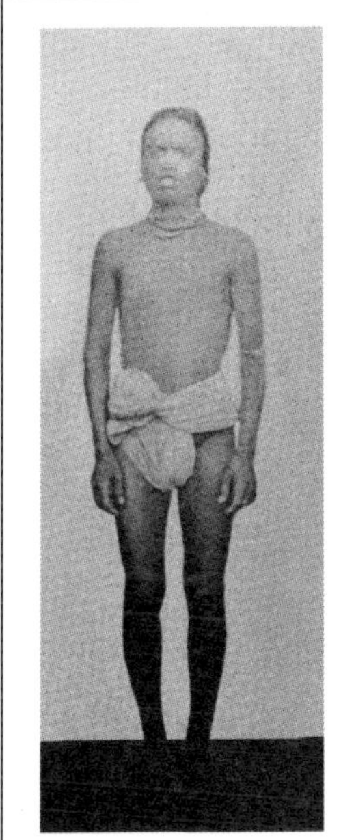

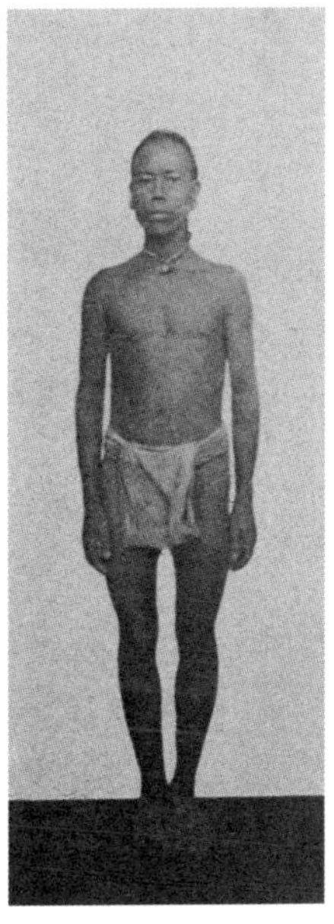
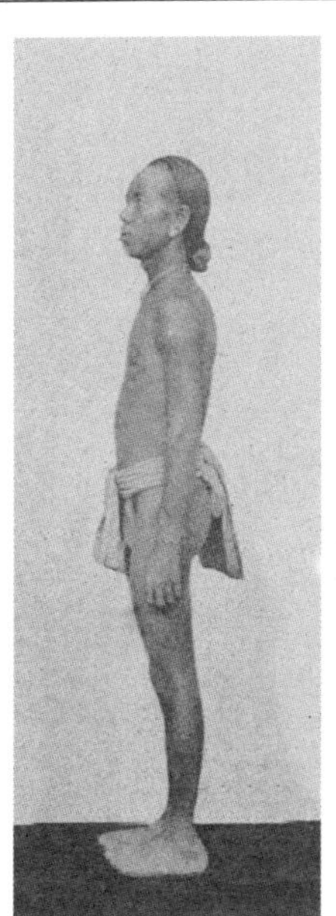

***Plate 4***. *'Pankho,' 1882. (Riebeck, 1885)*[1]

**Plate 5**. *'Group Picture of Ethnological Objects of the Hill Tribes in the Colony of Chittagong.' (Riebeck, 1885)*

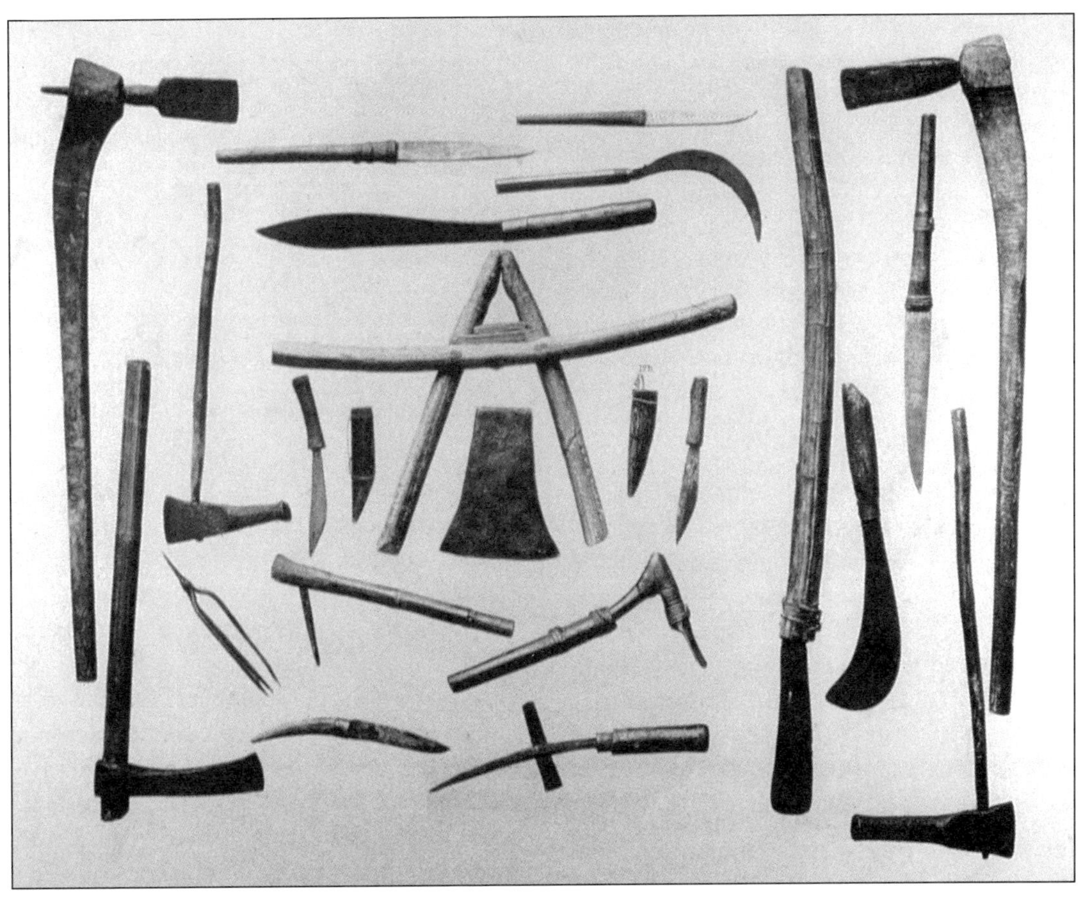

***Plate 6****. 'Implements of the Hill Tribes and from the Colony of Chittagong.' (Riebeck, 1885)*

In the early twentieth century, this trust in the objectivity of photography began to decline. It was realised that photographs can be placed at different points on a continuum from pure documentation to pure imagination. There was more awareness of the photographer's role in manipulating the visual image. With a declining belief in photographic objectivity, social scientists lost much interest in photography. The conservation, presentation and interpretation of 'ethnographic' images was given a lower priority.

It was not until the 1970s, with the emergence of visual anthropology, that photography became the focus of renewed interest. Now ethnographic photographs were scrutinised, not primarily for the objective reality they might represent, but as source material for a history of how reality was perceived and constructed in earlier generations. Today few observers can escape this inherent tension in photographs. Photographic images can serve to reconstruct situations in other times and localities but they can also serve to reconstruct notions of reality underlying their production. A moot question is how to resolve this tension. In the absence of generally accepted criteria for decoding historical photographs, or for linking them with written material, it often appears to be a question of personal judgement. In this book, we have read and contextualised photographs in different ways, and we have used contemporary texts to frame them. Sometimes we underscore the documentary value of the photographs we have selected, and sometimes we choose to emphasise what these photographs tell us about visions of reality. That ambivalence is inherent in the presentation of photographs, and other choices would have led to a different balancing of the documentary and the visionary.

### *Material Culture*

Physical anthropologists used photography to explore and categorise human variations. This has left us with large collections of images which show nude or semi-nude bodies, *en face* or *en profil*, lined up in the interest of advancing anthropological theory. Ultimately, this type of photography pointed to a sterile universe of brachycephalic and dolichocephalic indices.

Meanwhile cultural anthropologists did much the same thing with cultural material. Instead of lining up people to be photographed as if they were new recruits to the army, cultural anthropologists arranged cultural objects as if they were booty from a campaign of cultural conquest (**plates 5** and **6**). To them, material objects provided clues to illiterate and 'primitive' peoples in much the same way that written records provided clues to 'civilised' peoples. Adolf Bastian, founding father of German anthropology, once said that the objects brought to Europe from all corners of the world would at some future time serve as letters for the alphabet of the History of Mankind.

Ethnographic museums were to be the archives of primitive humanity, and ethnographic photography focused on the representation of their craft products, utensils, furniture, dress and ornaments. This type of photography was used to create inventories rather than documentation. Implements changed into objects, and culture was chopped up into categories such as 'woodwork,' 'metal objects,' and 'basketry.'

This approach is discernible in a number of photographs in this book, notably those by Riebeck, who combined an interest in physical and cultural anthropology (see our chapter 'Bodies and Costumes').

### *Controlling the Image*

Photographers were at pains to present reality in a controlled way. Photographs were usually conscious compositions, they were created according to a visual grammar, a European aesthetics and the technological requirements of the equipment at hand. When taking pictures of people in the Chittagong hills, photographers felt that they had to 'prepare' these people for the occasion (**plate 7**). It was not always easy to have them take up the 'right' position. When H.E. Kauffmann came across some women who spoke neither Bengali nor Arakanese,

> 'it turned out to be very difficult to make clear to them that they had to leave the shade and sit in the sunlight. Then I wanted to take a close-up of their heads with the oldest woman turning around to display her two-pronged comb. Immediately all three turned around, but what should I do with these three backs of heads, especially since the youngest girl was pretty enough to show her face in all its clumsiness and primitivity?' (Kauffmann, 17 December 1955)

Creating an aesthetically pleasing image required manipulating an often refractory reality. The effort to present hill people in this way sometimes failed; the intended effect, a portrait suggesting naturalness and composure, would not materialise. Instead, the result would be what we call a 'tribal portrait' (see chapter 'Portraits'). In this genre, anonymous individuals look into the

***Plate 7***. *Westerners preparing Mru women for a photograph. (Seifert, 1963)*

***Plate 8***. *The result, a 'tribal portrait.' (Seifert, 1963)*

lens, or more frequently away from the camera, with suspicion, embarrassment, or obedient awkwardness (**plate 8**). These images present a power struggle between controlling photographer and resisting subject.

## 1.2 From Culture-in-action to the Snapshot

Anthropological photography in the colonies was increasingly shaped by conscious efforts at standardisation. This was related to technical changes which made photography easier, more portable, cheaper and more common. Instruction manuals were published for handling photographic equipment and for making accurate observations. A general shift from inventarisation to documentation could be noticed. But:

> 'What should the traveller take pictures of?... We are shown mountains stretching far into the distance, pretty waterfalls, even some natives lined up like organ-pipes; but not one negative speaks of the true character of the country and the life of its inhabitants ... First one has to concentrate on the natives' activities. An unposed snapshot showing the labourer behind the plough or with a spade, the basket maker among his baskets, the weaver at the loom, is worth more than twenty waterfalls' (Neuhauss (1894, 18), quoted in Theye, 1990, 398).

Consequently, photographers were instructed to show culture-in-action:

> 'You should make pictures of all things which you cannot take with you, but above all of events and activities...Therefore do not make people pose but take photographs of them in natural poses and in their usual workplace. Moreover, the entire course of the labour process should be clear; you should make a series of exposures of all its stages' (Ackermann, (1914, 14), quoted in Theye, 1990, 398).

But anthropological photography and its conventions rapidly lost their importance as cameras came within easy reach, even in places as remote as the Chittagong hills. Westerners in the hills were missionaries, administrators and, after 1947, technical experts who had no need for anthropological manuals to make snapshots. To them, photography was not a tool in the pursuit of scientific accuracy. It was not public in the sense that they expected their photographs to be preserved in museums, research institutes, or books. Rather, photography was a personal matter. It served as a means of showing relatives and friends back home how you lived in a far-off place. And it might trigger memories in later life, as the Cannings had intended. Such snapshots remained private and were passed down from parents to children.

For others, the Chittagong hills became a site of romance and images of beauty. Claus-Dieter Brauns' photographs in this book are a good example. 'Motivated by a deep longing to break out of the pressures of technological society and to return to nature by experiencing "the unbridled freedom of primitive people,"' he came upon the Mru in 1963. They appeared to him to 'represent a tribal culture still closely tied to nature.' Over the years he returned several times and made some 6,000 slides. 'They are not intended to be purely scientific and functional documentary photographs, but rather seek at the same time to convey feelings—including all of those exotic and romantic sentiments which the Mru can awaken in occidental people' (Brauns and Löffler, 1990, 19, 21; **plate 9**).

Brauns' photographs have a clear message. They form a 'monument to the Mru' who are presented as living in a world of their own, unknown, inaccessible, in unbridled freedom —but ultimately threatened with extinction.

***Plate 9**. Mru woman harvesting paddy. (Brauns, 1971).*

## 1.3 Indigenous Photography

What about hill people as photographers? Although the oldest examples of photographs being taken at the initiative of people from the Chittagong hills date from around 1900 (e.g. the investiture photograph of Raja Bhuban Mohan Roy (1897) in our chapter 'How To Be a Raja'), these were taken in photo studios run by Bengali or European photographers. The earliest surviving photographs taken by hill people themselves appear to date from as late as the middle of the twentieth century (see our chapter 'Portraits'). These were for private consumption, their main concern the recording of family events. Professional photographers from the Chittagong Hill Tracts did not make their mark till the 1970s.

So far, no research has been done on the ways in which local photographers used the medium. In *Through Indian Eyes*, Judith Mara Gutman argues that:

> 'Indian photographers [of the nineteenth century] could and did adapt the equipment, adjust the light, and let their vision stream through the camera's lenses..., imposing their understanding of an extended reality on their photographs. They recycled a Western device into an Indian order, just as they restructured Britain's ceremonial structure of power and authority. But ultimately, the camera, especially in the twentieth century, changed some of India's visual patterns. As in the West, where the camera reinforced and spurred the overhaul of Western conceptual systems, in India, it first reinforced, then

> helped change indigenous systems...The camera spurred the creation of new imagery and new conceptualizations, but stayed within an Indian framework' (Gutman, 1982, 11; cf. Pinney, 1997, 92, 95-96).

Our collection does not appear to support the idea that there was a specific local way of using the camera. There is, of course, the problem of using the blanket term 'Indian' to cover the multitude of cultural frameworks in South Asia, and the related question of whether, or to what extent, the inhabitants of the Chittagong hills were part of a cultural unit called 'Indian civilisation' with distinct visual traditions. But more importantly, we have not found photographs by nineteenth-century hill people which might support, or indeed refute, Gutman's suggestion that cameras were used differently and that photography was informed by an indigenous conceptual system. Such connections remain to be explored, perhaps in a wider context, by future students of historical photography.

## 1.4 True Fiction?

A map is not the landscape it depicts, a description not the reality to which it refers. And yet they link us to realities 'out there.' Similarly, a photograph is merely a two-dimensional representation of a complex world which can be measured in length, breadth, depth and time. This book documents what photographs reveal about the complex world of the Chittagong hills between the 1860s and the 1970s. They are visual documents, images of a reality that has slipped away. They form a map of a landscape that can never be more than partly known.

But how to read that map? How can we be sure that our construction of the landscape makes sense? We explore the photographic record and relate it to the notions of reality which we think informed it. Our own way of ordering photographs, interpreting them and relating them to texts is merely another production of images. Reality is in the eye of the beholder.

*Map 1. The Chittagong hills in the sixteenth century. This map, made by João Baptista Lavanha in about 1550, shows a settlement called Chacomas in the area inhabited by the Chakma. Similarly, the nearby town of Codavascam is believed to refer to the region then ruled by Khuda Bakhsh Khan. (Barros, 1945-6)*

## Chapter 2

# MAPPING A REGION

The region which we now know as the Chittagong Hill Tracts appeared on the first known map of Bengal, dated about 1550 (**map 1**). It did not have a special name then; it was simply a section of the hill country linking India and Burma. In 1860 the British occupied it and made it a district of their colony of British India. It is they who named it 'Chittagong Hill Tracts' ('Parbotyo Chottogram' in Bengali).

The term *Chittagong Hill Tracts* indicates that the British saw these hills as an extension of the lowland to the west which they had ruled for over a hundred years. This lowland was (and is) known as Chittagong district, after the important port city of that name. In the same way adjacent sections of the hills were named after lowland districts. The hills to the south became the 'Arakan Hill Tracts' and those to the north 'Hill Tippera.'

Administratively, the Chittagong Hill Tracts were brought under the Province of Bengal, which covered all the land to the west. It was a district with a unique status. Unlike the lowland district of Chittagong, it was not a regular Bengal district. Unlike Hill Tippera, it was not an indirectly ruled 'Princely State.' And it was cut off administratively from the hill country to the south (Arakan Hill Tracts) and east (Lushai Hills), which became part of the Provinces of Assam and Burma, respectively (**map 2**).

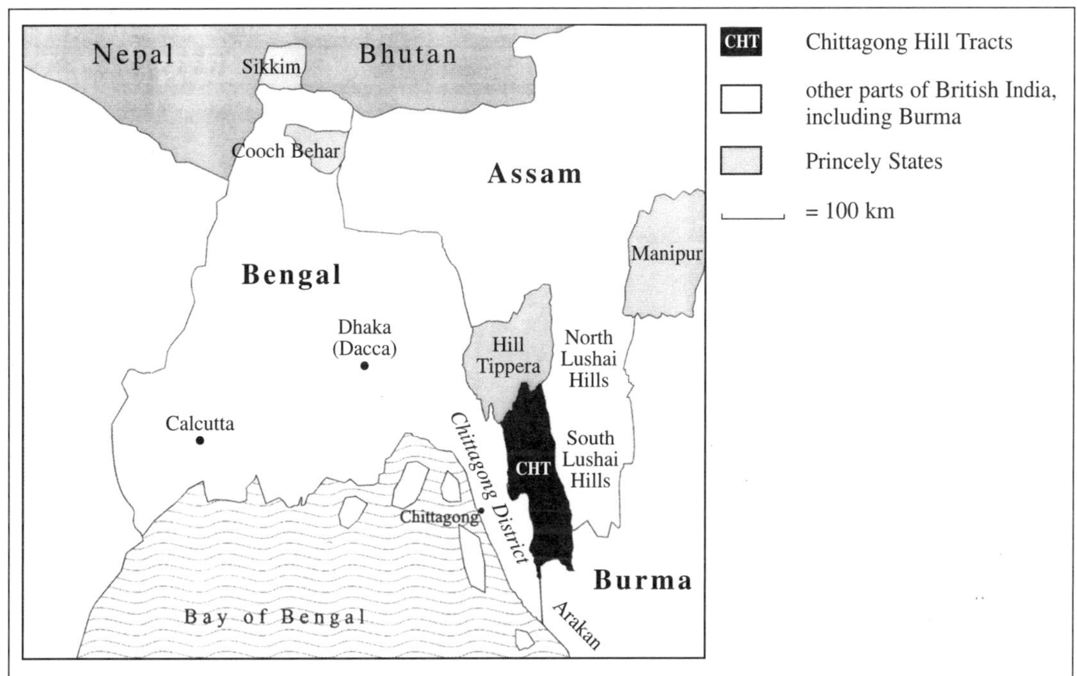


***Map 2**. The Chittagong Hill Tracts: political boundaries of 1900.*

These colonial decisions had far-reaching effects. Not only did the administrative divisions long survive colonial rule, they also determined a partition of the hill country between three postcolonial states. In 1947 the British left, and lowland Chittagong and the Chittagong Hill Tracts fell to Pakistan; the Arakan Hill Tracts were incorporated into Burma; and Hill Tippera (now Tripura) and the Lushai Hills (now Mizoram) became part of India (**map 3**).

The physical appearance of the Chittagong Hill Tracts changed dramatically in 1960, when the Kaptai Reservoir came into existence (**map 4**). In 1971 the Chittagong Hill Tracts, together with the rest of East Pakistan, separated from Pakistan to form the new state of Bangladesh.

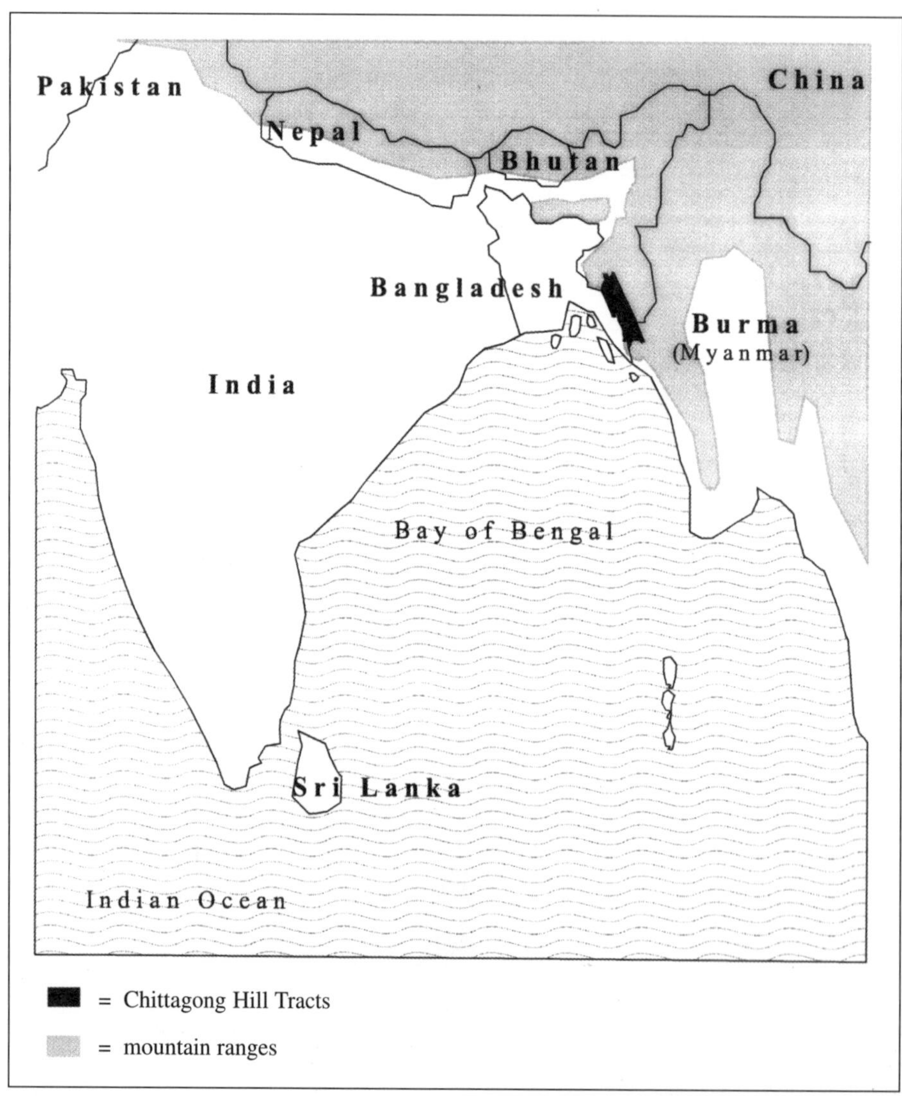


***Map 3****. The Chittagong Hill Tracts: postcolonial boundaries (from 1947 to 1971, Bangladesh was East Pakistan).*

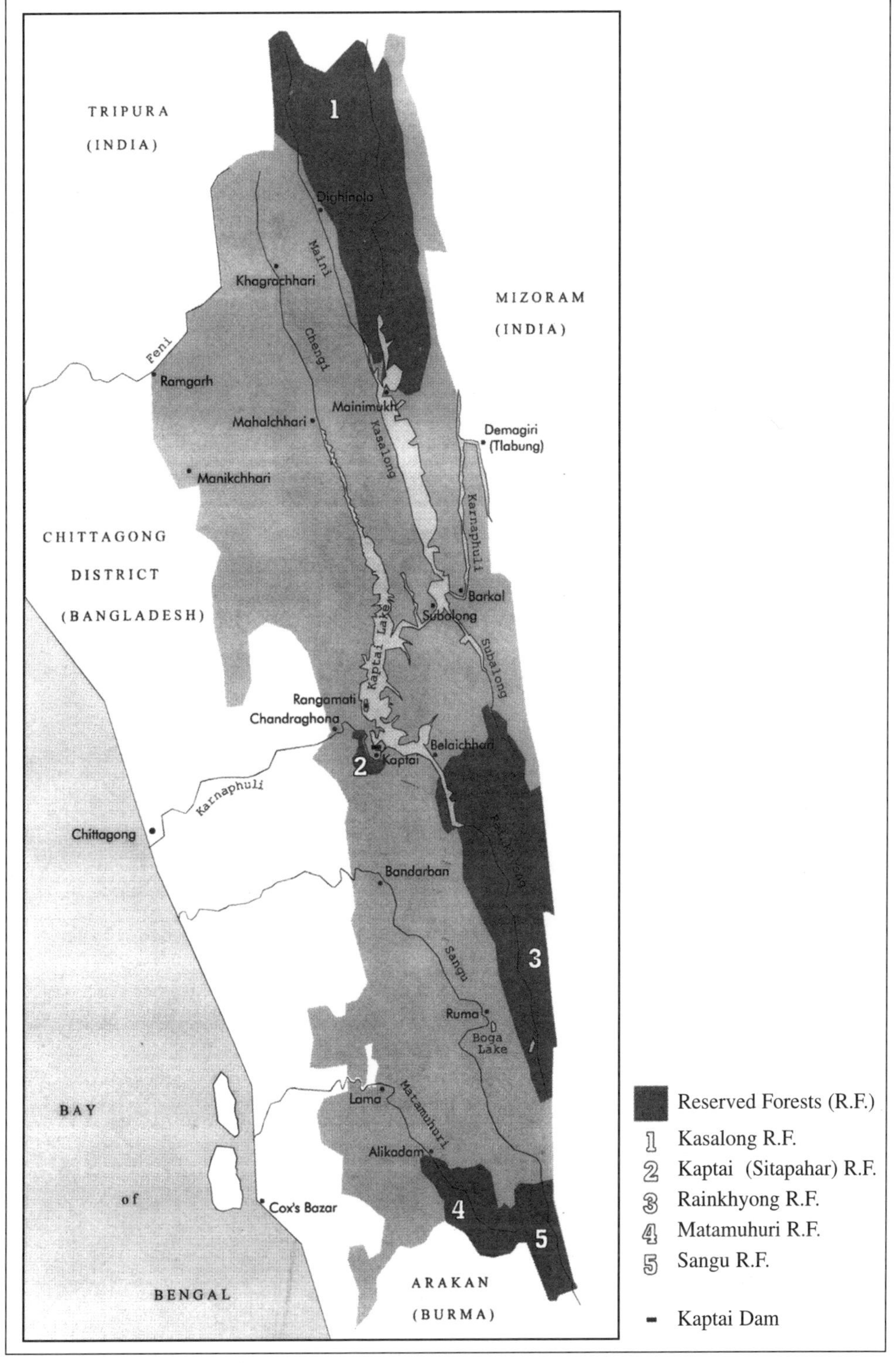


***Map 4**. The Chittagong Hill Tracts after the creation of Kaptai Lake (1960).*

***Plate 10***. *Laigoro, a traditional Khumi chief of the southern Chittagong hills. (Lewin, about 1867)*

*Chapter 3*

# CREATING A COLONIAL ARISTOCRACY

In 1860 the British occupied the hills to the east of Chittagong and annexed them to their colonial empire. For the first time in their history, the Chittagong hills were administered from Bengal. Before that time, political power in the hills had been dispersed among many chiefs (**plates 10** and **11**). These chiefs ruled groups of people rather than territories, and their followings ranged from several dozens to thousands of individuals. The most important chiefs lived in style. In 1798 the Scottish traveller Francis Buchanan described the most powerful independent chief of the southern hills as follows:

> 'Soon after my arrival I was visited by Kaung-la-pru, who is a stout little man with strong Burma features, and seems to be about fifty years of age. He came in a palankeen with many attendants, who appear to be in easy circumstances...The proper appellation for this Chief is Po-mang Kaung-la Pru. Po-mang [Bohmong] is his title, and signifies Captain. Kaung-la is his proper name; and Pru, which signifies white, is the name of the family. By three Women he has six Sons, and six Daughters...He has about twenty Hindoo Servants, and still more Mohammedans, his Dewan or Minister being of that Religion. The Domestic who takes care of his table is a Rajbunjee...Beside his numerous family, he has a great number of Ma-ra-ma slaves, that is, persons of the tribe who incur Debt go to him, and say, if you will discharge my Debt, I will become your slave...The House of the Chief is constructed like those of the other Joomeas, but is much larger than that of Aung-ghio-se [a lesser chief]. He has Chairs, Carpets, Beds, Mats, and other furniture' (Van Schendel (ed.), 1992, 87, 89, 91).

***Plate 11**. Taimang, a traditional Khumi chief of the southern Chittagong hills. (Lewin, about 1867)*

The British decided to give their new possession a special administrative status. Colonial rule was to be mediated through local dignitaries, each in charge of a section ('circle') of the hills. To this end, the British recognised only three chiefs. They chose those chiefs who were in control of the main entry points into the hills; other local power holders had to make do with subordinate positions in the new administrative structure. The three recognised chiefs ('tribal chiefs,' rajas) were the Mong Raja (seat at Manik-chhari, in the north), the Chakma Raja (at Rangamati, in the centre) and the Bohmong Raja (at Bandarban, in the south).[1]

The new district was named the Chittagong Hill Tracts. It consisted of the three chiefs' circles (and initially a khas mahal or government estate) and extensive forests which government 'reserved.' The administrative status of the district was unusual. A number of reasons prevented it becoming a 'Princely State' under indirect rule (such as neighbouring Tripura) or a regular district under the Government of Bengal (such as neighbouring Chittagong district). Its exceptional status was codified in the Chittagong Hill Tracts Regulation of 1900 which instituted a local system of tax collection with the chiefs at the apex. They presided over headmen who collected tax from each household and passed it on to their chief during a public ceremony each year. The chief then handed his circle's tax to the British authorities. Both headmen and chiefs received a commission on the collected tax and they were entitled to extra land. The chief also had jurisdiction over minor legal matters in his circle and could select headmen for the lowest administrative units (mauza) which the colonial regime had introduced in the hills.

Under colonialism, the position of chief was hereditary but the colonial authorities had a final say in which relative would succeed a deceased chief. The investiture of each new chief was a public display of the derived power of his office. After the demise of the colonial state in 1947, the rituals of power continued while the actual power of the chiefs was gradually restricted.

Photographs of chiefs are among the earliest surviving photographs from the Chittagong hills. Starting from the late 1860s, they show how radically the representation of power changed. **Plates 12** and **13** show some of the chiefs who were not made part of the colonial structure of administration and whose power would dwindle to a strictly local level.

**Plate 12**. *Khumi chiefs. (Lewin, about 1867)*

***Plate 13***. *'Purrikhet, Chief of the Kooki Tribe, Chittagong.' In the late nineteenth century many British still used the term 'Kuki' for a wide variety of groups living in the hill country east of Bengal and which they could not classify as either 'Chakma' or 'Magh' (= Marma). Purrikhet is depicted with his daughter. (Watson and Kaye, 1875)*

Early British observers were particularly impressed by the fact that some of the inhabitants of the Chittagong hills, including their leaders, wore few clothes. In 1873, when a group of Lushai chiefs was taken to Calcutta for the first time, they were photographed in long robes (**plate 14**). That Vanhnuaia, the Lushai chief seated on the left, did not always dress like this is clear from the description of a meeting between him and John Beames, the Commissioner of Chittagong, in Rangamati in 1878:

> 'He came to the Circuit House to see me on my arrival, but there was only one sitting-room, and there was a difficulty in admitting him as my wife and some other ladies were there, and Vanhoiya wore no clothes *at all*. A scarlet blanket was offered him but he refused to wear it. Eventually a compromise was arrived at. Two men walked in front of him holding up the blanket till he reached a chair into which he was pushed, and when he was seated the two retainers held the blanket before him all the while, so that only his head and hands were visible. In this position he harangued volubly and the interpreter translated. He swallowed a wineglassful of neat brandy and held out his glass for more, but Gordon ignored this and began to talk at him vigorously. He was a splendid animal—tall, muscular and active, with a keen, bright eye and a lordly demeanour. When we had finished our discussion and arrived at a satisfactory conclusion he rose to retire, and the blanket was then held behind him as he retreated. Though he would not wear it, he condescended to accept it as a present, as also a large glass tumbler which he took a fancy to' (Beames, 1984, 288-289).

***Plate 14**. Traditional Lushai chiefs on their first visit to Calcutta (1873): 'They went in due course to pay their homage to the Lieutenant-Governor...to whom they gravely bowed as to an equal, presenting him with the usual offerings of elephants' tusks and home-spun cloth...To the Calcutta idlers who came to stare at the wild men encamped on the "maidaun," they seemed but a handful of barbarians, with unkempt hair, clad in curious tartans, and armed with strange weapons; but to me, who had lived among them, and knew the nature of these men, and the authority wielded by them among their own people, it seemed a wonderful thing that I should ever have succeeded in persuading them to trust their lives in my hands' (Lewin, 1912, 311-312). (Lewin collection, 1873; cf. Whitehead, 1992)*

After colonial annexation, insignia of chiefly rank changed dramatically. By the 1880s the old ones, connected with precolonial political office, had already become collector's items. In 1882, Emil Riebeck, a German collector, bought the insignia of a Khumi chief (front) and a Bawm chief (back) (**plate 15**) and a goat-hair ornament worn by Shindu chiefs (**plate 16**; see also **plate 19**).

**Plate 15**. *'Ornaments of a Khumi headman and a Bawm headman, made of the tail feathers of a drongo.' (Riebeck, 1885)*

**Plate 16**. *'Insignia of goat's hair worn in the ear by Shindu headmen.' (Riebeck, 1885)*

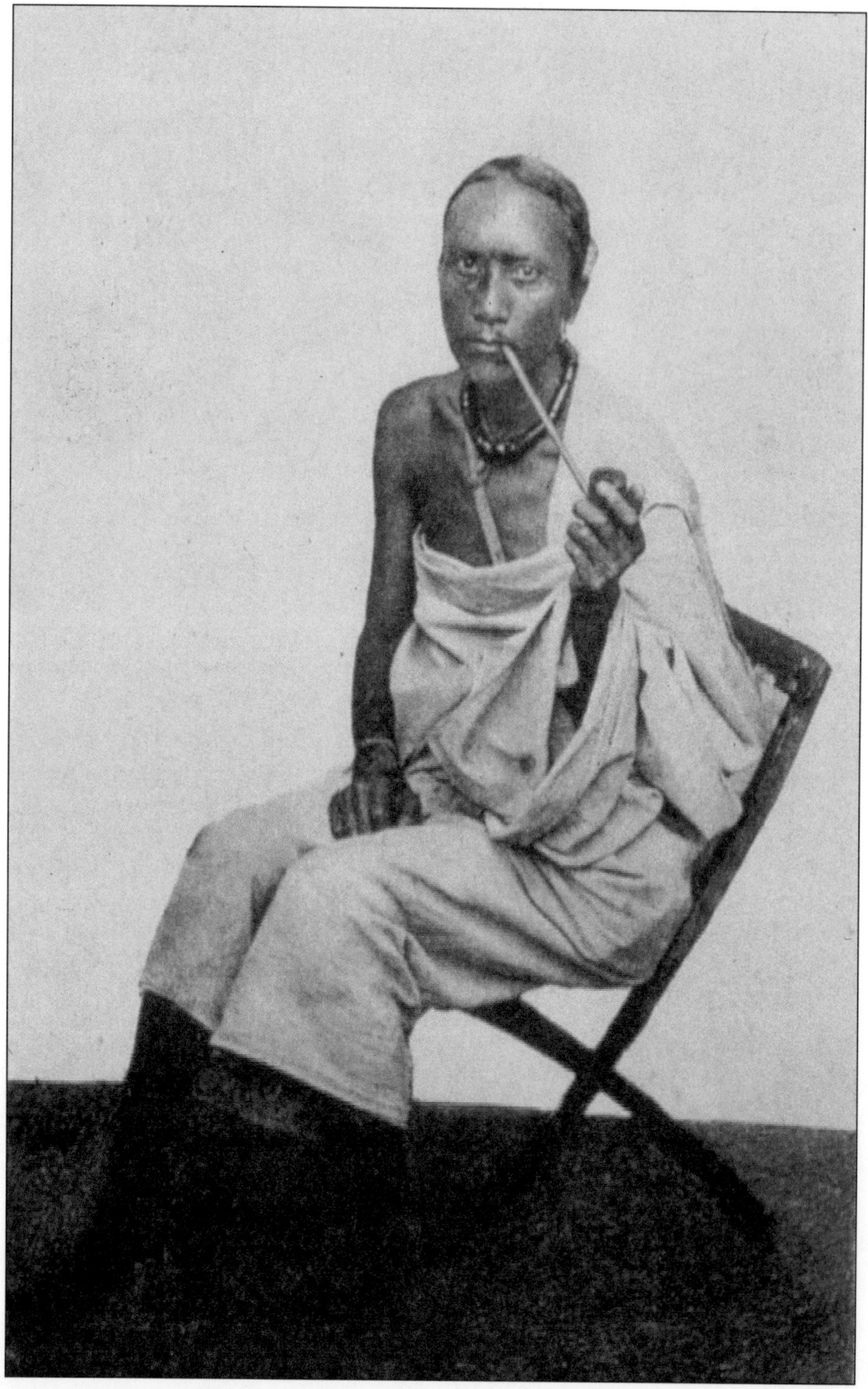

**Plate 17**. *'Lushai chief Pakhoma...He is wearing a large toga-like garment and around his neck a necklace of Burmese amber and the amulet made of a goat's beard tufts which a Lushai never takes off.' (Riebeck, 1885)*

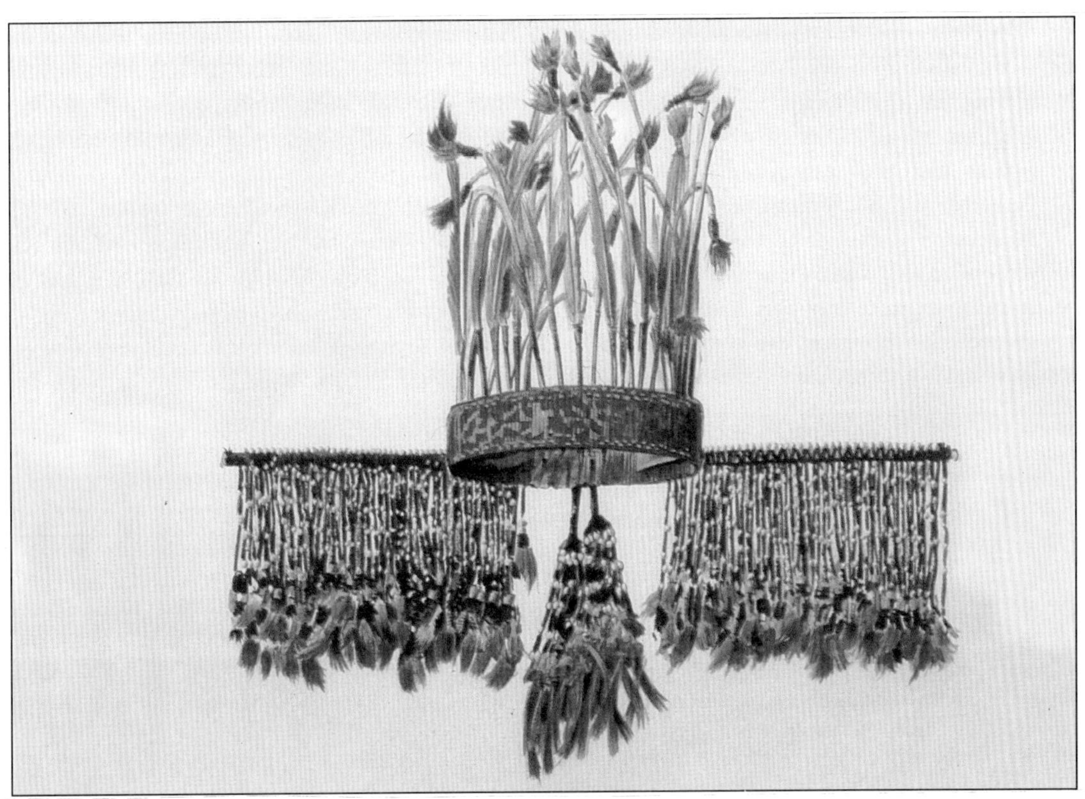

**Plate 18**. *'Headgear of Chief Pakhoma...worn as a sign of his rank during warfare.' (Riebeck, 1885)*

When Riebeck visited the village of Pakhoma, a Lushai chief in the eastern Chittagong Hill Tracts, the chief, pictured in **plate 17**, was most co-operative:

> 'The chief himself honoured us later by acting as our guide to every village house and, by putting in a word for us, facilitated the purchase of all kinds of objects. After all houses had been searched, he mentioned casually that he himself kept a valuable headgear, a symbol of his rank, so I immediately plied him with a large amount of brandy in order to make him part with it. In this I succeeded, although at first he would not let go of it. He also gave me a cloth woven by his small daughter, which, together with the headgear, forms the most valuable part of my Chittagong collection' (Riebeck, 1885, 7) (**plate 18**).

Although the old insignia were not recognised by the state and therefore lost their formal role, they continued to be used by local leaders well into the twentieth century. For example, in 1936 Deputy Commissioner W.J.H. Christie, on an official tour, was met by the headman of Ruilui village, Sakhaia, whom he described as a fine-looking old man [who] was wearing a kind of turban with several feathers stuck in it (Christie Papers, 1936).

**Plate 19**. *'Likebo, Chief of Boki Shendus.' (Lewin, about 1867)*

***Plate 20**. Raja Bhuban Mohan Roy, the Chakma chief, in ceremonial dress, 1897.*[1]
*(Ghosh, 1909)*

*Chapter 4*

# HOW TO BE A RAJA

Three chiefs of the Chittagong hills were recognised by the British as administrators under the colonial state. Henceforth they were known as the 'tribal chiefs' of the Mong, Chakma and Bohmong circles, or simply as the Mong, Chakma and Bohmong chief. The Government of Bengal did not recognise them as hereditary Indian princes, however, and the Chittagong Hill Tracts did not become one or more Princely (or Native) States.

T.H. Lewin, the first British Deputy Commissioner, 'saw as his first and paramount task the need to crush and extinguish the power of these chiefs,' and proceeded to restrict their military, political and financial powers. The Bohmong and Chakma chiefs opposed him by means of appealing against his court decisions, complaining to his superior about maladministration, and presenting petitions to the government. Lewin managed to replace Kong Hla Nyo, the Bohmong chief, by a more accommodating cousin, but he was no match for the formidable Chakma chieftainess, Kalindi Rani, an energetic, ambitious and clever widow who was described as 'a thorn in the side of government' (Hutchinson, 1906; Whitehead, 1992).

After Kalindi Rani's death in 1874, the Government of Bengal conferred the personal title of *raja* on the new Chakma chief, Harish Chandra, in order to underline his dependence on 'the pleasure of the paramount authority.' He was given a dress of investiture but no photographs of him survive. The first Chakma chief to be depicted in ceremonial dress was Bhuban Mohan Roy at the time of his investiture in 1897 (**plate 20**). In his brocade tunic, feathered turban and patent leather shoes, leaning lightly on one leg and a ceremonial sword, he presents himself to the camera as a self-assured colonial Indian prince, completely at ease in a late-Victorian photo studio. Later pictures (**plate 21**) show him in similar costume.

***Plate 21***. *Raja Bhuban Mohan. (Chakma Raja collection, about 1911)*

***Plate 22****. Chakma chief Raja Nalinaksha Roy. (Chakma Raja collection, 1937)*

It was Raja Nalinaksha Roy, Bhuban Mohan's son and successor (**plate 22**), however, whose style of dress became the family hallmark. Later his son would describe this photograph as follows:

> 'When [Father] had that photograph taken—with reluctance for he was shy and retiring but was unable to withstand his sisters-in-law's insistence—he was in his early thirties. He was dressed in his full regalia, sword, turban, aigrette on emerald and diamond diadem, gold achkan, diamond and emerald necklace and the gold necklace given by the Rajguru with a *pali mantra* in bold letters. It was in 1937. He had gone to Government House, Calcutta, in durbar dress for his investiture' (T. Roy, n.d.)

Nalinaksha was Chakma chief from 1935 to 1951. He was succeeded by his eldest son Tridiv Roy (**plate 23**) who was deposed by the Bangladesh government in the 1970s after choosing to remain in Pakistan (where he proceeded to become a government minister and ambassador). The Government of Bangladesh, honouring the tradition established with the investiture of Raja Harish Chandra in 1874, then installed his eldest son Devasish Roy as Chakma chief (**plate 24**).

During the British period, the Chakma chiefs presented themselves publicly as Indian princes. They took the South Asian nobleman as their role model, stressed a myth about their North Indian origins, became considerably Hinduised and established marriage links with prominent families of Bengal. For them, to be a raja was to be seen as members of the Bengal aristocracy.

**Plate 23**. *Raja Tridiv Roy, Nalinaksha Roy's son and successor. (Chakma Raja collection, late 1960s)*

**Plate 24**. *Raja Devasish Roy, Tridiv Roy's son and successor. (Chakma Raja collection, 1978)*

The Bohmong and Mong chiefs chose a different style. Their role model was the Burmese nobility, which was hardly surprising in view of the close historical, religious and linguistic links between the Marma and Burma. Moreover, Burma was an integral part of British India, ruled from Calcutta, till the late 1930s.

In a photograph published in 1906, the Bohmong Raja, Cho Hla Prue Chowdhury, is seen dressed all in white at a gathering in Bandarban (**plate 25**).

The fourth Mong chief, Ne Phru Sain, died in 1936 and his niece, Rani Nanoimah Devi, was installed as the fifth Mong chief. Shortly afterwards she posed for a studio portrait (**plate 26**), dressed in a *sari*-like garment.

She was married to a son of the Bohmong chief, Raja Cho HlaPrue Chowdhury. In a photograph of 1926, her husband, Kong Zaw Phru, presents himself to the studio photographer as a dandy, complete with Burmese silk *lungyi*, elegant piped velvet coat, walking stick and polished European shoes (**plate 27**).

***Plate 25****. The Bohmong chief, Raja Cho Hla Prue Chowdhury (dressed all in white and seated to the right of the small child) and retinue in Bandarban. (Hutchinson, 1906)*

***Plate 26****. The Mong chief, Rani Nanoimah Devi. (Mong Raja collection, 1938)*

***Plate 27****. Her husband, Kong Zaw Phru. (Mong Raja collection, 1925)*

**Plate 28** indicates how the three chiefs from the Chittagong Hill Tracts were integrated into the colonial power structure.

This gala picture probably was taken on the occasion of the coronation of King-Emperor George V in 1911. The Chittagong chiefs are seated close to the representative of the 'paramount authority' and his picture-hatted wife, and they are surrounded by other aristocrats and princes of India–all dressed in their most imposing finery.

The Bohmong chief, Cho Hla Prue Chowdhury (in white dress, centre of second row from the front in **plate 29**) sits next to the Chakma chief, Bhuban Mohan Roy (wearing a plumed white turban); the Mong Raja could not be present.

***Plate 28***. *Chittagong chiefs among Indian aristocrats. (Chakma Raja collection, 1911)*

***Plate 29***. Detail of **plate 28**.

**Plate 30** commemorates the visit of the Lieutenant-Governor of Bengal, Sir Lancelot Hare, to the Chittagong Hill Tracts in 1909. On **plate 31** the Bohmong Raja and his entourage are entertaining unidentified British officials in Bandarban, about 1910.

Incorporation into the colonial state also entailed the development of new symbols of political office. Among the symbols of aristocratic position which the Chittagong chiefs adopted was the family crest. **Plate 32** shows the elaborate crest of the Chakma chiefs, introduced at the time of Raja Bhuban Mohan.

***Plate 30****. The chiefs of the Chittagong Hill Tracts receiving Sir Lancelot Hare.*[2]
*(Bohmong Raja collection, 1909)*

**Plate 31**. *Bandarban. (Bohmong Raja collection, about 1910)*

**Plate 32**. *Crest of the Chakma Raja. 'The crest has two rampant elephants with a mounted cannon between them, and a pair of crossed swords. The motto in Sanskrit reads: "Fortune smiles upon the lion-hearted and the diligent"' (T. Roy, n.d.). (Chakma Raja collection)*

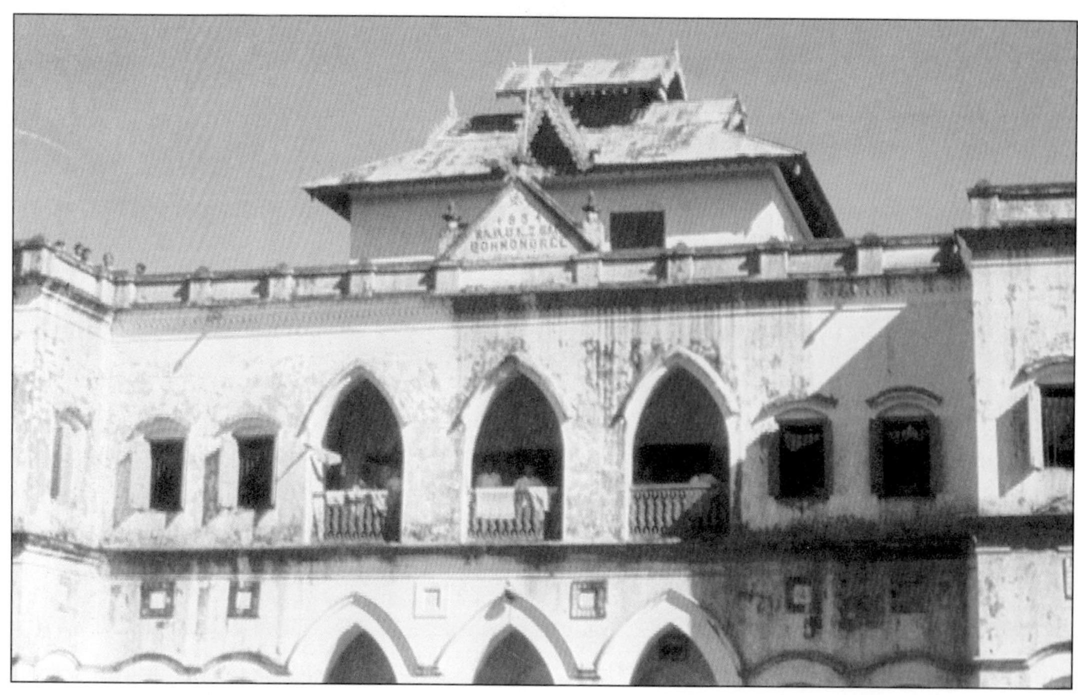

***Plate 33***. *The Bohmong rajbari in Bandarban. (Bientjes, 1962)*

***Plate 34***. *The old Chakma rajbari, built in the first years of the twentieth century, abandoned in 1960. (Chakma Raja collection)*

## Chapter 5

# THE PUBLIC DISPLAY OF POWER

Among the most visible acts of the chiefs was the annual *punya* (auspicious day[1]) or *darbar*, a public ceremony during which the headmen delivered the taxes to their chief. It also was a most important social gathering, with a bazaar, entertainment and religious ceremonies. The darbar became a favourite with photographers in the period after 1947 when this type of political theatre had been abolished in most of South Asia. Darbar photographs, with their romantic emphasis on the splendour of the chief's appearance, his retainers and guards, his ceremonial progress among the people, and the accompanying annual fair, recreate the fairy-tale qualities of this colonial survival.

The darbar was held in a special hall at the chief's mansion (*rajbari*, palace), which was built to impress by its grandeur (**plate 33**: Bohmong rajbari in Bandarban; **plate 34**: Chakma rajbari in Rangamati).

In 1961, the Chakma rajbari had to be abandoned as it became submerged in the newly-created Kaptai reservoir, and a new structure was built (**plate 35**).

***Plate 35**. The new Chakma rajbari. (Bientjes, 1962)*

***Plate 36***. *Raja Kyaw Saw Zen Chowdhury during his darbar at Bandarban. (Bohmong Raja collection, 1950s)*

During the darbar at Bandarban, the Bohmong chief and his retinue would leave the rajbari and proceed ceremoniously to the reception hall. An umbrella was held over the chief's head as a sign of his rank, and sword-bearers accompanied him. The chief and his officials wore tunics and Burmese-style head-dresses (*gaung-baung*) (**Plate 36-38**).

**Plate 37**. *His half-brother Raja Maung Shwe Prue Chowdhury, who succeeded him in 1959, moves through the crowd of spectators. (Taylor, 1964)*

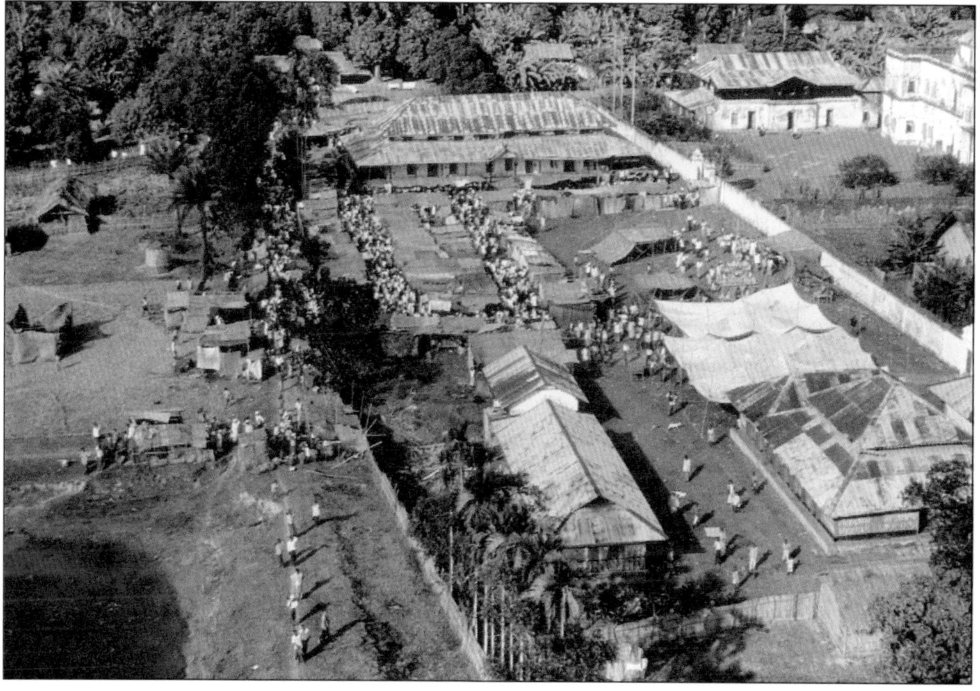

**Plate 38**. *The Bandarban fair during the Bohmong chief's darbar. (Lindsey, 1964)*

The Chakma chief's darbar at Rangamati was the most elaborate, most emphatically regal in style, and most photographed. That day, the chief would emerge from his mansion in full regalia.

> 'The liveried servants with the ankle-length red velvet coats waited on the top stair outside with the open golden umbrella for Father [the Raja] and the black and gold one for me [his heir, Tridiv Roy] ... The procession began with the guards leading the slow march. Father's ADC [aide-de-camp], in red flannel jacket with big brass buttons, black trousers and a black and silver turban marched three paces ahead and to the left of Father. My position was to Father's right, one pace behind, and behind both of us marched our umbrella bearers. After us came the rest of the Raj family, followed by the leading dewans and headmen... Two bands, one from Chittagong and another from Rajanagar [in Chittagong district, formerly the residence of the Chakma chiefs], alternately played in the courtyard in front of the Rajbari. The Hindu Bengali fishermen—the Doms, played their indigenous band consisting chiefly of drums and only one trumpet—like instrument called the shanai...The bands played a medley of film songs and highland music interspersed with the "Drunken Sailor" and other sea shanties ... The ceremonial guards in khaki trousers and jackets, and red and yellow fatigue caps, with martini action shotguns, stood at parade attention' (T. Roy, n.d.).

**Plates 41-43** illustrate this description. They show the ceremony in the late 1960s, when Tridiv Roy had become Chakma chief himself.

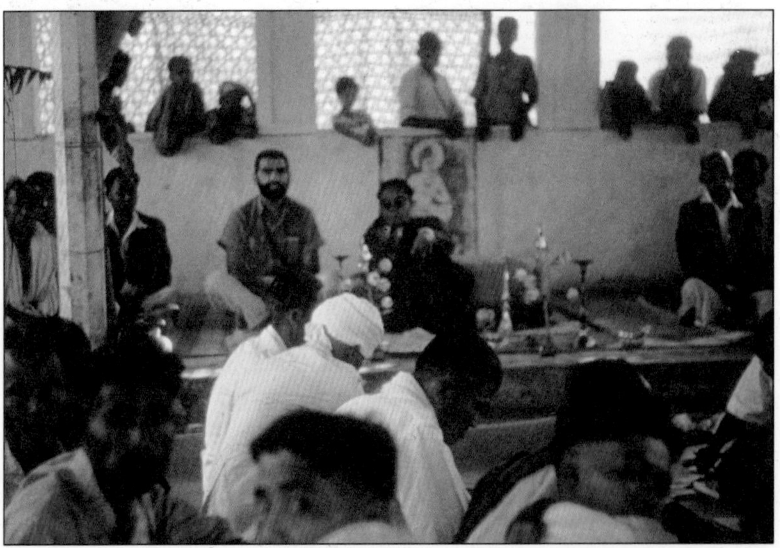

***Plate 39****. The Mong chief, Raja Maung Phru Sain (reclining, in western dress and dark glasses) in the Manikchhari darbar hall in 1961. Next to him is David Sopher, a visiting U.S. geographer. (Sopher, 1961)*

**Plate 40**. *Chakma chief leaving his mansion. (Anderson, 1968-70)*

***Plate 41***. *Ceremonial guards and band from Chittagong. (Anderson, 1968-70)*

***Plate 42***. *The procession. (Anderson, 1968-70)*

***Plate 43***. *The Dom drummers. (Anderson, 1968-70)*

The Rangamati punya would attract large crowds of spectators from villages and towns all over the hills as well as the plains. They came to observe the ceremony but also to participate in the Buddhist religious celebrations and annual country fair that were held at the same time.

The chief would then enter the darbar hall and take his place under a tinsel canopy. He would be surrounded by his dewans and headmen, his attendants and relatives, and a large crowd of visitors.

> 'For the occasion, all the headmen in the Chakma territory, covering half of the Chittagong Hill Tracts, assembled at their Raja's house... They, along with their entourage, were put up at the guest houses, temporary camps and some in the Rajbari itself... It was a national festival of the Chakmas and they converged from far and near. The harvest was in, and everyone was happy and in the mood for merry making at the festival, to wash away a year's troubles and sorrows. It was also an expression of national pride. During the festival there would be scuffles between the Chakma boys and Bengali boys when the Chakmas would take small revenge for the insults and humiliations they had suffered during the course of the year at government offices and bazaars' (T. Roy, n.d.)

The chief dressed in the style adopted during the colonial period (**plate 45**). Headmen would come up to their chief one by one, ceremonially present their swords to him in obeisance and offer him part of the annual tax (**plate 46**; cf. T. Roy, n.d.).

***Plate 44***. *Chakma chief Tridiv Roy in the darbar hall. (Skirrow, 1964)*

Important among the chief's retinue was his family, the male members of which dressed in festive tunics and turbans (**plate 47**). The umbrella bearers, seated behind their master, wore uniforms with the Chakma crest (**plate 48**). To the chief's right a dais was reserved for Buddhist monks. They had no connection with tax collection but they were of great symbolic importance as legitimisers of the chief's worldly power (**plate 49**).

***Plate 45***. *The Chakma chief with his brother. (Anderson, 1968-70)*

***Plate 46***. *Headman offering his sword to the Chakma chief. (Anderson, 1968-70)*

***Plate 47***. *Family members watching the darbar proceedings. (Anderson, 1968-70)*

***Plate 48***. *Umbrella bearers. (Anderson, 1968-70)*

***Plate 49***. *Buddhist monks attending the darbar. (Anderson, 1968-70)*

*Chapter 6*

# THE COLONIAL OVERLORDS

Despite the chiefs' public display of power, their jurisdiction was quite restricted. Large areas of the Chittagong hills were administered directly by the colonial Forest Department and the chiefs had no say over them. But even in their own administrative circles, various state functions were beyond their power.

*Defence* was one of them—for several decades after 1860 the eastern border of the Chittagong Hill Tracts remained turbulent, and it took several military expeditions to the Lushai Hills (now Mizoram, India) before British rule was established there. During this time the eastern border of the Chittagong Hill Tracts was also the eastern border of British India, and troops were stationed in several places in the district. Photographs and engravings of these troops, made in 1882, convey images of discipline, dedication and determination.

The British found their advance eastward blocked by the military power of the Lushai chiefs living in what is now Mizoram (India). Lushai would raid the Chittagong hills as well as the plains of Chittagong. It took several 'punitive expeditions' between 1849 and 1896 before the British broke the military power of the Lushai and controlled the Lushai hills. Till the early 1890s there was a real fear of Lushai invasions of the Chittagong Hill Tracts and military posts were maintained along the eastern border. That discipline was upheld even in the farthest-flung outposts of empire was demonstrated ostensibly by these posed pictures of a double row of Gurkha border

***Plate 50.*** *'A sergeant of the border troops... armed with a Snider gun and the dreaded national weapon of the Gurkhas of Nepal, the kukri [curved knife]... On his breast he wears a decoration of the Lushai expedition.' (Riebeck, 1885)*

***Plate 51**. 'Major Pughe heading a group of border soldiers in Rangamati. The men—Gurkhas from Nepal, Manipuris and Assamese—wear white drill summer uniforms.' (Riebeck, 1885)*

***Plate 52**. 'Group of non-commissioned officers of the border corps at Rangamati, in the usual black uniforms.' (Riebeck, 1885)*

troops pointing their guns eastward (**plate 53**), men standing to attention outside the small border post at Sirte Tlang overlooking Demagiri (now called Tlabung; **plate 54**), and the orderly scene inside that border post (**plate 55**).

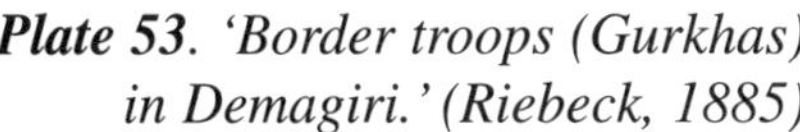

***Plate 53***. *'Border troops (Gurkhas) in Demagiri.' (Riebeck, 1885)*

***Plate 54***. *'Border post at Sirtay.' (Riebeck, 1885)*

***Plate 55***. *'Inside the border post at Sirtay.' (Riebeck, 1885)*

The state's monopoly of violence was, however, less absolute than in the Bengal plains where the peasantry was thoroughly disarmed: many villagers in the hills retained arms, e.g. these 'Kukis with guns,' a photograph published in 1906 (**plate 56**).

***Plate 56***. *'Kukis with guns.' (Hutchinson, 1906)*

***Plate 57****. Water colour by T.H. Lewin, Superintendent of the Chittagong Hill Tracts. 'The Superintendent's bungalow, provided rent-free by Government, ... was small, containing only a sitting-room and a bed-room, with bath and store-room; the situation was beautiful, and it was my delight to sit and work at a table in the verandah with all this new and lovely scenery spread out before me.' (Lewin, 1912, 186). (Lewin collection, 1867)*

The chiefs' power was also circumscribed by the fact that they were under the control of the *bureaucracy*. From the 1860s onwards, British officials with considerable powers resided in the district. They oversaw the chiefs' doings and formed the vanguard of an extensive and expanding state bureaucracy with which the chiefs and the other inhabitants of the Chittagong hills had to come to terms. For example, British officials collected rent from plough cultivators; the chiefs were only allowed to collect tax from people practising *jhum* (shifting cultivation) in their circle. This was a major reason why the chiefs were opposed to an expansion of plough cultivation in the hills. At first the district headquarters were at Chandraghona (**plate 57**) but they were soon transferred to Rangamati (**plate 58**).

***Plate 58****. Water colour by T.H. Lewin. (Lewin collection, about 1872)*

This is how the Commissioner of Chittagong described relations between the hill chiefs and Europeans in the 1870s:

> 'Rangamati is...a small place on a plateau surrounded on three sides by the river, about 300 feet above the water, chosen by us on account of its impregnability. It consists of a small native bazar, the lines and parade ground of the Regiment, and some six or seven roomy bungalows on piles, with walls of mats and thatched roofs. Major Gordon and Mr Crouch met me at the landing-place in full uniform. The Regiment presented arms, and from a cliff over our heads a salute of eleven guns was fired. It seems I was *ex officio* Agent to the Viceroy for the Eastern Frontier and so entitled to a salute...The next day the Mong, the Bohmong, and the Chakma Raja with a large concourse of followers arrived to pay their respects to the Mong Gri (= Great Chief, i.e. Commissioner) ... the whole multitude came up before me one by one and saluted by going down on all fours and touching the ground with their foreheads' (Beames, 1984, 280-281).

The early administrators lived in huts built in the local style by local people. In 1872 T.H. Lewin indicated his wish to stay at Sirte Tlang, above Demagiri, to Lushai chief Rutton Poia and:

> 'the men of his tribe had speedily constructed there a rough but comfortable house, in Lushai style...[it] was made of rough unhewn logs, plastered outside with mud, and the walls inside covered with bamboo matting, very comfortable in its way, but decidedly savage' (Lewin, 1912, 306) (**plate 59**).

By the early 1880s, however, government bungalows were sizeable structures of bamboo and wood (**plates 60** and **61**).

***Plate 59***. *Water colour by T.H. Lewin, 1872. (Lewin collection)*

***Plate 60***. *'Bungalow of Deputy Commissioner Forbes in Rangamati.' (Riebeck, 1885)*

***Plate 61**. 'Group of Lushai men and women before the government bungalow in Demagiri. They had gathered there to get rice from the British government. Most of the women are sitting on the ground behind their big baskets, with their pipes in their mouths ... On the verandah are the Bengali servants of the government bungalow,' photographed in 1882. The Lushai hills had been struck by one of their rare 'bamboo famines.' With intervals of 45 to 60 years, large numbers of* muli *bamboo would come into flower at the same time, leading to a population boom among bamboo rats which, after consuming the bamboo, would polish off the field crops, leaving the human population without food. 'Millions of voracious rats had descended on their paddy fields, obliterated the harvest, and forced them to seek refuge in British territory where they were given basic food.' (Riebeck, 1885)*

By 1910, the district headquarters, Rangamati, was still no more than an overgrown village attracting few visitors. A rare photograph of that period shows that by this time government officials lived in brick bungalows (**plate 62**).

***Plate 62**. Rangamati, about 1910. (Baptist Missionary Society)*

The fact that these officials ruled in the name of the British monarch was symbolised in various ways, e.g. by celebrating the Silver Jubilee of King George V in 1935. As part of the festivities a boat race was organised on the Karnaphuli river at Rangamati (**plate 63**).

***Plate 63**. 'Boat race at Rangamati, 1935.' (Christie, 1983)*

High colonial officials rarely visited the Chittagong Hill Tracts but in 1935 the Governor of Bengal, Sir John Anderson, decided to make a ten-day tour,

> 'with his complete staff and their wives, his sister and his daughter and a retinue of about a hundred persons. It was a great honour,' wrote John Christie, the Deputy Commissioner, 'but also a severe strain on the resources of a poor district and an unusual load of responsibility on its multi-purpose Deputy Commissioner. I had a nightmare about this visit, that I should somehow be late for the Governor's arrival in my district. It was one of those terrible nightmares that come true...The Governor had decided, without warning us, to leave Chittagong earlier than had been planned. No doubt security had something to do with it, for terrorism was still a hazard in Bengal, and Sir John Anderson had already been a target... I sometimes have that nightmare still.'

Christie had been ordered to provide essential supplies and had prepared as best he could; but the visitors consumed the 300 eggs he had collected within a day.

> 'It was then that the Chittagong Hill Tracts Armed Police had to go into action. I sent them into the villages with orders to produce one thousand eggs by nightfall, which they did. I did not conceal from His Excellency the act of extortion (although the eggs were supposed to be paid for) which his rapacious staff had made necessary, and H.E. replied, with a very straight face, "Very well, we must ration ourselves for eggs from now on"' (**plate 64**).

***Plate 64***. *'Darbar at Rangamati, 1935, Sir John Anderson's visit.' (Christie, 1983)*

Apart from this, the district authorities had prepared the excursion well.

> 'We built four separate camps of bamboo huts, complete with banqueting halls and decorated archways. The party moved between them in a triumphal progress, on elephant-back and on foot ... [The last of the twelve elephants] had the menial task of carrying from camp to camp, exposed to public view, two of those useful pieces of domestic furniture known as thunder-boxes. They were reserved for the use of the Governor and his sister; the rest of us had to make do with holes in the ground' (Christie, 1983, 53-54) (**plate 65**).

***Plate 65**. The Governor's elephants in front of Chandraghona hospital. (Bottoms/Maslen collection, 1935)*

The elephants which carried the Governor's party around the Chittagong Hill Tracts were regularly employed by the *Forest Department*. After colonial annexation, jurisdiction over large parts of the Chittagong Hill Tracts had been taken away from the chiefs and given to this government department. In the 1870s, an observer reported:

> 'The tangled maze of hills in which they [the Marma] live is densely wooded and contains a great deal of valuable timber. It had been placed under the charge of the Forest Department. A department of any kind in India always assumes that the world exists solely for the use of itself, and considers that anything that interferes with the working of the department ought to be removed... Dr Schlich, the Head of the Forest Department, calmly proposed that the whole Mugh and Chakma population should be removed from their native hills! He did not say where they were to go to. He merely said, in the true departmental spirit, "These people destroy the trees, therefore let them be sent away." Of course, the district officers and the Commissioner strongly opposed this view. The Commissioner (my predecessor, not me) even went so far as to say that if trees and Mughs could not live together, he thought it would do less harm if the trees were removed, which caused Dr Schlich to foam at the mouth and utter bad words' (Beames, 1984, 282) (**plate 66**).

***Plate 66***. *Forest Department elephants. (Starke, 1960)*

***Plate 67***. *Memorial to T.H. Lewin. (Lewin collection; cf. MacDonald, 1988)*

Although many British administrators passed through the Chittagong Hill Tracts in the course of almost 90 years of colonial rule, not many left a lasting impression. An exception was Thomas Herbert Lewin (1839-1916), who was not only the first Deputy Commissioner of the district (as well as administrator of the Lushai hills), but also a man of action, soldier, linguist, writer, artist and musician. In 1921, shortly after his death, a memorial stone was erected in his honour at Demagiri (now Tlabung). A fragment of the inscription read:

> 'The people knew him as Thangliena, Tom Lewin, & honoured him as a chief. They called him the Lushais first white friend. They built a house for him voluntarily in token of his devotion. Their children now have voluntarily brought stones here .. to the memory of Thangliena' (**plates 67** and **68**).

IN MEMORY OF
LT COLONEL TOM HERBERT LEWIN. B.S.C.
ONCE SUPERINTENDENT OF THESE HILL TRACTS
BORN 1839. DIED 1916.
HE CAME TO THIS PEOPLE IN 1865.& WORKED AMONG THEM & FOR THEM FOR NINE YEARS.WHEN LOSS OF HEALTH COMPELLED HIM TO RETURN TO ENGLAND.
THE PEOPLE TRUSTED & LOVED HIM FOR HIS SYMPATHY & SENSE OF JUSTICE.FOR HIS UNTIRING INTEREST IN THEIR WELFARE & FOR HIS INTREPID & DAUNTLESS COURAGE.
HE TRAVELLED IN THEIR UNKNOWN LAND,VISITING THEIR CHIEFS THEIR VILLAGES & THEIR HOMES,ALONE & UNAFRAID.
HE WAS THE FIRST TO INTERPRET & WRITE DOWN THEIR LANGUAGE,PREPARING THE WAY FOR SCHOOLS & PROGRESS.
HE STUDIED & IMPROVED THEIR AGRICULTURE & THEIR LAWS & HELPED THEM IN ALL THEIR DIFFICULTIES.
THE PEOPLE KNEW HIM AS THANGLIENA. TOM LEWIN. & HONOURED HIM AS A CHIEF.
THEY CALLED HIM THE LUSHAIS FIRST WHITE FRIEND.
THEY BUILT A HOUSE FOR HIM VOLUNTARY IN TOKEN OF THEIR DEVOTION.
THEIR CHILDREN NOW HAVE VOLUNTARILY BROUGHT STONES HERE,NEAR WHERE HIS HOUSE ONCE STOOD & HAVE HELPED THE ONE WHO KNEW HIM BEST OF ALL & WHO KNEW HOW HIS HEART WAS EVER WITH THIS PEOPLE TO BUILD UP THE STONES TO THE MEMORY OF
THANGLIENA.


***Plate 68****. Text on the Lewin memorial.*
*(Lewin collection; cf. Whitehead, 1992, viii)*

***Plate 69**. 'Children's Songs and Waving Flags Greet East Pakistan's First Lady ... Blue-shirted tribesman in center makes a gesture of respect.' (Shor and Shor, 1955)*

***Plate 70**. 'The installation of the new chief of the Chakma tribe which took place on March 2, 1953.' The installation of Raja Tridiv Roy took place in Rangamati. (Bernot, 1953)*

## Chapter 7

# PAKISTAN AND THE CHIEFS

In 1947 British rule came to an end. British India was partitioned to form two new states, India and Pakistan. The Chittagong Hill Tracts were awarded to Pakistan, which was remarkable in view of the rationale for Pakistan: to provide a homeland for South Asia's Muslims. Muslim-majority areas of British India were to be awarded to Pakistan and other areas to India. The population of the Chittagong hills, with fewer than two percent Muslims, were astounded to find themselves included in Pakistan.

The state of Pakistan retained the Chittagong Hill Tracts Regulation of 1900, which had underpinned the district's unusual administrative status during the colonial period, and with it the ceremonial role of the chiefs and their subordinates.[1] Symbols of Pakistan began to appear: **plate 69** shows villagers at Baradam waving Pakistani flags and expressing their allegiance to the Provincial Governor's wife, Lady Noon.

The chiefs and headmen of the Chittagong hills were smoothly integrated into the new state structure, and this was striking in view of the simultaneous abolition of the rights of *zamindars* (landlords/tax-collectors in the Bengal plains) who were seen as colonial feudal grandees. The same democratic sentiment fuelled a movement among the hill people which sought to abolish the hereditary offices of chief, *talukdar*, *dewan*, and so on. It did not succeed in winning the support of the state; some of its protagonists even saw themselves forced into exile in India (Chakma, 1985-86).

The postcolonial state publicly gave its stamp of approval to the chiefs and their colonial office when it installed a successor to a deceased incumbent. In the 1950s this happened in both the Chakma and the Bohmong circles (**plates 70** and **71**).

One consequence of the reaffirmation of the chiefs' position by the state of Pakistan was that the hierarchy of office holders on which the chiefs depended was also retained. This meant that people in the Chittagong Hill Tracts lived under systems of taxation, local authority and political control which differed sharply from those in other parts of East Pakistan (**plates 72-74**).

***Plate 71****. The new Bohmong chief, Maung Shwe Prue Chowdhury, was installed by the Commissioner of the Chittagong Division, Mr Taraf Ali (standing), in Bandarban in 1959. (Bohmong Raja collection)*

***Plate 72**. Shortly after his inauguration, the new Bohmong chief, Maung Shwe Prue Chowdhury, posed with his office staff in Bandarban. (Bohmong Raja collection, 1960)*

***Plate 73***. *Inauguration ceremony of a young Marma village headman during the Pakistan period. (Löffler, 1956)*

***Plate 74***. *During a Rangamati darbar in the 1960s, headmen were waiting to hand over collected taxes to the Chakma chief. (Anderson, 1968-70)*

**Plate 75**. *'President Ayub with the three tribal chiefs of the Chittagong Hill Tracts at the foundation-stone laying ceremony of the new town of Rangamati, District Headquarters of the area.' (Rajput, 1965)*

The position of the Chittagong chiefs in the state of Pakistan was symbolised by their assisting the President of Pakistan, Ayub Khan, in laying the foundation stone of the new town of Rangamati (**plate 75**).

However, the pomp and circumstance had to cover up a great deal of bitterness and anger. A new town had to be built because the old town was being inundated in the name of development. The Pakistan government had decided to go ahead with the Kaptai hydroelectric project which created a large lake. Neither the chiefs nor the population of the Chittagong hills were asked for their opinion about this intervention in their lives. The political realities behind the ceremony were such that the Chakma chief was not even able to save his own house, let alone his town, from the effects of 'development.' The rajbari was left to crumble in the rising waters of the Kaptai reservoir (**plates 76** and **77**).

***Plate 76***. *Chakma rajbari, Rangamati. (Sopher, 1961)*

***Plate 77***. *Chakma rajbari, Rangamati. (Smith, 1962)*

That the political sands were shifting could also be deduced from the prominence of Pakistani officials at the darbars (**plates 78** and **79**), and the following incident at the reception in honour of Queen Elizabeth II of Britain at the Chittagong Circuit house:

> 'We [the Chakma, Bohmong and Mong chiefs] were to be the first to be presented to Her Majesty as she entered the pandal. The Deputy Commissioner was placed after the three Chiefs. Just as the Queen arrived, this gentleman, a Mr. Chowdhury, hopped out of his place and stood to my right. I saw the other Chiefs exchange a swift glance' (T. Roy, n.d.) (**plate 80**).

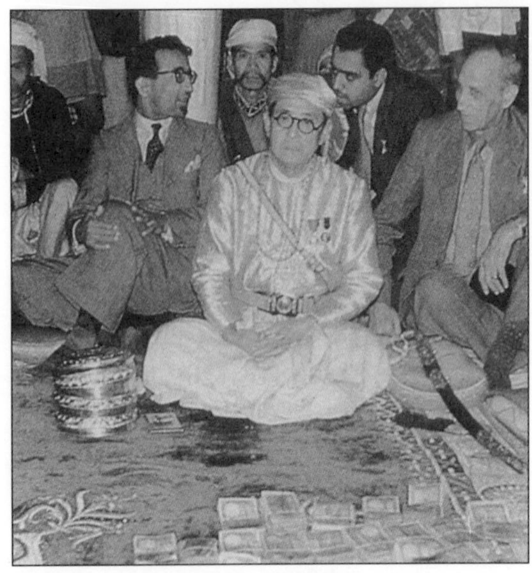

***Plate 78***. *Bohmong chief and officials. (Kauffmann, 1955)*

***Plate 79***. *Chakma chief and officials. (Sigl, 1960s)*

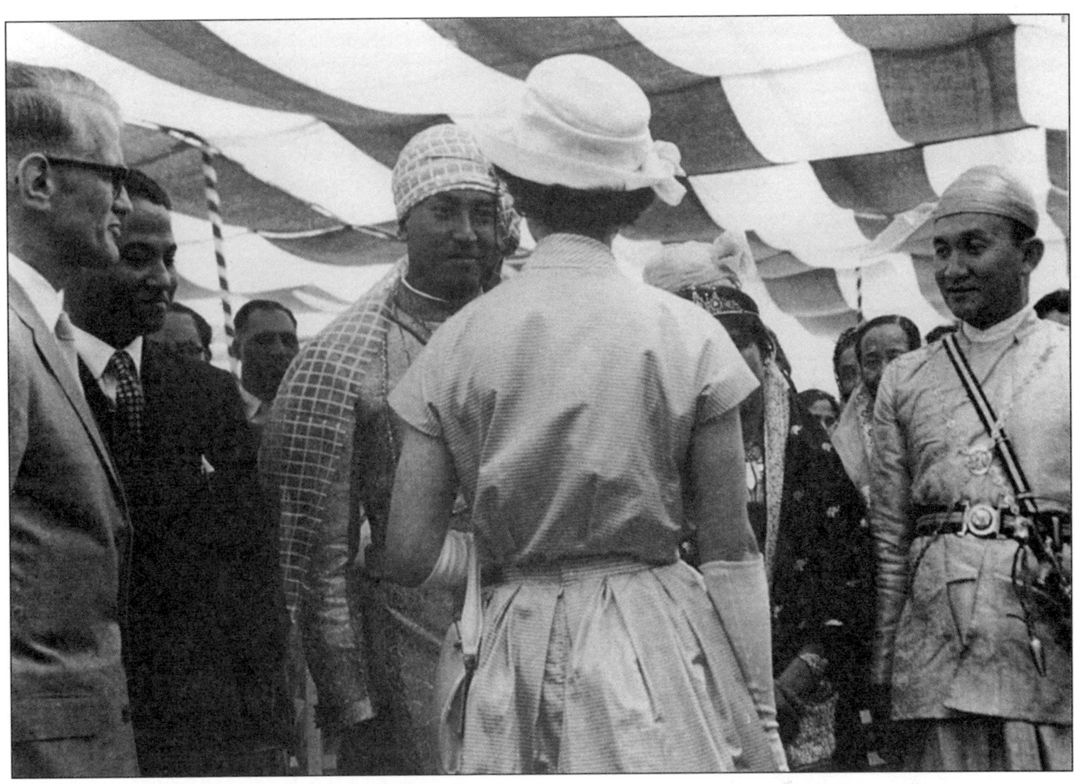

***Plate 80***. *The chiefs being presented to Queen Elizabeth. (Meier, 1961)*

The chiefs were particularly worried about discrimination against hill people in the administration:

> 'Ninety percent of government functionaries posted to the Chittagong Hill Tracts were Bengalis who, barring notable exceptions, apart from lining their own pockets, set about the Bengalisation of the Tracts. In the recruitment to Class I and II services, not even 5% was taken from amongst the hill people although there were qualified candidates. Even in Class III and IV jobs plainsmen were given preference' (T. Roy, n.d.).

The changing political climate induced the chiefs to search for a more 'modern' political role. Changing their appearance once again and donning business suits, they sought elected office in Pakistan and preferred to present themselves as modern administrators even in their role as local hosts. The Mong chief would dress in business suit for formal state occasions, and the Chakma chief also often was seen in Western dress (**plates 81** and **82**).

The same change could be observed in the Bohmong chief who, during the 1960s, held several ministerial posts in the East Pakistan Cabinet. In four photographs published in the Bengali magazine Pak-Somachar in 1965, he is seen taking the oath at Government House in Dhaka, delivering a speech to electors ('Basic Democrats') at Rangamati, praying with other Buddhists for Pakistani victory in the 1965 war with India, and, together with Cabinet colleagues, donating a cheque to the War Fund. A photograph of 1968 captures him being presented to the Chinese prime minister at Dhaka airport (**plates 83-87**).

***Plate 81***. *The Chakma chief, showing Gen. Azam Khan (Pakistan's Secretary for Rehabilitation) around a Chakma village, mirrored his guest's dress. (Pakistani Khobor, 1959)*

***Plate 82***. *When Governor Abdul Monem Khan came to Rangamati to distribute clothes to the poor, the Chakma chief dressed in a smart Western-style suit. (Pak-Somachar, 1967)*

***Plate 83***. *'At Government House, the Hon. Abdul Monem Khan is seen leading the oath-taking ceremony for new Ministers. Abdul Hai Chowdhury and Mr. Maung Shwe Prue Chowdhury are seen taking the oath.' (Pak-Somachar, 1965)*

***Plate 84****. 'The Provincial Minister for Health and Social Welfare, Mr. Maung Shwe Prue Chowdhury, giving a talk to Basic Democrats in Rangamati.' (Pak-Somachar, 1965)*

***Plate 85****. 'At the initiative of the Association for the Propagation and Development of Buddhism, a special prayer was held...at Kamlapur Buddhist temple against the Indian attack and in favour of Pakistani victory. The Provincial Minister for Health, Labour and Social Welfare, Mr. Maung Shwe Prue Chowdhury, also participated in the prayer.' (Pak-Somachar, 1965)*

***Plate 86**. 'The members of the Provincial Cabinet donating a cheque worth one month's salary for the War Fund to Governor Monem Khan.' (Pak-Somachar, 1965)*

***Plate 87**. East Pakistan Governor Monem Khan presenting Minister Maung Shwe Prue Chowdhury to Chinese Prime Minister Liu Shaoqi at Dhaka airport. (Bohmong Raja collection, 1968)*

***Plate 88***. *Mru man in jungle. (Brauns, 1970)*

*Chapter 8*

# INNOCENCE AND CHARM

Almost all Westerners who visited the Chittagong hills were touched by the gentleness of the local people. They often thought of these people as living in a direct and harmonious relationship with nature—unlike Westerners who had lost their touch. One of them, C.D. Brauns, repeatedly visited the hills with the explicit purpose of meeting 'man living in peace with nature,' and his evocative photographs reflect this perspective.

Many photographs and writings on the Chittagong Hill Tracts project a vision of innocence and charm. They make a sharp distinction between the photographer ('civilised' but alienated from nature) and the photographed (still in tune with the rhythms of nature and the flow of life). Nostalgia and romanticism are core elements of this dominant view of life in the hills.

## 8.1 A Rustic Paradise

The people of the Chittagong hills were often likened to children living happily and playfully in a benevolent jungle environment. The long-standing use of the Marma terms *toungtha* ('children of the hill,' for the groups living on the ridges of the hills) and *kyoungtha* ('children of the river,' for the groups living in the valleys) supported this notion. These terms were persistently employed by writers in English and eventually found their way into the official literature on the Chittagong hills (e.g. Ishaq ed., 1971, 44).

Life in the jungle was seen as easy and relaxed. People were surrounded by the sounds of the jungle and the sunrays playing on leaves and grass (**plate 88**).

Work—a few laborious days in the swidden fields perhaps, or spinning and weaving at home—was seen as really more a pastime in spectacularly beautiful surroundings, a brief interruption of the quiet flow of time, than a burden. Productive activities were also more than just labour; they carried the connotation of contemplation, being part of the web of natural relations (**plate 89**). In the words of T.H. Lewin:

> 'Although the clearing of a patch of dense jungle is no doubt a very severe labour, yet the surroundings of the labourer render his work pleasurable...the hillman works in the shade of the jungle that he is cutting; he is on a lofty eminence, where every breeze reaches and refreshes him; his spirits are enlivened and his labour lightened by the beautiful prospect stretching out before him; while the rich and varied scenery of the forest stirs his mind above a monotone. He is surrounded by his comrades; the scent of the wild thyme and the buzzing of the forest bee are about him; the young men and maidens sing to their work, and the laugh and joke goes round as they sit down to their mid-day meal under the shade of some great mossy forest tree...and it is not to be wondered that the hill people have a passion for their mode of life' (Lewin, 1869, 11).

Nature was seen as bountiful, providing the material for musical instruments, things to play with and beautiful flowers to

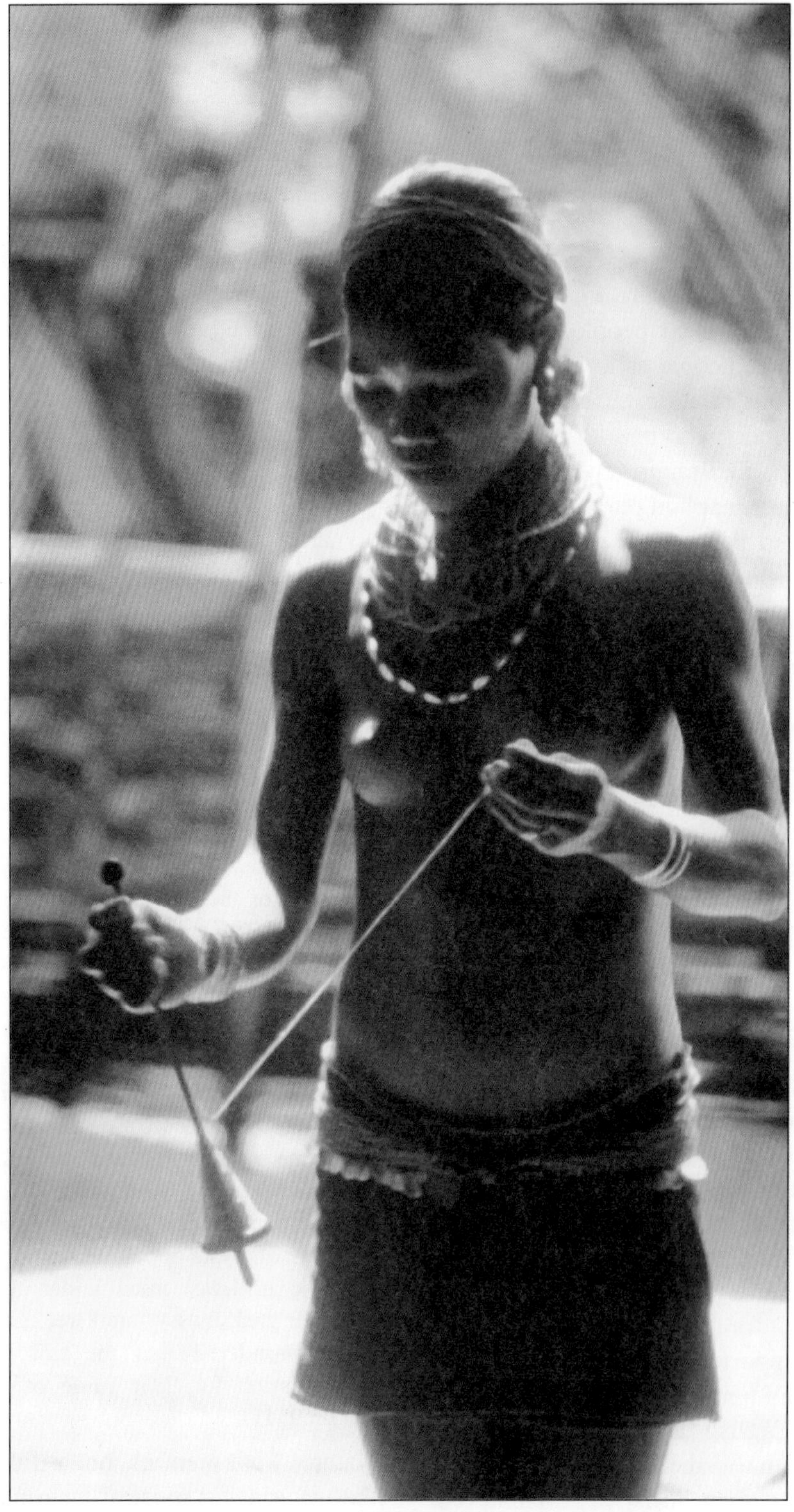

***Plate 89**. Woman spinning cotton. (Brauns, 1970)*

embellish life (**plates 90** and **91**). The hill people's wishes and desires were thought to be few: a loin cloth, a knife and a gun sufficed to make them masters of their jungle world. (**plates 92** and **93**). As the anthropologist H.E. Kauffmann noticed:

> 'How modestly and simply do these people spend their days. Secluded from the world and in deepest peace they let life stream by. Not driven by haste or impatience, nor rushed by sensations, they pass their time with occupations that afford them the bare necessities of existence' (Kauffmann, February 4, 1956).

Hill people were pictured as open, yet shy and philosophical (**plate 94**)—and never alone, always embraced by the care and affection of parents, relatives and the wider community (**plate 95**). This vision of a simple, innocent and happy jungle life far removed from ordinary worries survived for decades; it remains a dominant motif in written and visual representations of the Chittagong hills.

***Plate 90***. *A Mru boy, Chimbuk. (Taylor, 1968)*

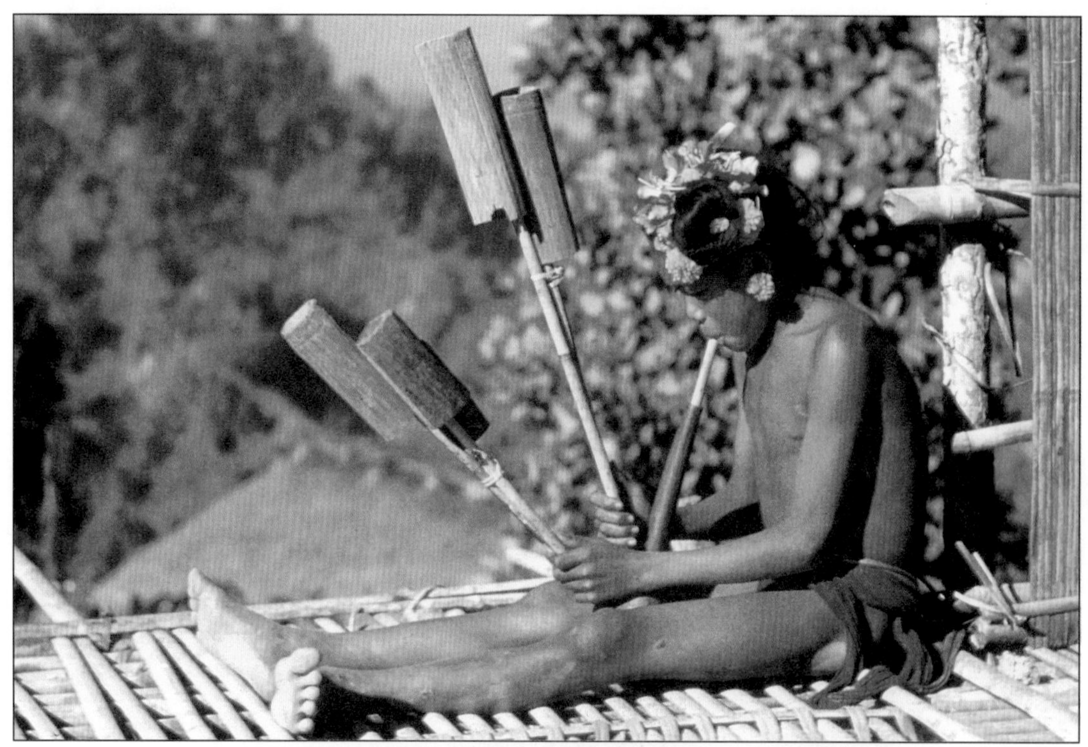

***Plate 91**. Mru boy with mouth organ. (Brauns, 1969)*

***Plates 92** and **93**. Mru with knife and gun. (Seifert, 1963)*

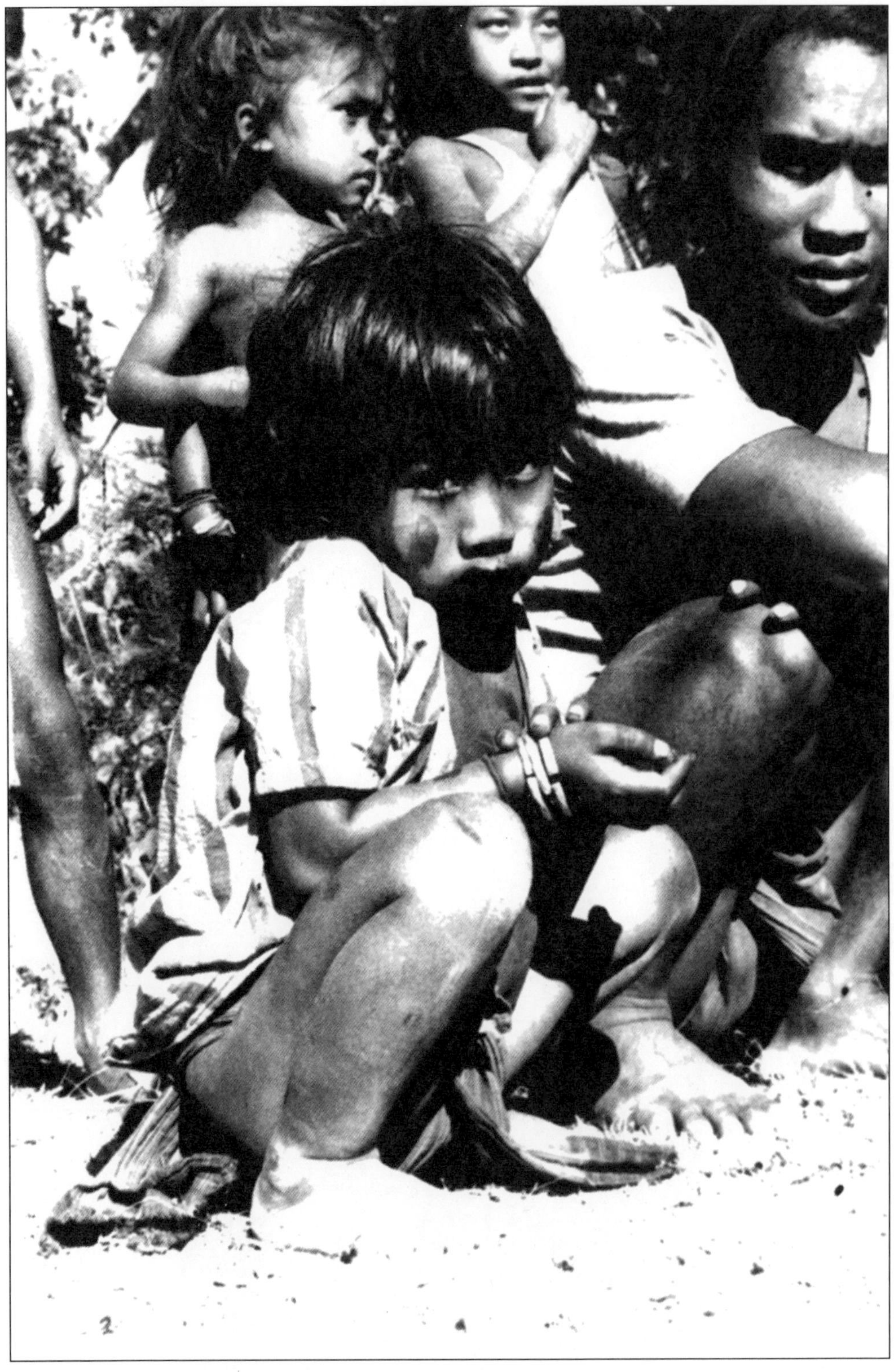

***Plate 94***. *Shy Mru child. (Seifert, 1963)*

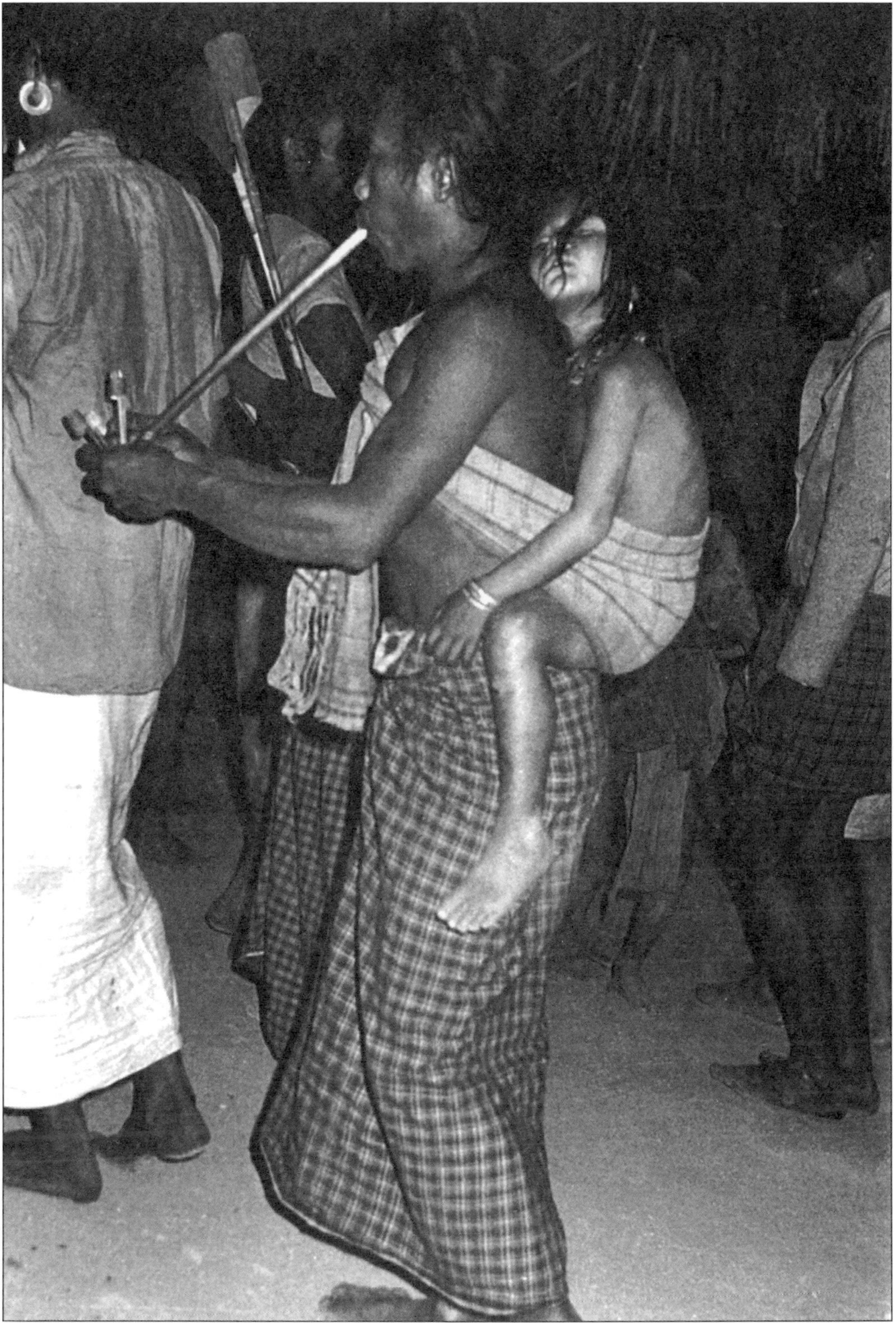

***Plate 95**. Father and daughter dancing. (Seifert, 1963)*

## 8.2 The Lure of the Simple Life

T.H. Lewin was the first to point to the attractions of this life of happy innocence. In a letter to his Aunt Harriet, written from Chandraghona in 1867, he spoke of the:

> 'blue hills, the deep dark valleys, the lights and shades of the brilliant sun on the gorgeous tints and varying outlines of the forest scenery ... [the] people here are to my taste—Ah heavens if you knew the delightful change it was to me ... to find myself among a race whose normal condition is that of truthfulness and who positively make love as God intended it should be made' (Lewin letters, April 13, 1867).

Having returned from a jungle trip some months later, he wrote to his Aunt Jane that:

> '[For weeks] I had been leading ... the life of the village people ... sleeping on the floor of a bamboo house ... and yet I was content with the simple wild life and found happiness in the unrestrained intercourse I had with the people.' (Lewin letters, July 10, 1867).

This happiness was closely linked to his growing detachment from British ways of life:

> 'The ties which bind me to England grow looser I think--at least as I gain friends (a thing unknown to me before) that I do not long to go home and that I even contemplate with some degree of pleasure the possibility of my passing my life among my Hill people ... and again the faded conventionalism and the stale vices of European life have no charms for me in comparison with the freedom of my Hills and their people. I am now thank God beginning to make entrance into their inner life to break down the generally inseparable barrier which difference of race and colour raises up between us English and our subjects out here ...Now I live as a Hill man...I live as a Hill chief--I go bare foot and there is nothing a Hill man can do--no fatigue which he can endure that I also have not experienced. My text is--I am a man like you--I eat your food--wear your dress and feel as you do ... See here this is the life--We cut our joom--I have cut mine this year, our joom supplies us with cotton for clothes which are woven by the women--with rice and vegetables for our food ... My house is surrounded by some 6 to 8 families of stalwart young men and their wives. They call me Father and are not afraid to let me see and come into contact with their wives and daughters' (Lewin letters, April 25, 1868).

This eagerness to break down the barrier between 'us English and our subjects out here' came across in the images he created. In **plate 96** Lewin presents himself as 'Herbert Tongloyn [=Tom Lewin],' in the manner of an oriental pasha, surrounded by armed men, a loose turban on his head, clad in Burmese-style jacket and sarong, and a gun on his knees.

In **plate 97** we see a barefoot Lewin swearing a solemn oath of friendship with Khumi chiefs Teynwey and Yuong. During this river-side ceremony a young gayal heifer was thrown down and its neck fastened to a stake. One end of the cord by which it was bound was held by Teynwey and his followers, the other by Lewin. Yuong then took a mouthful of liquor from a cup and blew it out in a spray over the sacrifice, another mouthful over Lewin, and a third over Teynwey and his company. After invoking the spirits of the air and the water, and killing the animal, Yuong took some of the warm blood and smeared it on everybody's foreheads and bare feet. As he did so, he invoked the wrath of the spirits on the head of him who should be untrue or unfaithful (Lewin, 1912, 166).

***Plate 96**. 'Herbert Tongloyn & his men'; this was the name T.H. Lewin used during his exploration of the southern Chittagong hills in 1865. (Lewin collection, 1865; cf. Lewin, 1912, 149)*

***Plate 97**. 'The Oath at Teynwey's Village on the Koladyne.' Water colour by T.H. Lewin, 1866.*

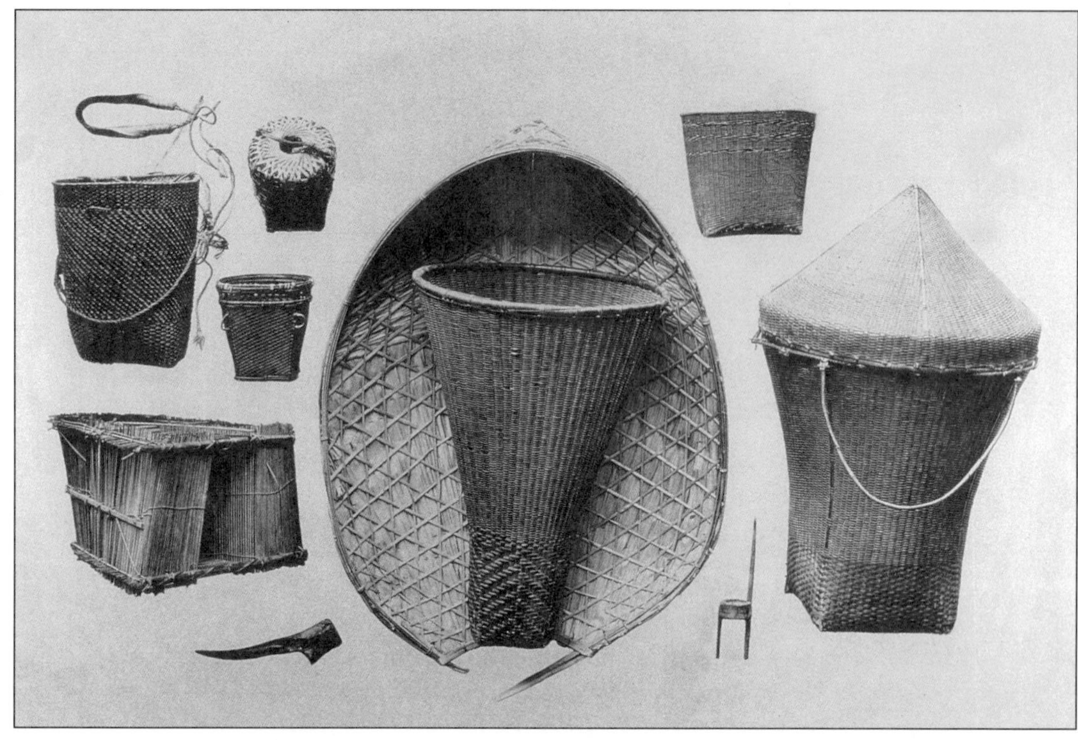

***Plate 98***. *Bamboo baskets and utensils collected in 1882.*[1] *(Riebeck, 1885)*

## 8.3 Bamboo and Flowers

In idyllic descriptions which seem to echo memories of pre-industrial English country life, Lewin expressed the closeness of hill people to nature in terms of bamboo and flowers (**plate 98**).

> 'The bamboo is literally the stuff of life. He builds his house of bamboo; he fertilizes his fields with its ashes; of its stem he makes vessels in which to carry water; with two bits of bamboo he can produce fire; its young and succulent shoots provide a dainty dinner dish; and he weaves his sleeping mat of fine slips thereof. The instruments with which his women weave their cotton are of bamboo. He makes drinking cups of it, and his head at night rests on a bamboo pillow; his forts are built of it; he catches fish, makes baskets and stools, and thatches his house with the help of the bamboo. He smokes from a pipe of bamboo; and from bamboo ashes he obtains potash. Finally, his funeral pyre is lighted with bamboo. The hillman would die without the bamboo, and the thing he finds hardest of credence is, that in other countries the bamboo does not grow' (Lewin, 1869, 9-10).

A century later, bamboo still played a central role in the life of many people in the Chittagong hills (**plates 99** and **100**).

***Plate 99***. *Bamboo house. (Brauns, 1970)*

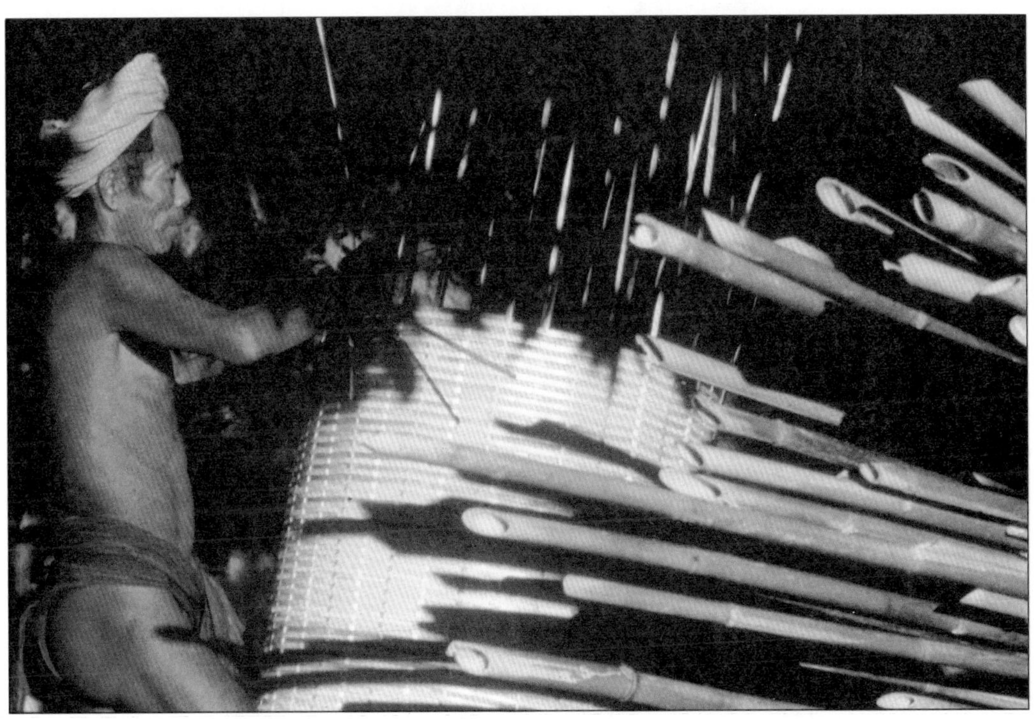

***Plate 100***. *Working bamboo. (Brauns, 1970)*

Outside observers usually felt that in the hills, in stark contrast to the plains, nature served human needs completely and did not demand regular and disciplined labour. Poverty was not a constant threat and there was time to enjoy nature's beauty:

> 'A Magh, if well-to-do, is extremely indolent, and will only do such work he is compelled to. Given a sufficient number of cheroots to smoke, and a comfortable spot on which to recline, he is quite content to laze away the whole day ... He can, however, be trusted not to do a stroke of work more than the necessities of his family life require. The Magh is a happy-go-lucky fellow, easily pleased and of a most independent nature... He is also of a poetical nature and can turn out crisp lines, full of local colour and apt rhyme. He has a child's love for anything bright—especially flowers: and they occupy a very important position in his devotions and love passages' (Hutchinson, 1906, 111-112).

> 'Men and women both among the Khyoungtha are passionately fond of flowers; it is the offering of women to the gods, of men to their mistresses. The young maidens wear constantly in their hair the graceful white or orange-coloured blossom of the numerous orchids with which the forest abounds; and a young man will rise long before dawn to climb the loftiest hills and trees to win his sweetheart's smile by bringing her a flower that others do not possess. The males generally stick a bunch of flowers and sweet-smelling herbs into the turban or through the lobe of the ear' (Lewin, 1869, 46).

Not only natural flowers but also ear-rings ('ear flowers') made of silver were highly valued (**plate 101**).

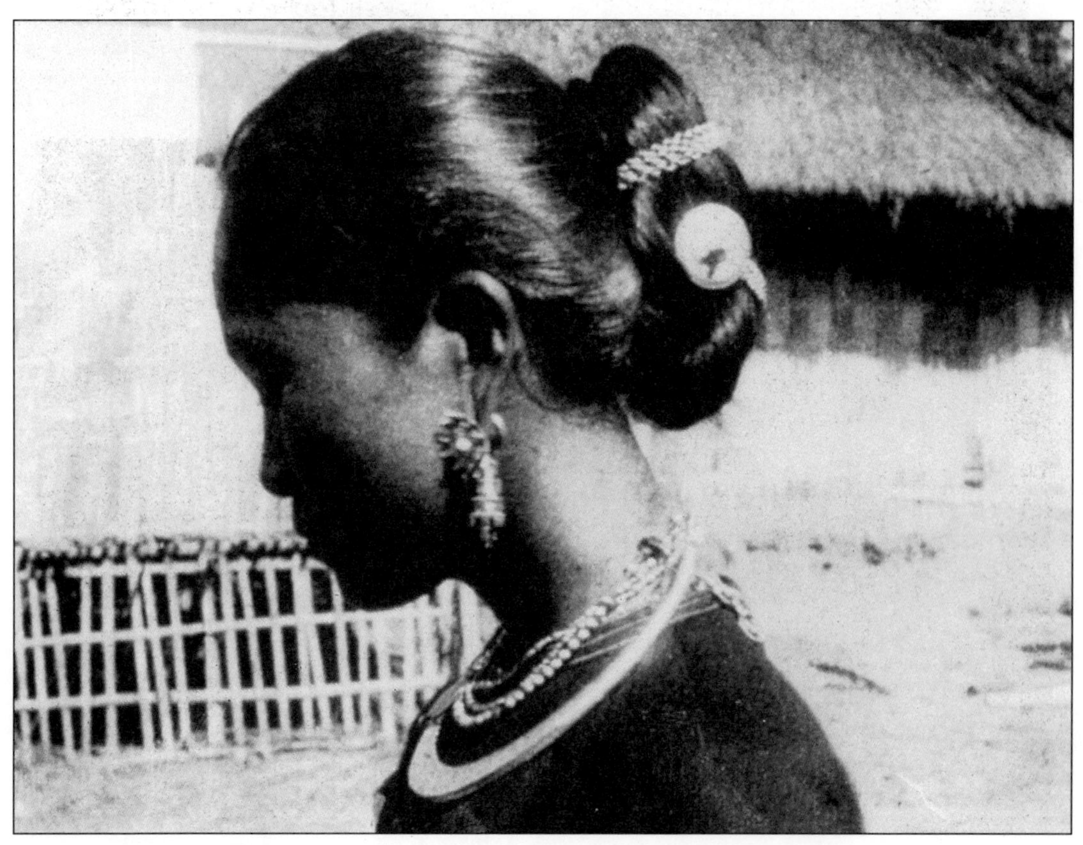

***Plate 101**. Marma woman with silver ear-rings. (Konietzko collection, 1927)*

## 8.4 Dreams of Erotic Licence

It was not only charm and innocence which Westerners detected in the people of the Chittagong Hill Tracts. They also observed customs which they interpreted as sexual wantonness. In line with nineteenth-century European assumptions about the sexual behaviour and morality of 'uncivilised' people, Europeans often projected onto the hill people an unrestrained sexuality that was never there. They reacted variously: rejection, disgust, fascination, admiration and attraction were all there. John Rawlins noted down wild stories circulating about the Lushai [Kukis] in the late eighteenth century. He registered mainly incredulity: 'a man may marry any woman, except his own mother' (Rawlins, 1790, 188). Writing over a century later, Hutchinson struck a more disapproving note:

> 'The Magh girl is a most fascinating little body, possessing generally a very pleasing face [but if] we judge them by our ideas, the standard of morality among them is low. A chaste maiden life is a very rare exception, and no sense of shame or wrong is ever attached to the lives that these young girls live' (Hutchinson, 1906, 113-114).

Lewin, on the other hand, wrote extensively and admiringly about the sexual customs of the hill people:

> 'Great license is allowed before marriage to the youth of both sexes, between whom intercourse is entirely unchecked...According to European ideas, the standard of morality among the Khyoungtha is low. It is not thought a crying sin for a maiden to yield to the solicitations of her lover before marriage; indeed, a girl generally has had two or three sweethearts before settling down to wedded life. The intercourse between the sexes before marriage is almost entirely unrestricted ... This practice, however immoral as we should consider it, produces no ill effect among them, but, on the contrary, acts rather beneficially than otherwise ... marriages in the hills are unions of inclination, and not of interest' (Lewin, 1869, 47, 77).

Remarkable for his time, Lewin advocated broadmindedness rather than censure:

> 'The relations that should exist between the sexes is one of the most important problems of the day, and it is therefore interesting to note the, to us, somewhat strange customs prevailing among these tribes. We cannot condemn them on the score of indecency, for to the pure all things are pure. Our present notions of sexual decorum are highly artificial. The question of more or less clothes is one purely of custom and climate ... If it were the custom for the legs of horses and dogs to be clothed, it would assuredly in a short time be stigmatized as gross indecency were they to appear in the streets without trousers ... [Under enlightened guidance] let the people by slow degrees civilize themselves. With education open to them, and yet moving under their own laws and customs, they will turn out, not debased and miniature epitomes of Englishmen, but a new and noble type of God's creatures' (Lewin, 1869, 117-118).

## 8.5 Power, Sexual Exploitation and Shame

Colonial and postcolonial rule was, however, far from innocent regarding relations between the sexes. The erotic universe was highly gendered, and ideas about the 'looseness' of morality in the hills were easily translated into male behaviour which targeted hill women. Kauffmann quoted in his diary an Excise Officer in Ruma who reminisced about the colonial period:

> 'It used to be a great time for the Masters. Whenever a civil servant travelled, he would summon the *karbari* [leader] of a village and order, apart from food, a girl for himself and each of his retinue. Contradiction was out of the question, this was simply the way things were done' (Kauffmann, January 12, 1956).

But times changed and resistance to such institutionalised rape grew:

> 'In recent years, however, when Aung Shwe Prue was S.I. [Sub-Inspector of Police], he and other members of the Bohmong family went around and told the Magh [Marma]: "Be proud, you are as worthy as they are, don't be compliant, don't give them chickens, don't give them eggs or *modh* [rice spirit], and, above all, don't give them your wives and daughters"' (Kauffmann, January 12, 1956).

During the Second World War the Japanese conquered Arakan, and allied forces prepared to counter them in the Chittagong hills:

> 'Especially the American soldiers were said everywhere to have gone ruthlessly for the female section of society, and this induced the natives to hide their womenfolk. The Bohmong chief coldly refused a high-ranking British officer's demand to supply women to his forces, saying: "Perhaps elsewhere, but not in my country"' (Kauffmann, December 26, 1955).

Nevertheless, the sexual exploitation of hill women continued. In the late 1960s local people told Wolfgang Mey that whenever a high official in the Bandarban area 'needed' a woman, he would give word to a village headman, who had to see to it.

***Plate 102**. Marma women near Bandarban. (Laurence, 1961-63)*

## 8.6 Flirtation and Inhibition

The anthropologist Kauffmann commented upon his strong attraction to women in the hills. His efforts at flirting with young girls were, however, met with shyness, if not fear. At a Bengali-Burmese theatre performance in Polika near Ruma Bazar in 1955, he offered cigarettes, betel and tea to a Marma girl whom he liked. 'When she felt my eyes resting upon her, she quietly and measuredly raised her eyes, met mine for a moment and bashfully lowered her head to one side.'

He compared the modesty and bashfulness of the Marma girls with the 'exhibitionism' of women back home:

> 'These Magh women with their red lungis falling right down to the ground and tightly hugging their slim hips, and their dark blue jackets, radiate a particular appeal when they come tripping along quickly. Their Mongoloid eyes, which are set in softly rounded yellow-brown faces with flat noses and high cheekbones, glance shyly and furtively, as they smile uncertainly ... All women, even prostitutes, are, by our standards, simply unbelievably bashful, and allow no man to look at even the least of their intimate charms...The exhibitionism of [Western] women with their shorts, bikinis and other exposure of the body would meet with a terrified rejection here, and would never find acceptance...On the road, we passed various Magh girls who, shy and fearful, made way for us, or even ran away like hares with all signs of horror ... and when [a girl] passes our bungalow and looks quickly in our direction, she sends smiling glances which signal to men that she is experienced in love matters' (Kauffmann, December 17, 1955; January 12, 15 and 17, 1956) (**plate 102**).

What hill people thought of such interpretations has not been recorded. It is important to realise that there were large cultural differences between groups in the Chittagong hills. From the Marma perspective, the behaviour of some other groups seemed unguarded. For example, a Marma student taking photographs among the Mru wrote the following caption in English on one of them: 'Mro tribe. Mother and child. They always line up bearly [=bare-breasted]. Shame is not fact for their' (**plate 103**).

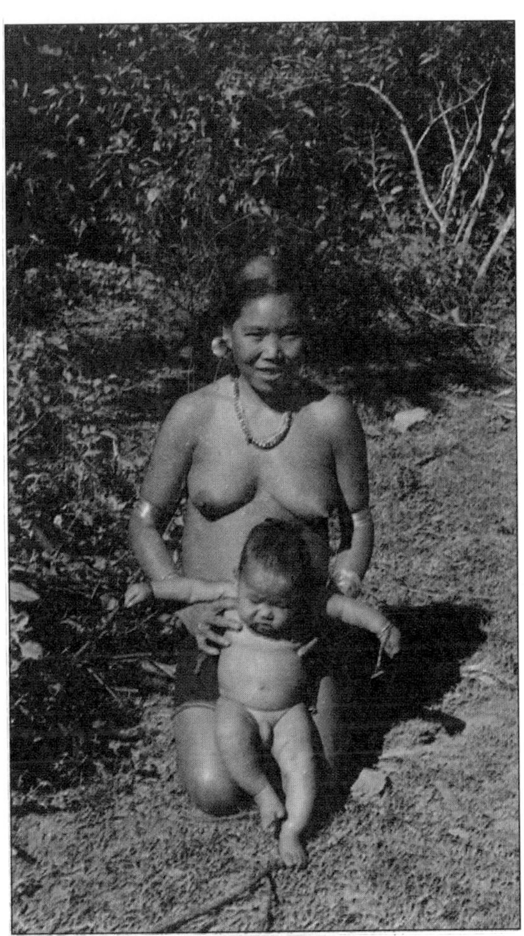

***Plate 103***. *Mru woman and baby. (A. Mong Akhyai, 1990s)*

## 8.7 Brown Saheb's Burden?

This nostalgic, romantic and intensely personal sensitivity to the charm and innocence of the Chittagong Hill Tracts appears to have been a particularly European concern (**plate 104**). Bengalis generally did not share it at all, as Kauffmann found out during lengthy discussions with Bengali officials in the hills. Far from waxing lyrical about a presumed bond between hill people and nature, they insisted on the need for them to raise the living standard of these 'poor and unhappy hill cultivators.' Kauffmann lamented that the Pakistan government would not 'tolerate that there are citizens in its territory whom outsiders could call primitives or even savages' (Kauffmann, February 4, 1956). He pointed out that rapid cultural change could lead to a total breakdown, but officials held a different view:

> 'Mohammed Akhter Hussain [Officer in Charge at Bandarban], looking rather wild but an expert in languages and the Koran, forcefully pointed out to me that Islam has the mission to bring religious beliefs to all people, and these tribes up there in the hills did not possess even a trace of religion—therefore they were not yet proper human beings' (Kauffmann, January 15, 1956).

Generally speaking, Bengali officials and intellectuals shared the paternalistic view that they were the natural guardians of the hill people who, they imagined, needed their guidance. Progress, brought to the hills by well-meaning Bengalis, would lead the hill people out of superstition and darkness, and into a new age. Such ideas were most forcefully expressed by Abdus Sattar:

> 'once educated they [the hill people] stay clear of the dark alleys of tribal cults and enter the fold of civilized religions with overall improvement in their society and way of life' (Sattar, 1975, 6; cf. Van Schendel, 1992 and Mey, 1991b, 102-106).

As self-appointed handmaidens of progress and modernity in the Chittagong hills, most Bengali officials broke with the European inclination to see the Chittagong Hill Tracts as a pastoral idyll—a place of peace, beauty, simplicity and freedom. The romantic view of the hills which runs through the photographic record from its earliest beginnings did, however, survive in a new and commercialised form: photographs intended to build up a tourist industry in the Chittagong hills (see chapter 'Developing the Hills').

***Plate 104***. *Mru girl. (Seifert, 1963)*

***Plate 105***. *Field-Marshal Earl Roberts of Kandahar on his charger Vonolel, named after Lushai chief Vanhnuailana. Painting by C.W. Furse, circa 1893-1900.*

*Chapter 9*

# BODIES AND COSTUMES

When representing the people of the Chittagong hills, outsiders (both Western and Bengali) have consistently stressed nakedness. Nakedness carried connotations of primitiveness, indecency and sexual titillation. In 1801 John MacRae reported a 'Kooki tradition' according to which they and the Marma were the offspring of the same father who had two sons by different mothers. While the Marma are the descendents of the eldest son, who was well looked after by his mother, the 'Kookies' are descended from the youngest son who:

> 'was neglected by his step-mother, who, while she clothed her own son, allowed him to go naked; and this partial distinction being still observed, as he grew up, he went by the name of *Luncta*, or the naked ... [And these] *Kookies*, or *Lunctas* (as they are also called) are the least civilized, of any people we as yet know, among these mountains' (MacRae, 1801, 184).

Nakedness also suggested people who still formed part of nature, as John Beames, the Commissioner of Chittagong, indicated in his memoirs. He describes how Lushai chief Vanhnuaia [Vanhoiya] came to the Circuit House in Rangamati in 1878:

> 'there was a difficulty in admitting him as my wife and some other ladies were there, and Vanhoiya wore no clothes *at all*. A scarlet blanket was offered to him but he refused to wear it ... He was a splendid animal—tall, muscular and active, with a keen, bright eye and a lordly demeanour' (Beames, 1961, 288-289; cf. chapter 'The Colonial Overlords').

This strong association between 'natural' man and animal was also echoed by Field-Marshal Earl Roberts who was involved in the first military campaign to subdue the Lushai (Mizo). He named his horse after a Lushai chief (**plate 105**); in a further twist, the horse was later treated as a human being when it was decorated for its service to the British Empire.[1]

### 9.1 Studying Human Bodies

The naked body also became an object of scientific study. In 1882 Emil Riebeck travelled in the Chittagong hills at the request of Adolf Bastian, founding father of German anthropology and director of the Ethnographic Museum in Berlin. Riebeck, following Bastian's theories, wanted to identify common human traits in different cultures. The bodies of men and women were made the object of disinterested scrutiny. Analysis of anthropometric data was expected to yield insights into the constitution and distribution of 'races.' By reducing 'primitive' people to their bodily essence it was hoped to find out what made them so different from the Western observer. To this end, Riebeck could not simply take photographs of people as he met them in the Chittagong hills: he had to prepare them for the Western scientific eye by having them almost undressed, lined up in an orderly manner and deprived of any social context. There was no need to identify the individuals beyond their 'tribal' label; the women as Lushai and the men as Tippera (**plates 106** and **107**).

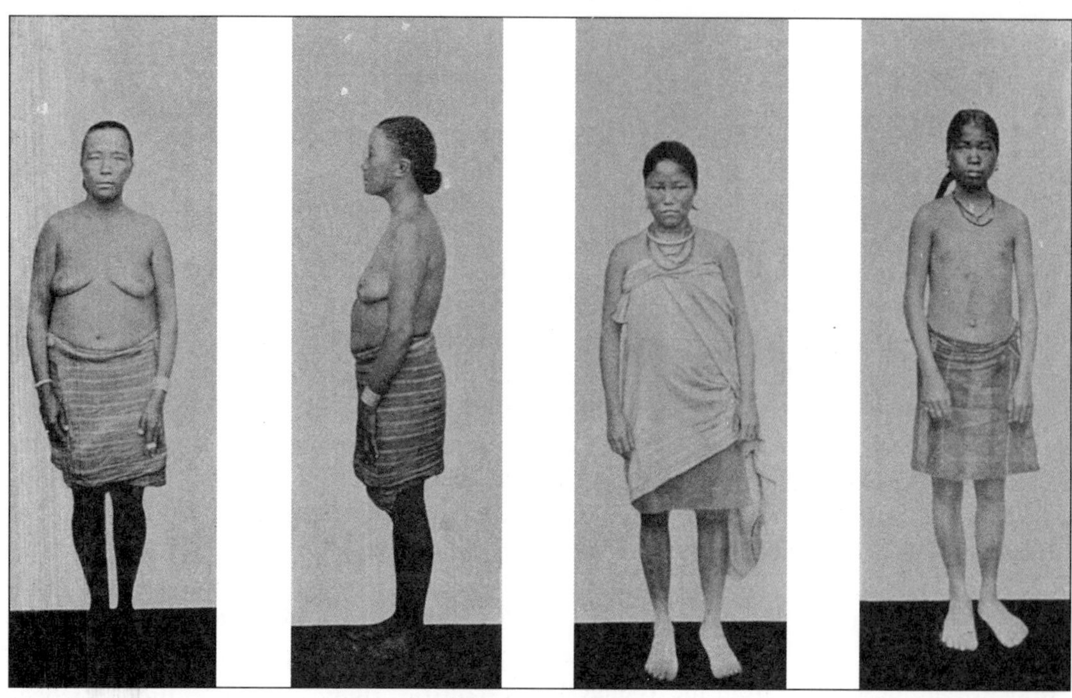

***Plate 106***. *'Lushai.' (Riebeck, 1885)*

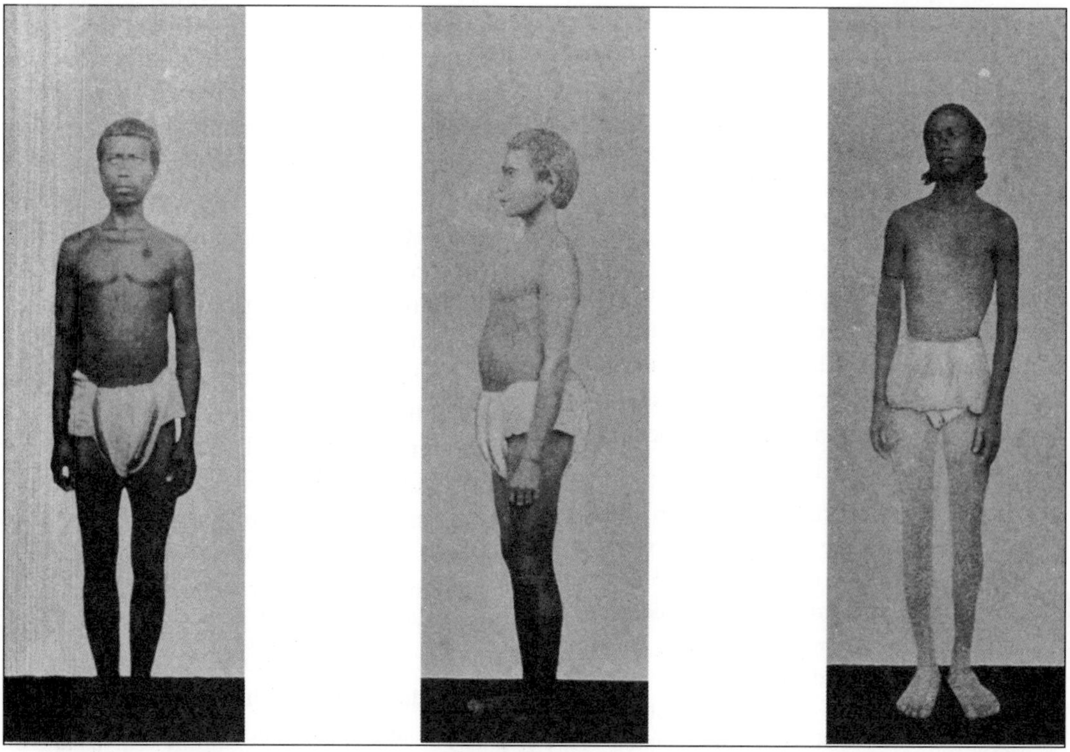

***Plate 107***. *'Tipperah.' (Riebeck, 1885)*

***Plate 108**. 'Kúkis, male and female.' (Dalton, 1872)*

But primitiveness was not indicated only by nakedness; it could also be expressed by 'exotic' dress. In 1872 Dalton published a book in which individuals were used as examples of their group (e.g. **plate 108**). To Riebeck, textiles were also material evidence of primitivity and he collected beautiful samples (**plate 109**).

This approach soon gave way to two others. With the establishment of 'Pax Britannica,' an administrative mood took over and near-naked people were displayed in a more matter-of-fact manner. Hutchinson published a photograph captioned 'Khyengs standing in the verandah of their house' without further comments (**plate 110**). He was, however, not always uncritical of local dress styles: 'No particular attention is shown by them to the demands of decency in the matter of clothing' (Hutchinson, 1906, 132).

Meanwhile, changes in anthropological theory led to a functionalist approach to the people of the Chittagong hills. In 1927 a German couple, Julius and Lore Konietzko, spent a short time in the hills and acquired a remarkable ethnographic collection of mainly Marma and Chakma objects. Lore Konietzko described their mode of operation in her diary:

> 'First we make photographs: the village, the bamboo fences round the fields, and women and men in their homespun clothes and their rich glass beads and silver ornaments ... All wear blue saris with two broad red stripes and coloured borders, a striped cloth tightly round the breast and ... silver bangles on their arms' (Mey, 1991a, 434).

**Plate 111** indicates this shift in perspective. Instead of completely isolating people for measurement, as Riebeck had done, the Konietzkos put them in a context. Nakedness played no role in these photographs (it rarely did when Western women were present) but all the more attention was given to clothes. On Marma dress, Lore Konietzko wrote:

> 'The women wear beautiful multi-coloured homemade cloths round the waist, a striped

**Plate 109**. *Marma, Kumi, Ka-khyen and Lushai textiles and Shindu ear ornaments collected in 1882.*[2] *(Riebeck, 1885)*

***Plate 110***. *'Khyengs standing in the verandah of their house.' (Hutchinson, 1906)*

***Plate 111***. *Marma women from a village near Rangamati. (Konietzko collection, 1927)*

cloth over the breast, and a colourful silk jacket on festive occasions. Their hair is combed back and tied in a knot high at the back of the head, held together by silver chains, and they wear a broad coloured silk or cotton band round the forehead ... thin anklets, many smooth silver rings, one upon the other, on their forearms and a broad richly ornamented bracelet round the upper arms, worn over the blouse. Round the neck a heavy silver necklace and a simple gold chain with glass beads and rupee coins, and in the ears broad silver tubes with broad rims, to which rich pendants are attached' (Mey, 1991a, 430).

These photographs were still highly posed (**plate 112**). People were grouped in order to document the authenticity and use of the ornaments and clothes which the Konietzkos collected.

This particular way of placing persons was less evident in the photographs taken by J.P. Mills in 1926. He was:

> 'temporarily seconded to the Bengal Government to look into and make recommendations for the administration of the Chittagong Hill Tracts. In two months he travelled nearly five hundred miles, mostly on foot, producing a detailed and wide ranging report. As was his habit, he naturally took the opportunity to find out as much as possible about the tribal people who he encountered' (Hobson, 1996, n.p.).

In Mills' photographs the stress on people as displayers of finery was less pronounced. In his representation of the hill people he stressed neither their nakedness nor their dress. He presented them in their natural and cultural setting (**plate 113**). At times, however, he would isolate individuals with a view to showing particular cultural traits or techniques (**plates 114** and **115**).

***Plate 112***. *Julius and Lore Konietzko posing with villagers in the Chittagong Hill Tracts. (Konietzko collection, 1927)*

**Plate 113**. *'Pulika. The headman & family, son with pellet bow.' (Mills, 1926)*

**Plate 114**. *'Basanta Kuki Para, the mode of wearing the hair.' In his diary Mills wrote: 'Saw some Bunjogi Kukis + took their photos. Hair done in big bun on top of head.' (Mills, 1926)*

***Plate 115**. 'A group of women.' (Mills, 1926)*

## 9.2 Nakedness as a Postcolonial Theme

Nakedness appears to have had no particular significance for administrators and anthropologists of the late colonial period; for them it simply belonged to the 'way of life' of people in the hills. As time went by, the topic became much less prominent in writings and photography. It resurfaced, however, with the changing power relations after 1947. The Chittagong Hill Tracts, which had been ruled separately and had been largely out of bounds for Bengalis during the colonial period, suddenly came into view when Pakistan gained independence. The presence of Bengalis and West Pakistanis increased rapidly, and with it a new confrontation between local and Islamic notions of decency.

The Chittagong Hill Tracts formed an anomaly in Pakistan, a state based on the Muslim right to self-determination. In 1947, Muslims made up less than 2 percent of the population of the Chittagong hills. Moreover, although Pakistan harboured other groups which it identified as 'tribal' (e.g. the Pakhthuns or Pathans in West Pakistan), these shared the Islamic moral code. Only on the fringes of East Pakistan could one find peoples whose lifestyle was far outside the code of decency prescribed by Islam.

The notion of 'primitivity,' which had become discredited and obsolete in anthropological discourse, now reappeared in Pakistani popular literature as a concept to explain the hill people's way of life. They were seen as uncivilised, ruled by 'superstitions' rather than religious beliefs, without history, and, in the words of Abdus Sattar, a prolific and widely sold author on the subject, 'of deep interest to any one who wants to discover man in his raw form' (Sattar, 1971, 4).

> 'The district of Chittagong Hill Tracts is...a cradle of human evolution. In the grooves of its forests and lonely recesses of hills abound diverse wild tribes, crude, primitive and aboriginal' (Sattar, 1971, 191).

> 'The ripples of civilization into these hills have not yet penetrated beyond its surface. We, the inhabitants of the town and plainland have very little idea of this strange and new world peopled by these aboriginals, although they are our countrymen—the citizen of Pakistan...All drive must be made to educate the tribes to enable them to smash through the sociological frontier' (Sattar, 1971, ix, 6).

Sattar is at pains to underscore the 'primitivity' of the hill people, and nakedness is a symbol that will shock a Muslim readership. For example, he makes the wild claim that the Shendu:

> 'remain barely covered. Men wear loin-cloth and women do no more than hide the private parts of their body. But in the dense forest it is not unlikely to find entirely unclothed Shendus adults' (Sattar, 1971, 269).

In 1971 the Subdivisional Officer of Bandarban Subdivision similarly used nakedness as a symbol of wildness when he explained to Wolfgang Mey why the Chittagong Hill Tracts were closed to foreigners:

> 'There are wild elephants, and the natives go almost naked. We cannot guarantee the security of tourists.'

During the same year Claus-Dieter Brauns, many of whose photographs have been included in this book, spent some time with the Mru in the southern hills.

> 'Then the thing happened which I had always feared: policemen came in order to take me from the village. In Lama a West Pakistani security officer awaited me. He appeared to be well informed about my photographic activities and indicated that it was forbidden to do mission work in the mountains and to take pictures of 'unclothed natives.' The only thing which might be permitted, he said, was

> the taking of group pictures at the bazaar. I showed him a few black-and-white photographs, which were immediately burned' (Brauns and Löffler, 1990, 21).

In other words, primitivity was re-invented in the Pakistan period, and nakedness and superstition were two of its basic aspects. Sometimes nakedness was mildly ridiculed; the caption of **plate 116** was 'Tippera youth in full dress' (but notice the cloth at his feet).

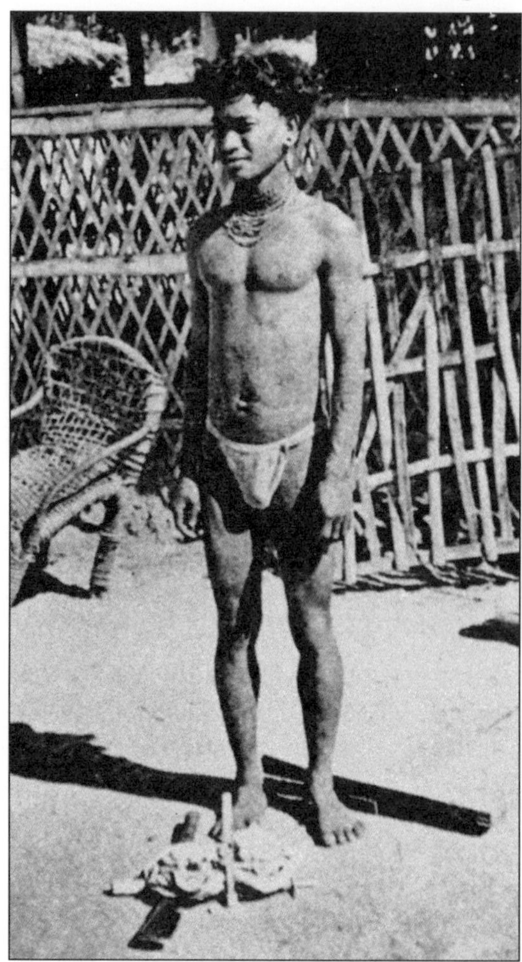

***Plate 116***. *'Tippera youth in full dress.' (Diettrich, 1960)*

Nakedness had to be treated with circumspection: photographs of topless women never appeared on the covers of books but as illustrations of primitivity in the text. This eye-catching symbol was naked proof of the need to civilise and clothe these people, or—to use the term which emerged during this period and would spread like water-hyacinth through the literature on East Pakistan/Bangladesh—the need to 'develop' them. As A.B. Rajput put it:

> 'with the present pace of development in East Pakistan, the tribesmen are bound to benefit in the not too distant future ... It will, of course, be of interest to watch how the tribal folk react to a revolutionary change in their outlook when the development projects in various fields offer them better opportunities for living and mixing freely with comparatively more advanced people belonging to the same land' (Rajput, 1962, 19).

In the mid-nineteenth century, nakedness had been a symbol of wildness; a century later it had become a symbol of underdevelopment.

What the 'unclothed natives' meanwhile thought of all this remains unrecorded. They did not have cameras. But the gaze of the Mru man in **plate 117** speaks volumes. To him it was the nudity of the Western visitor, and not his own, which was a sight to behold.

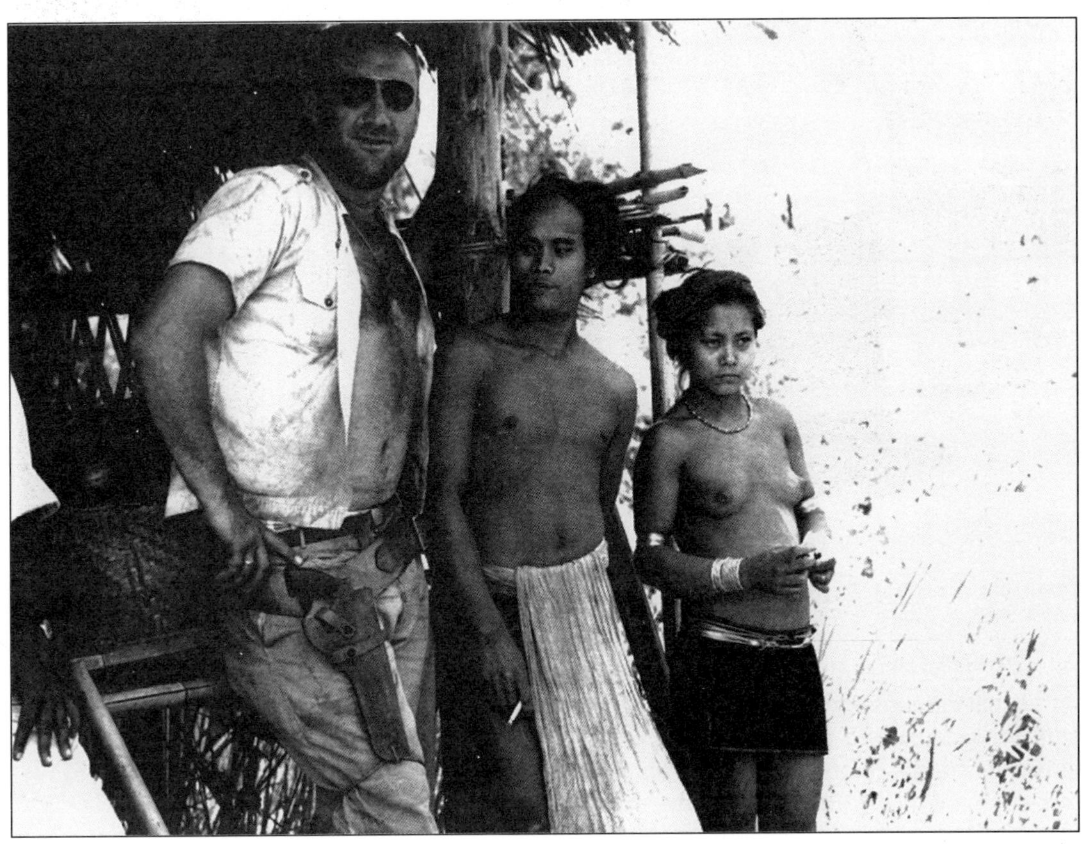

***Plate 117***. *Mru couple and European visitor. (Seifert, 1963)*

***Plate 118***. *Women, Khagrachhari. (Recter, 1965)*

## 9.3 Covering up

As social circumstances in the Chittagong hills changed, so did the dress styles of the different groups. Some of these changes involved covering more of the body. In **plate 118** Chakma women in Khagrachhari are seen to have adapted their traditional dress, consisting of pinon (skirt) and khadi (breast cloth), by adding blouses. The khadi's function has changed from cover to decoration.

Covering the body could also be a protective measure. Mru women were never shy to be photographed in nothing but their short wan-klai, a 'piece of cloth which comes down only to the knees and is open on the left side and has an embroidered centre of above six inches width from top to bottom' (Sattar, 1971, 230), as **plate 119** shows.But with the increasing number of Bengalis in the hills, they began wearing coloured or white cloaks, bought at the bazaar (**plate 120**). These were used, among other things, 'to protect us from the eye of the Bengali.'

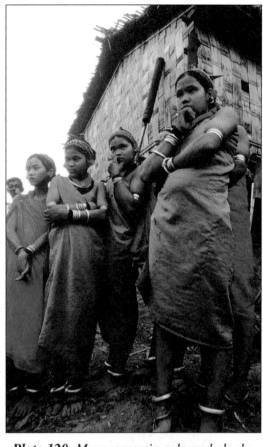

***Plate 120***. *Mru women in coloured cloaks.*
*(Brauns, 1974)*

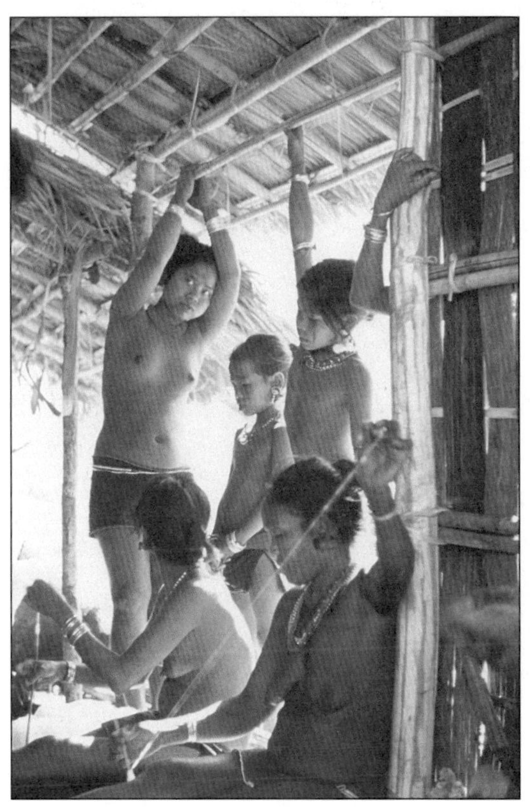

***Plate 119***. *'Family group in hut,'*
*Chimbuk. (Band, 1968)*

***Plate 121***. *Mru feast. (Belitz, 1976)*

What Mru women meant by 'protection from the eye of the Bengali' was indicated by a confrontation documented in **plates 121-126**. Harry Belitz and his Bengali guide Karim visited a Mru village where a festive dance was being held. During a short interval, when the girls were having fun, the guide interfered. He ordered them to remove their breast cloths. A short argument ensued among the girls. Some complied and some did not, but the festive mood was gone. Karim also asked Belitz to take a photograph of himself with a topless Mru girl, and later ordered 20 extra copies to show around. That night he indulged in rice beer and tried his best to conquer one of the Mru girls.

Karim exhibited the ethnocentric behaviour that made the Mru fear Bengali visitors. For him the Mru village was obviously a place which he judged by his own standards; where women went around bare-breasted, they could not be anything but loose. Hence the code of decency by which he lived at home was not operative and he could indulge in what were sins under that code (watch scantily dressed dancing women, have them photographed as sex objects, drink alcohol and perhaps engage in some extramarital sex) without fear of retribution.

***Plates 122-126****. Mru feast and Karim's intervention. (Belitz, 1976)*

A somewhat similar encounter took place between Western holiday-makers and a group of Mru villagers in 1963. Here the erotic element is perhaps more equally balanced with the desire to portray nakedness as part of the 'authentic' Mru costume. In **plates 127-129** we see how a male visitor induced some Mru women to take off their wraps and expose their bare breasts for a snapshot. The women were visibly annoyed and uncomfortable but too intimidated to refuse. In the final picture we see the man standing in a dominant position, facing the camera. The women look down, clutching their wraps, feeling shy and unhappy.

Not only Mru women but also Mru men took to covering their bodies more, especially when they went out of their own circle, e.g. to visit towns. **Plate 130** shows Mru men at the annual fair in Bandarban. Whereas Lushai chief Vanhnuaia had refused to wear a blanket to cover his nudity in order to please the Commissioner of Chittagong in 1878 (see above), Mru villagers in East Pakistan could not afford such a debonair attitude. If they were to protect themselves against ridicule and censure, they had to get 'better dressed.'

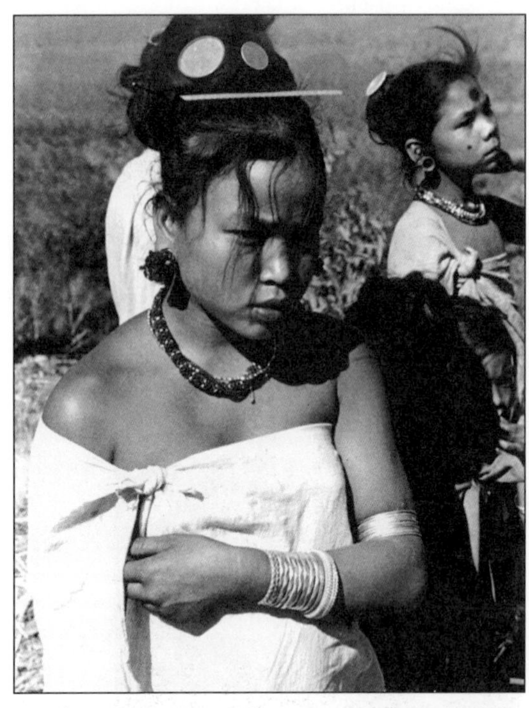

***Plate 127***. *Mru villagers. (Seifert, 1963)*

***Plate 128***. *Mru villagers. (Seifert, 1963)*

***Plate 129****. Mru villagers and Western visitor. (Seifert, 1963)*

***Plate 130****. 'Mru tribesmen attending the mela with rather more clothes than usual,' Bandarban. (Taylor, 1968)*

***Plate 131**. Pangkhua dance group, Rangamati, about 1960. (Rajput, 1962)*

***Plate 132**. Pangkhua dance group. (Sigl, 1965-69)*

## 9.4 Folklorisation

The process of Pakistani nation-building led to cultural pressure on the hill people to develop 'correct tribal costumes.' Such costumes should be colourful, distinctive of each separate group and, above all, in line with majority notions of decency. The outcome was the invention of several variations of the full-body costume.

A major catalyst was the command performance. Dance groups were regularly required to enliven state occasions at Rangamati or Chittagong, and to entertain officials and their guests. It was important that they should not offend the feelings of propriety of their audience.

> 'In a dance performance, usually half a dozen unmarried girls and a dozen or so instrument players participate...The dancers put on jingling anklets of aluminium to keep time and produce a musical effect by their footwork. The dress remains the usual wrap of dark-blue home-spun, except on occasions when they have to give a performance before outsiders. The girls then are asked to drape their bodies with shawls or sheets of cloth in which they naturally feel quite awkward' (Rajput, 1965, 12).

This period saw fanciful additions and adaptations to traditional dress. In the 1950s, a group of Pangkhua dancers would occasionally come to Rangamati to give performances (**plate 131**). Their dress is markedly different from that of another Pangkhua dance group, photographed some ten years later (**plate 132**), which combines old and new elements (e.g. bright yellow and blue skirts) intended to please a non-Pangkhua audience.

A photograph of a Mru group is particularly instructive (**plate 133**). When the President of Pakistan visited Kaptai in 1969, this group performed for him. In a real context, Mru men blow mouth organs facing a row of dancing women (see our chapter 'Religions of the Hills'). Here the women danced in front of the men, facing the public. The clothes were provided by the authorities. The men wore a kind of sarong instead of their loin-cloth and the women long white skirts and red jackets. This photograph highlights the transformation of cultural expressions into folklore, and dress into costume.

***Plate 133**. Mru dance group performing during the President's visit to Kaptai. (Sigl, 1969)*

The arbitrariness of nation-building and its link with outward appearance is illustrated in **plate 134**. The Bawm have strong cultural ties with the Lushai (Mizo), the vast majority of whom live in Mizoram. After 1947 Mizoram (then called the Lushai Hills) became part of India. In 1968, as in every year, a 'tribal dance competition' was held in Bandarban to celebrate Pakistan Day. The girls of the Bawm village in which Almut Mey and Wolfgang Mey lived practised Lushai dances for several days to prepare for this event. They moved to the rhythm of hymn-like Lushai songs, accompanied on a guitar. The girls wore the Lushai *puan* and Western-style blouses. On their heads they each wore a crown with a green crescent, the symbol of Pakistan. Nothing was traditional about all this, and yet this group won the first prize in the competition for its 'tribal dance performance.' The authorities were pleased with them.

Cultural pressures induced hill people to invent a dress style that suppressed those aspects which to Bengali perceptions appeared to be the most 'primitive' and embarrassing. This process is continuing today. The Taungchengya women shown in **plate 135** still wore *pinon* and *khadi* but the function of the khadi (breast cloth) was taken over by a white blouse. The khadi was used as a shawl, rather in the way Bengali women wear a shawl. The head was covered by a cloth.

The three Khumi women shown in **plate 136** wore fanciful red dresses which did not resemble traditional Khumi dress in any way. Decorative silver belts, chains, turban-like head-cloths and red beauty spots on their foreheads completed the outfit.

Folklorisation was the outcome of adaptation to criteria of decency imposed by powerful outsiders. By inventing, and experimenting with, new informal 'tribal uniforms,' hill people tried to get away from the stigma of 'primitive nakedness' and link up with modernity. This was done in various ways. The most common was to create a *modernised 'traditional costume*,' the result of negotiating between the old cultural style and new elements of respectability. The blouses of the Taungchengya women above are a case in point.

A second option was to reinvent completely one's outer appearance and come up with a truly *modern costume* which was still specific to each group. The Khumi women had chosen this option.

Finally, one could do away with the outward markers of one's group altogether and adopt *Bengali or Western dress*. This was more common among men than among women. It was closely linked with the status provided by formal education and state or private-sector employment. Elite hill women educated in Bengali ways would occasionally choose this option, particularly for public appearances, or when they lived outside the Chittagong Hill Tracts (see our chapter 'Lifestyles').

***Plate 134***. *Bawm girls practising for Pakistan Day, Munnuam village. (A. Mey, 1968)*

***Plate 135***. *Taungchengya women at Bandarban fashion show. (A. Mong Akhyai, 1996)*

***Plate 136***. *Khumi women at Bandarban fashion show. (A. Mong Akhyai, 1996)*

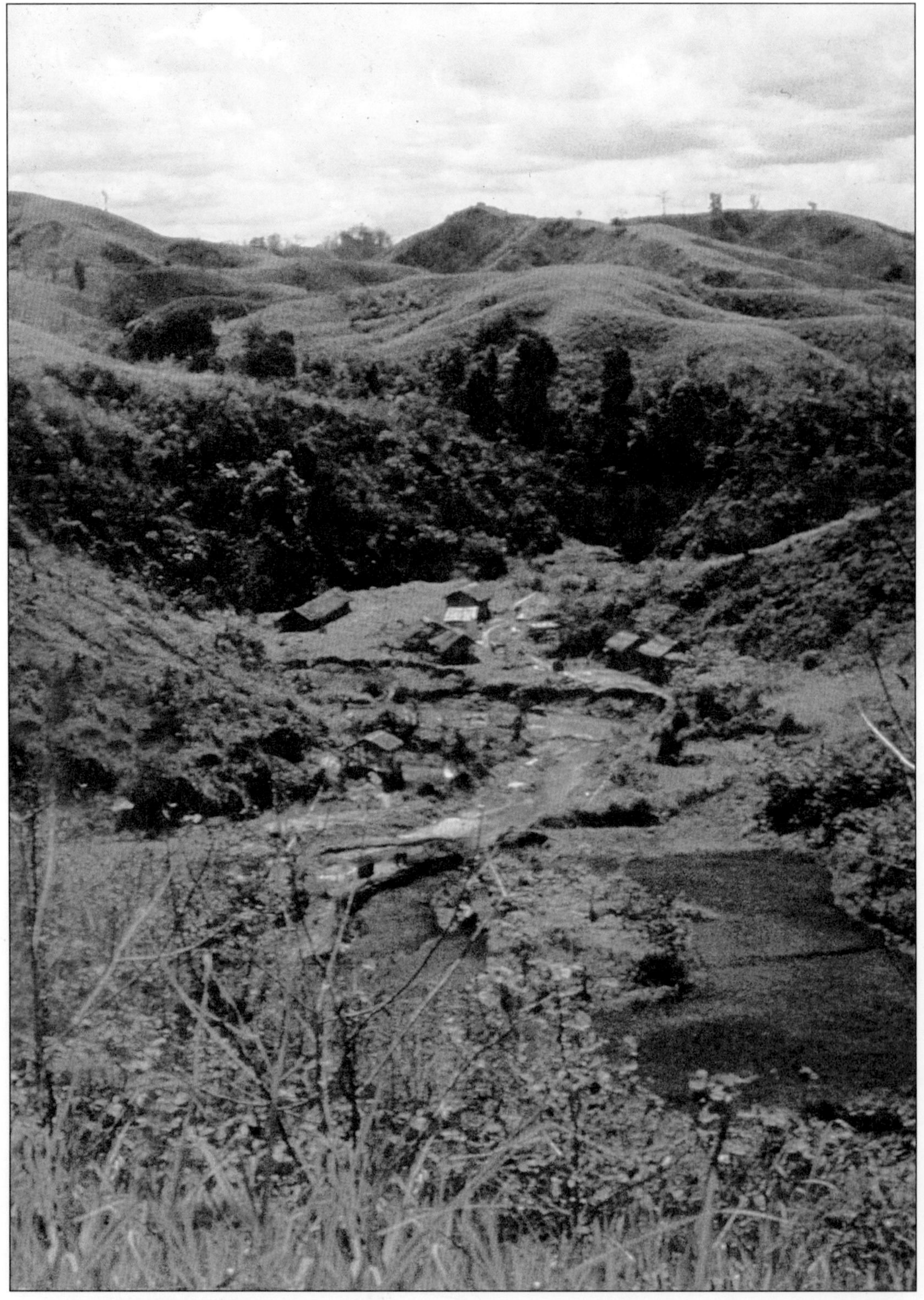

***Plate 137***. *Pekua village in the Kaptai valley. (Wahlquist, 1977)*

*Chapter 10*

# IMAGES OF NATURE AND DESTRUCTION

The scenic beauty of the Chittagong hills has often been described in glowing terms. A typical description is provided by Hutchinson:

> 'The scenery throughout the District is very picturesque, the mixture of hill and valley densely covered with forest and luxurious vegetation, yields the most beautiful and varied effects of light and shade. To be viewed at the best it should be seen from the summits of the main ranges, where the apparently boundless sea of forest is grand in the extreme. The cultivated area of the valleys, dotted here and there, appear as islands, carpeted with emerald green, cloth of gold, or sober brown according to the season of the year. The rivers slowly meandering on their way to the sea, now shimmering like liquid gold, and again reflecting in heavy dark shadows every object within reach, all combine to make a picture not easily forgotten' (Hutchinson, 1909, 2).

Undoubtedly, the Chittagong hills have at times displayed such majestic natural beauty but their history has also been one of persistent human interference with the ecosystem. Three types of interference stand out: hill agriculture *(jhum)*, state-sponsored exploitation of forests, and the creation of the huge Kaptai reservoir.

### 10.1 Jhum Cultivation

The traditional method of land use in mountainous areas all over South and Southeast Asia is shifting cultivation. In the Chittagong hills, plough cultivation and horticulture were also practised. Shifting cultivation exerts pressures on the natural environment but has been sustainable for many centuries. The annual cycle, which dominated economic and social life in the Chittagong hills, began during the months of January and February with the selection of a patch of jungle or fallow land and the cutting down of trees and other vegetation. Sometimes scaffolding was used to fell particularly big trees (**plate 138**). The final clearing of the new field, or *jhum*, took place in late February (**plates 139** and **140**).

The undergrowth and logs were allowed to dry until April when they were set on fire (**plate 141**). During those weeks many patches of forest were on fire, and thick clouds of smoke would darken the sky. Shortly before the monsoon rains set in, the cultivators began planting and sowing various crops (**plate 142**).

During the rainy months that followed, weeding was the primary activity. Most villagers, except for old people, would move to temporary field huts to do this work and protect the crops from animals (**plate 143**). The various crops did not ripen at the same time. Rice was harvested in September and brought to the field huts (**plate 144**). The Mru used their feet for threshing the paddy, which was then brought to the village for storage (**plates 145** and **146**).

After the harvest, the fields were left to themselves and undergrowth and bamboo would soon cover the soil. Given a sufficiently long fallow period, the soil would recover completely. **Plate 147** shows a field after having been left fallow for three years. Earlier, the fallow period would last

***Plate 138**. Felling a big tree prior to jhum cultivation. (Wahlquist, 1977)*

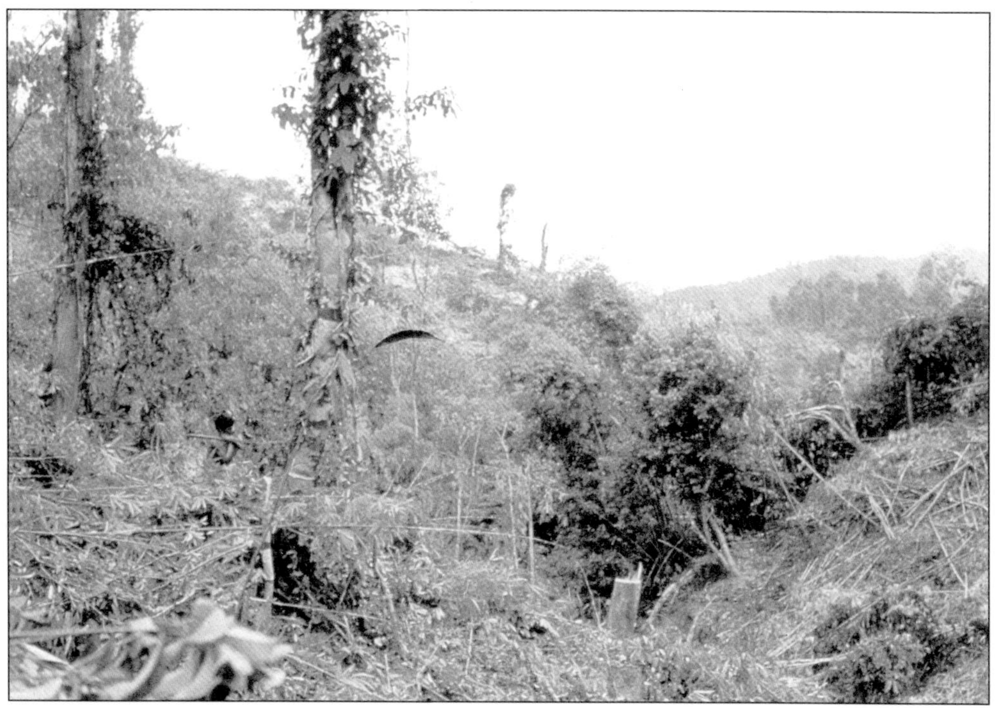

***Plate 139***. *Newly cut jhum field, upper Alikhyong valley. (Wahlquist, 1977)*

***Plate 140***. *Final clearing of a jhum field. (Wahlquist, 1977)*

***Plate 141***. *Burning fields. (Seifert, 1963)*

***Plate 142***. *Mru sowing a hill field. (Löffler, 1957)*

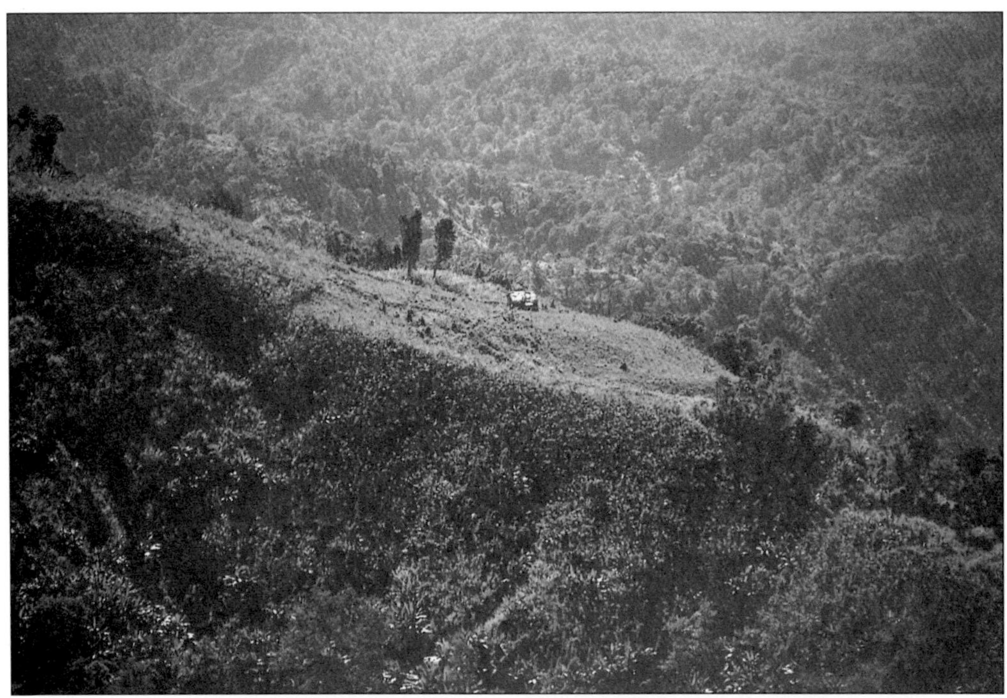

***Plate 143**. Field with temporary field hut. (W. Mey, 1990)*

***Plate 144**. September: harvesting paddy. (Brauns, 1971)*

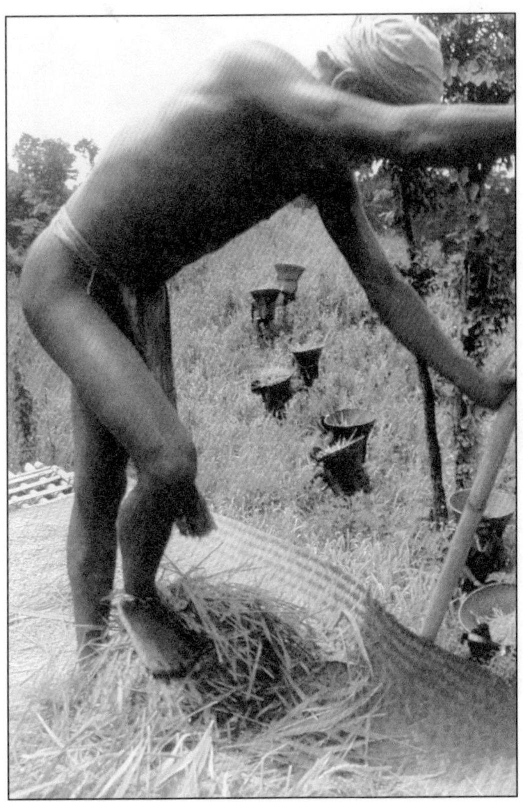

***Plate 145**. Threshing the paddy. (Brauns, 1971)*

from 10 to 15 years. Under such circumstances, jhum cultivation was not detrimental to soil fertility, although most trees in the plots were eventually cut down. Yields from these fields were remarkably high and T. H. Lewin noticed that hill people spent only half as much time on their fields as plains cultivators.

**The jhum controversy**. The colonial authorities were much opposed to shifting cultivation. This was deplored by R. H.S. Hutchinson, Superintendent of the Chittagong Hill Tracts, who wrote:

> 'There seems in past years to have been an unaccountable aversion on the part of the authorities to Juming and this has been a great deal due to misconception of the actual facts at issue ... The objections to Juming are (1) the waste of forest produce; (2) the tendency to encourage the nomadic habits of the Hill Tracts. The value of the forest produce depends entirely on the facilities available for removing the same from its site and placing them on the market ... In the Chittagong Hill Tracts this can only be done by means of the existing waterways. The extreme hilliness of the district and its intersection by numberless small streams and the sandy nature of the soil render the construction of cart roads extremely difficult and in cost prohibitive ... Government had reserved over one-fourth of the area of the district as closed forests in which no cultivation is allowed: these are situated on the principal waterways and are in themselves more than sufficient to meet the requirement of trade. If juming were abandoned the hills of the interior would lie idle, instead of as at present supplying food and valuable produces

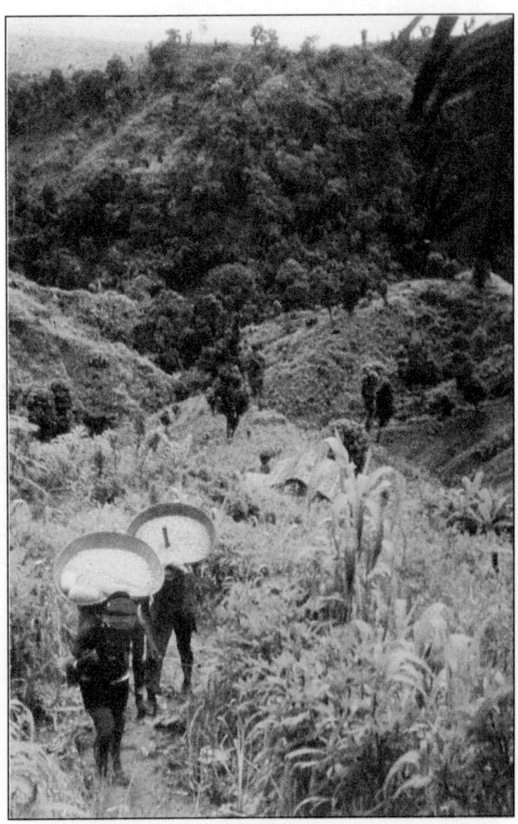

***Plate 146**. Taking the threshed paddy to the village. (Brauns, 1971)*

for sale to the inhabitants of the District and being as well as source of considerable revenue to Government. The hills are covered for the most part with bamboo forest, and this is always selected by preference for juming. The bamboo has a great recuperative power and in seven years the land jumed is ready for rejuming ... And consider the advantage to the hillman. In an ordinary year he will secure an ample supply of rice for his own requirements, and a surplus for sale, in addition to yams, pumpkins, melons, chillies and Indian corn to vary his diet and for barter. He will get enough cotton to supply all the household requirements, and in addition have plenty over to sell, the price of which added to the sale price of his sesamum crop will give him the wherewithal to lay in a supply of necessaries and to purchase ornaments ... As regards the supposed tendency t1o encourage the nomadic habits of the hill tribes the great majority of the villages in the District are permanent and have occupied their present site for a great number of years' (Hutchinson, 1909, 66f).

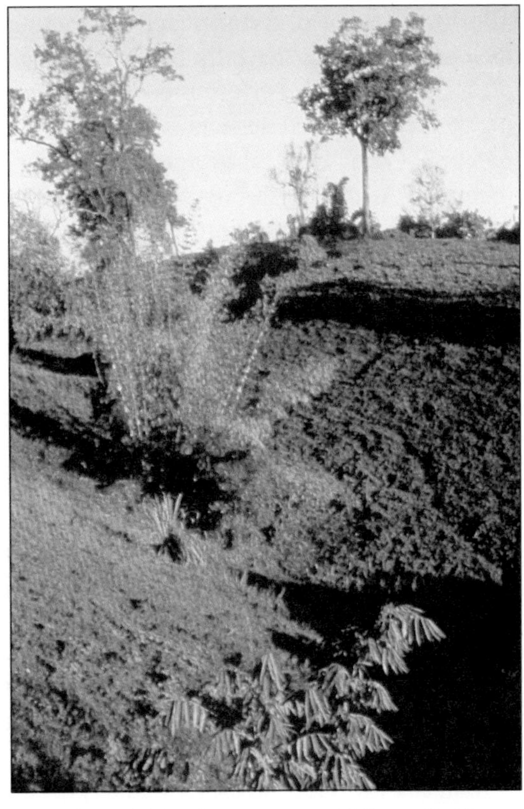

***Plate 147***. *Three-year-old jhum field. (Wahlquist, 1977)*

Administrative measures blocking the cultivators' access to a large portion of the

***Plate 148***. *Illicit jhum field, Rainkhyong Reserved Forest. (Wahlquist, 1977)*

hills (the reserved forests) and restricting their movement in the hills had put serious pressures on hill agriculture. Population increase exacerbated these pressures, and the outcome was land shortage and 'over-jhuming.' At the beginning of the twentieth century, parts of the northern hills were already overjhumed; in other parts of the hills the critical point of overjhuming and soil exhaustion was reached in the 1950s and 1960s. Even in remote areas, yields dropped at an alarming rate, and wherever possible the affected population took to wet-rice farming and the production of citrus fruits and other cash crops. But this option was not open to everyone. Many entered the reserved forests and cut their jhum fields there. **Plate 148** shows illicit jhuming in a Reserved Forest. Now jhum agriculture was considered not only anti-development, but also somehow anti-national.

> 'Control of the harmful Jhumming practice rampant in the Unclassed State Forests should go a long way to divert their energies towards more useful national work' (Kermani, 1953, 48).

**Plate 149** illustrates land use in the Chittagong hills. On the right is an intact forest, next to it the overgrown jhum field of an earlier season, and on the left a new field.

***Plate 149**. Three stages in shifting cultivation. (Anderson, 1968-70)*

***Plate 150**. Overgrown jhum field. (W. Mey, 1990)*

By the 1970s and 1980s, the fallow period had dropped to two to three years in many places. In fields which were taken in production after too short a fallow period weeds would proliferate and make cultivation impossible (**plate 150**).

## 10.2 Exploitation of Forests

Shortly after 1860, when the Chittagong hills were annexed to the British Empire, the state began to exploit their forest produce. In 1871 almost the entire area was declared a 'Government Forest.' In 1871-72 the first experiments with teak plantations were carried out. In 1874-75 two forest reserves were demarcated, followed by five more up to 1883. Thus in twelve years one-third (3,500 square kilometers) of the entire area was taken away from use by cultivators and put under the Forest Department.

It was a highly profitable concern. At the beginning of the twentieth century the annual expenditure for the Forest Department establishment in the Hill Tracts amounted to Rs. 2,712 while the revenue derived from licences to export timber to the plains was Rs. 86,902 (Hutchinson, 1906, 30-31). Timber was used as sleepers for the railways in the plains (railways were never constructed in the Chittagong hills) and for ship-building in the port of Chittagong.

**Timber extraction**. Timber could not be extracted without work elephants. These were captured locally and tamed. Government *kheddas* (elephant capturing operations) were regularly held. T.H. Lewin described one of these:

> 'The khedda was an ingenious sort of trap; a thin fence of bamboo was first constructed, in shape like a fan, extending onwards (at its broadest being, perhaps, four miles wide), but as this thin fence narrowed in, it increased in size and strength, changing from split bamboos to whole bamboos, and so on, until at length it became a stout fence or palisade of young tree trunks. At the narrowest end, where the two sides of the fan approached to a point, the khedda was constructed. This was a great circle of some fifty yards in diameter made of stout tree-trunks set close side by side, end on in earth, buttressed outside with supports, the whole being firmly bound together and fastened with withes of tough green cane ... An entrance was left, four yards in width, above which hang a heavy portcullis garnished on the inner side with sharp bamboo spikes, which could be dropped into place at the critical moment by cutting the rope.
>
> ... At early dawn thirty men had been sent to the head of the valley by a *détour*, with orders to drive the herd down to the khedda...As the sun rose all preparations had been completed, and far away up the valley we heard the shouts of the men, mingled with the noise of shots and drums, as they drove the herd down on us ... In front of all came a huge tusker, who seemed to dominate the whole herd, so large was he. They pushed forward in hot haste until they reached the main stockade, and here, for a moment they hesitated. The noise, the shouts, the explosions of fire-arms were redoubled; the leader turned, trumpeting with unlifted trunk, as if conscious of his danger, but the smaller elephants hurried timorously past him, entered the stockade, and, after a slight hesitation, he followed them. At this moment [Captain] Hood cut the cord, and down fell the portcullis' (Lewin, 1912, 302-303).

***Plate 151***. *Khedda in the Chittagong hills. (Noon, 1953)*

Later, tame elephants with men on their backs would enter the enclosure. The men would tie the hind legs of the wild elephants which were then led out of the khedda and bound with strong ropes to big trees. In due course, the animals were tamed and put to work in the jungle.

Kheddas were organised till the early 1960s; after that the number of wild elephants in the Chittagong hills decreased dramatically. **Plate 151** shows a khedda. Tame elephants at work can be seen in **plates 152** and **153**.

In addition to government exploitation of the forests, permits were farmed out to private contractors. Cutting timber had always been an aspect of the hill people's economy. Under colonial law, hill people were the only citizens who could obtain timber permits to cut trees in the Chittagong hills. It had become a long-standing practice, however, for hill

***Plate 152***. *Work elephants at Rangamati. (Konietzko collection, 1927)*

***Plate 153***. *Logging with elephants, Alikhyong Khal. (Wahlquist, 1976)*

***Plate 154**. Felling at Rangapahar. (Bientjes, 1963)*

people who had been issued a timber permit to sell it to Bengali contractors right outside the Deputy Commissioner's office. Some of these contractors worked on a large scale.

Most logs were brought to collection points (**plates 154** and **155**), floated down the reservoir and brought ashore in Rangamati or Kaptai; both places developed into important receiving centres (**plate 156**) where logs were cut to size, put on trucks, and taken to Chittagong town (**plate 157**). By the early 1990s logging had reached such intensity that logging trucks could be observed leaving Rangamati in the direction of Chittagong every ten minutes.

Excessive logging not only depleted the reserved forests but also led to further ecological damage. Where the protective vegetation had been removed, the soil was exposed to the monsoon rains and eroded

***Plate 155**. Log storage area, Kasalong Reserved Forest. (Bientjes, 1963)*

***Plate 156***. *Bringing logs ashore, Kaptai. (Bientjes, 1961)*

***Plate 157***. *Logging truck. (Band, 1970)*

***Plate 158***. *Landslide. (Anderson, 1968-70)*

rapidly. This resulted in landslides, and the loose soil was washed down the slopes and carried by rivers into the Kaptai reservoir (**plates 158** and **159**). As a result, the reservoir silted up rapidly; in the early 1990s authorities confirmed that in its 30 years' existence it had lost about 25 percent of its volume due to siltation .

**The industrial use of bamboo**. When the paper mill in Chandraghona came into production in 1953, large quantities of bamboo were needed annually. Forest areas were demarcated and the mill acquired the right for 99 years to extract its raw material from these areas. The manager of the mill organised inspection tours far into the interior to oversee the work and to identify areas of bamboo to be cut down (**plate 160**). The bamboo was sorted, cut and floated down rivulets and rivers till it reached the Kaptai reservoir (**plates 161** and **162**).

***Plate 159***. *Eroded forest soil. (W. Mey, 1990)*

Bundles of bamboo were put together to make small rafts, and once these small rafts

***Plate 160**. Paper mill manager on inspection tour of bamboo extraction areas. (Meier collection, 1955-61)*

reached the reservoir they were rearranged to form enormous floats (**plate 163**).

The mega-rafts were often photographed; they had to be moved by winches and during the long journey down the reservoir the operators made the rafts their home, building small huts and cooking their meals on them (**plate 164**). When the rafts reached Kaptai, they were broken up, hoisted over the dam and floated down the Karnaphuli river till they reached the paper mill at Chandraghona (see chapter 'Developing the Chittagong Hills').

Apart from the large-scale extraction of timber and bamboo, other kinds of forest produce were exploited by small traders. Thatching grass was one of these (**plate 165**). Another export was stone. The plains of Bengal being alluvial,

***Plates 161**. Sorting bamboo. (Meier collection, 1955-61)*

***Plate 162***. *Transporting bamboo. (Meier collection, 1955-61)*

***Plate 163***. *Bamboo raft on Kaptai lake. (Sandercock, 1964-65)*

**Plate 164**. *'Tiffin time for guard who will ride raft to Kaptai, CHT.' (Welsh, 1963)*

**Plate 165**. *Transporting thatching grass. (Sandercock, 1964-65)*

***Plate 166***. *Small stream in the Chittagong hills. (Belitz, 1990)*

***Plate 167***. *Loading stones on truck, southern Chittagong hills. (Belitz, 1990)*

hardly any stone was to be found there. In order to obtain gravel for road-building in the plains, bricks had to be broken. Stone, a more durable material, was much preferred. In the Chittagong hills, the beds of rivulets are full of stones (**plate 166**).

As roads were built, lorries could push much more deeply into the hills and collect stones from these rivulets (**plate 167**). The ecological impact of this export was considerable: with the stones removed, the speed of the water in the river beds increased enormously, especially during the rainy season, and erosion intensified.

## 10.3 The Kaptai Reservoir

The construction of the Kaptai dam led in 1960 to the creation of a huge reservoir, usually known as the Kaptai Lake, in the central and northern Chittagong hills. Its effects on the ecosystem have been profound. The spectacular scenic beauty of the lake (**plate 168**) could not hide the fact that it was a catastrophe for thousands of hill cultivators. Not only did it flood 650 square kilometers of valley land (40 percent of the arable land in the area), it also displaced about 100,000 people whose houses and villages were submerged. The reservoir deeply affected the pattern of human life in the hills. The death of the old days was symbolised by the great Buddha image of the main temple at Rangamati; it was drowned and for years would re-emerge during the dry season, until it finally crumbled and disappeared forever (**plate 169**).

In the same way, the ecological damage caused by the Kaptai dam was symbolised by the branches of dead trees which stuck

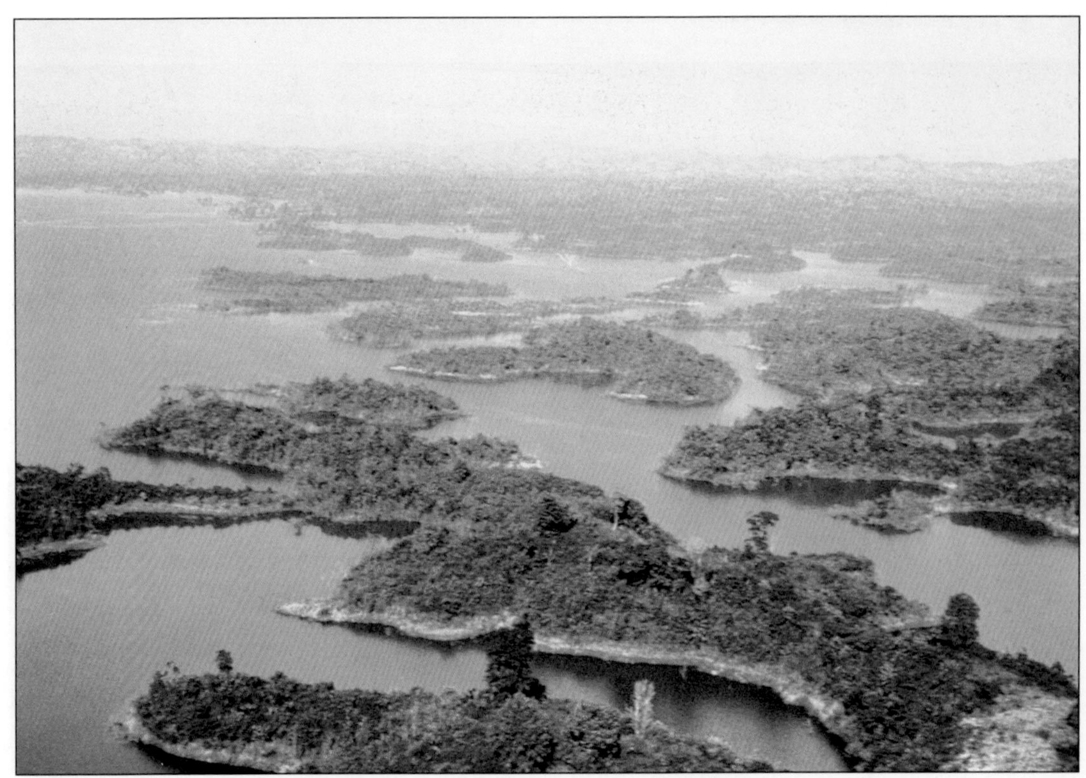

***Plate 168****. Islands in the Kaptai reservoir. (Recter, 1965)*

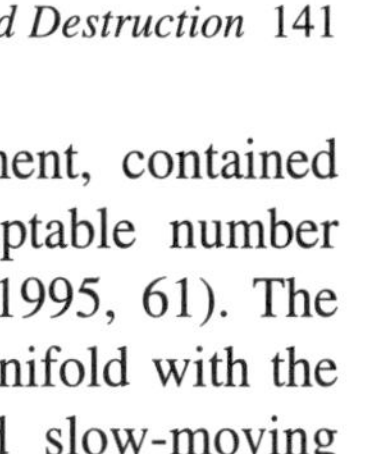

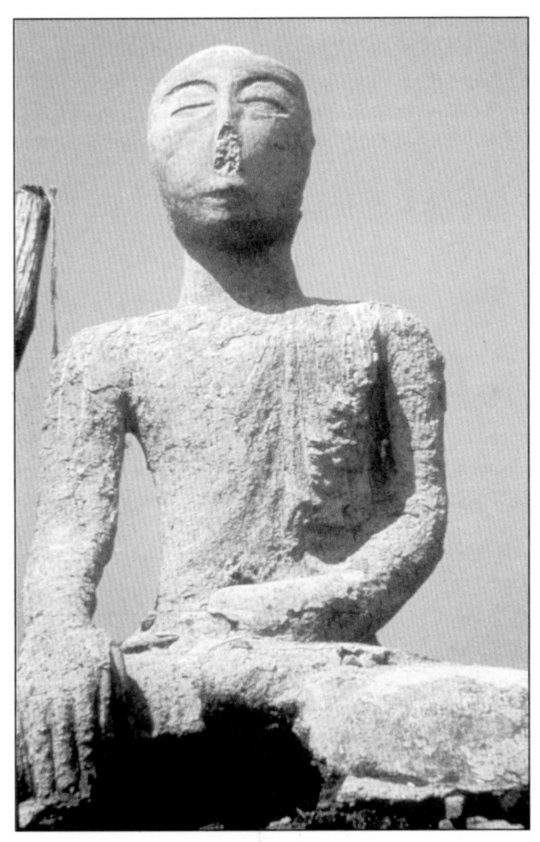

***Plate 169**. The Buddha, re-emerged from the Kaptai reservoir during the dry season. (Anderson, 1968-70)*

out of the water when the reservoir was low (**plates 170**) and by the spectacle of devastation and decay which was offered by flooded jungle areas (**plate 171**).

The ecological damage of the Kaptai project went far beyond inundation. Water pollution became a serious hazard. Fertilisers and pesticides, used to combat decreasing soil productivity, were washed down from the fields and more than 5 tons of human excrements and other waste were reported to flow into the lake each day. As 85 percent of the population living around the lake depended on its water for drinking, cooking, washing and bathing, health risks increased sharply. Even the drinking water in Rangamati town, supplied by the Public Health Engineering Department, contained far over 10 times the acceptable number of bacteria (Chakma et al., 1995, 61). The risk of malaria increased manifold with the huge body of stagnant and slow-moving water in the reservoir.

Water pollution also affected life in the water. Although no fish cultivation was undertaken in the lake during its early years, the fish population grew naturally. Many displaced cultivators who had settled on the shores took to fishing with the result that these resources began to decrease (**plate 172**). The Fisheries Department later released fish fry but with little success, partly because of the increasing use of fertilisers and pesticides around the lake. In 1966 the share of big fishes in the total fish population was 78 percent, by 1993 it had come down to 2 percent (Chakma et al., 1995, 62).

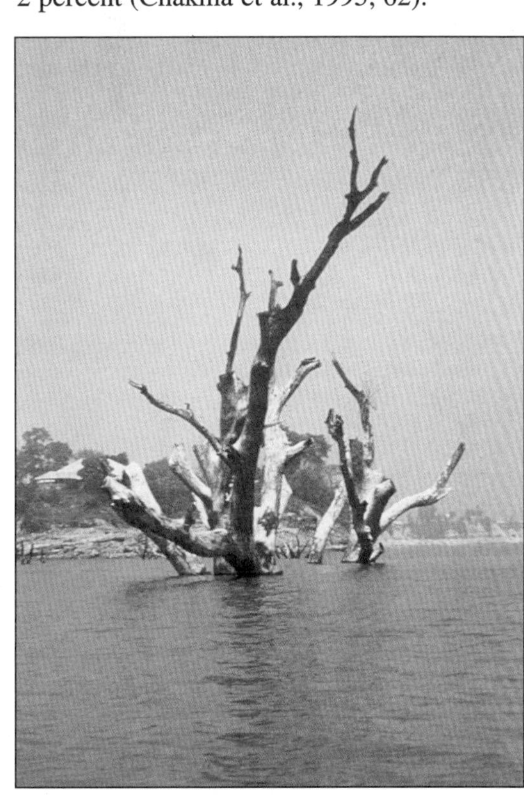

***Plate 170**. Submerged trees, Kaptai lake. (Anderson, 1968-70)*

***Plate 171***. *Flooded forest, Kasalong Reserved Forest. (Bientjes, 1963)*

***Plate 172***. *Fishing in the Kaptai reservoir. (Sandercock, 1964-65)*

***Plate 173***. *The World Wildlife Fund's expedition came across a Reticulated Python: 'Three strong men had to hold [it] up while it was being examined.' (Hosking, 1966)*

***Plate 174***. *The Slow Loris, a nocturnal primate of the Chittagong Hill Tracts. (Hosking, 1966)*

**Wildlife.** In 1966, the Pakistan Government invited the World Wildlife Fund to study the status of wildlife and habitats in the Chittagong Hill Tracts. Reporting on their visit to the Kassalong Forest, they recounted its manager's account of recent history:

> 'It was a sad story. In 1954 the reserve had been planned to embrace 800 square miles around the Kassalong River and Maini headwaters. Work on the Kaptai Dam project began in 1960 and by 1963 the area of the reserve, having lower priority, had been reduced to 500 square miles under Pakistan's Second Five Year Plan. Later, it was twice further reduced and by the time the flooding of the dam was completed only 172 square miles of the original reserve remained. Most of the best forested valleys were drowned and although the water rose slowly, considerable loss of wildlife occurred. Many Elephants, Tigers and various species of deer which escaped drowning were unable to retreat across the 3,000-foot ridge of the Lushai Hills to the east, and therefore moved either north to Assam, or west across the Kassalong River into Tripura. Some of the best remaining land along the margins of the flooded area was then taken over for tribal cultivation and ten square miles were planted with Government controlled plantations. Under present plans, an additional thousand acres per annum were to be taken from the reserve for planting Teak. A monoculture of Teak, however desirable commercially, is a death-knell to wildlife conservation. No species of deer or monkey can find food in such vegetation, and they are forced to abandon the area. In the absence of deer, Tigers and Leopards turn to preying on cattle and goats around the villages and are therefore soon shot ...The establishment of marsh vegetation on the banks was inhibited by the thirty-foot fluctuation in the water level, and ducks were therefore relatively uncommon ... Tigers and wild Indian Elephants had become rare and

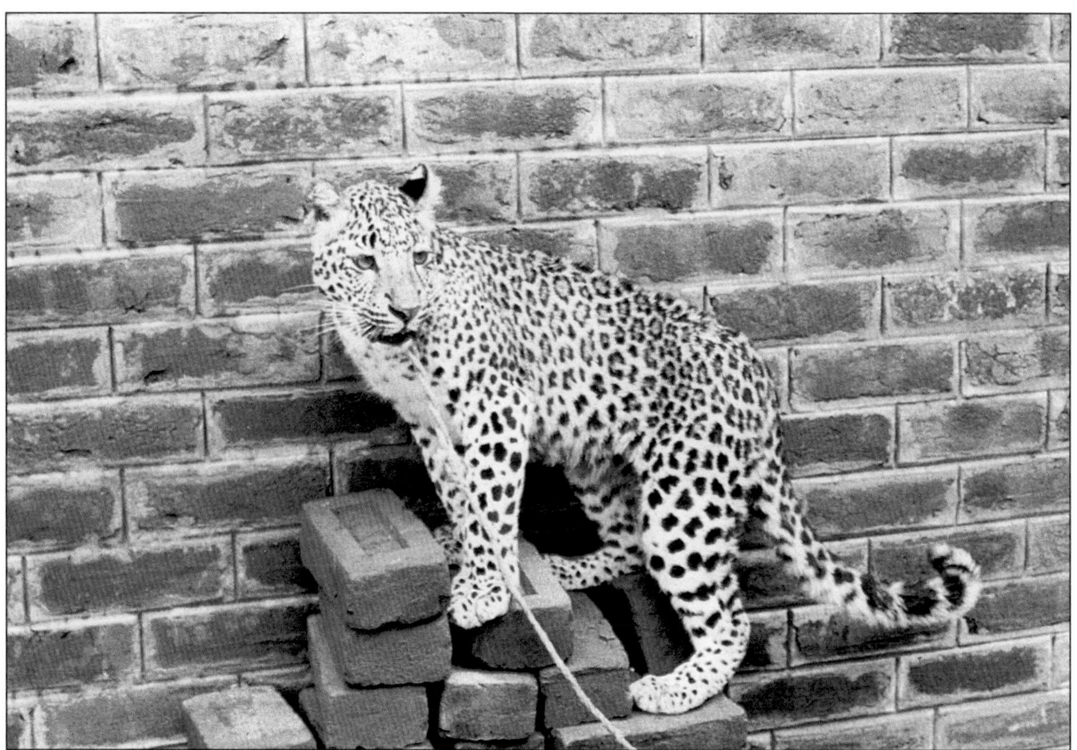

***Plate 175****. A rare captive leopard at Kaptai. (Bientjes, 1961)*

the Marsh Crocodiles had all been killed ... Obviously what had once been planned as a major jungle reserve had now lost all prospect of fulfilling its proper function' (Mountfort and Hosking, 1969, 105-106; cf. Mountfort, 1967) (cf. **plates 173-175**).

The photographic record of the Chittagong Hill Tracts abounds with pictures of natural beauty. And yet, the combined result of excessive logging, overjhuming, population dislocation and flooding was a transformation in the appearance of the hills.

In 1860, when the Chittagong hills were annexed to the British Empire, they formed a heavily forested and sparsely cultivated region intersected by numerous rivers. By the 1970s, they had come to look like a hilly park draped around a giant lake (**plate 176**). Although the scenery was still charming and the tourist literature might continue to rave about 'a world of panoramic beauty Mother Nature has so lavishly unfolded' (Bangladesh Tourist Handbook, n.d., 21), it is important to understand the stark realities behind this apparent charm. Almost everywhere the forests had been depleted and the soil was so degraded that agricultural yields had declined and in many place only minor shrubs and weeds would grow. The natural regeneration of the Chittagong hills will take a very long time, if it can be achieved at all.

***Plate 176****. A view of the Chittagong Hills. (Brammer, early 1960s)*

*Chapter 11*

# RELIGIONS OF THE HILLS

Much of the everyday religious life of the Chittagong Hill Tracts was never represented in photographs. This was partly because photographers were unfamiliar with the religious meanings attached to certain objects and forms of behaviour, and partly because they were not particularly interested in what were widely regarded as marginal if not 'corrupted' belief systems which did not really merit close scrutiny. Nevertheless, the visual record shows an enormous richness of religious practices. These co-existed, combined and transformed themselves in ways which remain to be explored.

In the Chittagong hills two kinds of religion could be distinguished. On the one hand there were religious traditions which focused upon maintaining harmony amongst the spirit, human, animal, plant and mineral worlds to which we all inescapably belong. Such traditions have been called 'community religions.' Examples of community religions in the Chittagong hills were the belief systems of the Bawm, the Pangkhua, the Mizo (Lushai), the Mru and the Khumi.

But there were also examples of 'universalistic religion,' characterised by teachings recorded in sacred books, a desire to know God and thereby transcend an unsatisfactory world, and the possibility for outsiders to join by way of conversion. Examples of universalistic religions were the Buddhism of the Chakma and Marma, the Hinduism of the Tripura, and more recently the Christianity of Mizo, Bawm, Pangkhua and Khyeng.

***Plate 177**. Drawing on a Lushai amulet. (Riebeck, 1885)*

## 11.1 Community Religions

The material expression of community religions was often unobtrusive and drew little attention from photographers. Relatively little is known about the meanings of sacred objects such as amulets (**plates 177** and **178**). The spirits of waters, woods and specific localities could interfere with human life. In order to appease them, sacrifices were offered to them. To this end, bamboo platforms were often erected; here rice, flowers and vegetables were offered to the spirits (**plate 179**).

***Plate 178**. Talisman put up outside a Lushai village, tied with white thread, to ward off disease. (Riebeck, 1885)*

But sacrifices or amulets were not always sufficient:

> 'In case of epidemics, the custom of quarantine, or, as it is called "khang," is universal among them ... A sacrifice is offered, and the village is encircled with a fresh-spun white thread. The blood of the animal sacrificed is then sprinkled about the village, and a general sweeping and cleansing takes place, the houses and gates being decorated with green bough' (Lewin, 1869, 78).

If a disease could not be overcome in this way, the entire village would be abandoned—a remedy which was still occasionally resorted to in recent years (**plate 180**).

There was one aspect of community religions in the Chittagong hills which considerably interested photographers: the *sacrificial feast*. Those who wanted to build up influence, qualify for the office of village head, or express their gratitude to helpful gods, would invite relatives, fellow villagers

***Plate 179**. Bamboo platform for sacrifices. (A. Mey, 1968)*

***Plate 180**. Deserted Mru village. (A. Mey, 1968)*

***Plate 181**. A Mru sacrificial feast: making bamboo decorations. (Brauns, 1970)*

***Plate 182**. Mru dancing during a feast. (Brauns, 1970)*

and honoured persons to an impressive feast of merit. Another reason might be to ward off the envy of spirits or other villagers after an exceptionally good harvest.

The cattle feasts of the Mru were particularly well documented by C.D. Brauns; we reproduce a few of his photographs to give an impression of their richness. During these feasts a cow, bull, or, exceptionally, gayal (*mithan*, another bovine species (*bos frontalis*)) was sacrificed. In preparation, women would make rice beer and liquor and men would repair the old mouth organs, practise tunes, and make bamboo decorations (**plate 181**).

On the ceremonial ground a cage was built in which the sacrificial animal was kept during the two-day ritual. Nearby a stand for the big gong was erected, and a miniature altar with vegetable offerings to the spirits. Beer and other alcoholic drinks were placed underneath. On the first day, the musicians walked several times around the animal and then the festive dance would commence with the blowing of the mouth organs (**plate 182**). In the afternoon, people performed sacrifices to the spirits, followed by more dancing around the animal. Afterwards, the young men invited the girls to share rice beer with them, and drinking continued into the night.

The next morning saw more ceremonious walking around the animal and dancing accompanied by mouth organs. Again the spirits were invoked and finally the animal was killed (**plate 183**). It was then dragged to the host's house, cut up, cooked and distributed.

After a sumptuous meal, the consumption of numerous pots of rice beer (**plate 184**) and concluding rituals, the guests returned to their villages.

***Plate 183****. Mru sacrificing an animal during a feast. (Brauns, 1970)*

**Plate 184**. *Men drinking rice beer. (Brauns, 1970)*

**Plate 185**. *'Khumi village (Taunglung). Khumi brave and skull gallery in headman's house—gayal and buffalo.' (Sopher, 1961)*

***Plate 186**. After the Lushai and Pangkhua became Christians they no longer erected stones; but the Christianised Bawm continued the custom in the form of concrete memorial 'stones' for deceased family members. (A. Mey, 1968)*

Among the Khumi, the animal's skull was kept as a symbol of achievement (**plate 185**).

These feasts served, among other things, to transform agricultural surplus into more durable 'goods' like cattle and pigs, and then to distribute these among all group members. In this way, economic equality was (re-)established. The feast created and confirmed important social links on which one could fall back in times of need. It played a crucial role in regulating social relationships and maintaining harmony in the spiritual world.

Feast-givers distributed material wealth to others and gained social prestige and merit. In the 1950s the anthropologist Lorenz Löffler met an old Mru man who was very poor but who was known locally as 'Raja of the Hills': he was a great feast-giver. Those who organised a good feast could mark their achievement by erecting stones of various sizes (**plate 186**) but this was done much less frequently than in other parts of the region, e.g. Nagaland. In the Chittagong hills forked posts were more common symbols of feast-givers' achievements (**plates 187** and **188**).

### *Boga Lake*

High up in the hills east of Ruma, and rarely photographed, the small Boga Lake has always been held in awe (**plate 189**). When visiting, according to Raja Tridiv Roy:

> 'You are advised not to gasp in wonderment and blurt out: "How enchanting! What a beauty!" or any such thing. Save your breath. Let the senses seep in the impressions the eye relays. Ranges of hills leading away, receding, layer against layer into the wilds of Burma and Mizo Hills...At the root of [an]

**Plate 187**. *'A forked post is set up outside the house of a man who has done a mithan sacrifice. A stylised mithan [gayal] head is carved below the fork.' Basanta Kuki Para, a Pangkhua village near Subalong. (Mills, 1926)*

***Plate 188****. The village head of Nilkop Para and his brother, standing in front of a forked post, demonstrate festive dress and an iron spear used for gayal sacrifices. (Sopher, 1961)*

> age-gnarled Jarul [tree] people offer coins, light candles, release pigeons, or in silent reverence stand and stare. These votive offerings to the Spirit of the lake may not be appropriated. People say that those who do are subject to dire consequences—like vomiting blood, for example. Those that know caution visitors to avoid voicing aloud their feelings at the first glimpse of this mountain lake. You would do well to abide by the stricture ... There is a stillness all around, a placidity not unmixed with a subtle foreboding flavour of some powerful all pervasive spirit—sombre, watchful ...' (Roy, 1972, 49-51).

According to the legend of origin, Boga Lake was created after the inhabitants of a Khumi village killed and ate a deity which appeared to them in the form of a snake-like dragon. An earthquake followed, the hillside caved in, and the village was destroyed. In its place formed a deep lake whose name means 'sacrificial offering' (Roy, 1972, 51-53).

In the early years of the twentieth century, Hutchinson visited the lake with the Bohmong Chief and 200 Marma on the occasion of 'an annual puja—sacrifice or sacred festival—to the spirit of the lake, who is supposed to influence the fate of the Jums.' He was struck by the great depth of the lake and the fact that 'there are absolutely no fish in the lake and a few live specimens that were brought by the Bohmong speedily came up dead when released in its waters.'

The puja performed by the Bohmong Chief 'consisted in erecting a bamboo altar in the water and decorating it with marigold

***Plate 189**. Boga Lake. (Sandercock, 1964)*

flowers and placing thereon a cocoanut, rice and a few other articles while one of the followers mumbled certain incantations invoking the blessing of the spirit' (Hutchinson, 1906, 10-13).

## 11.2 Universal Religions

The most important universal religion in the Chittagong hills was Buddhism which first spread from the Bengal plains and much later from Arakan and Burma. Over time, Chakma, Marma, Taungchengya, Sak, and Khyeng came to identify themselves as Buddhists. Many Tripura considered themselves Hindus. Islam, for centuries the majority religion in the Chittagong plain, never reached the hill people. Christianity was a relative newcomer; in the twentieth century it spread predominantly among followers of community religions.[1]

***Plate 190**. Offering to appease Ganga, the river goddess, Kaptai reservoir. (A. Mey, 1970)*

The Buddhism of the hills was generally of little interest to outsiders. Often they could

***Plate 191****. Buddhists wishing to earn merit could erect a water stand to offer water to any thirsty passer-by. (Anderson, 1968-70)*

not make sense of it and described it as a 'debased' or 'corrupt' form. Actually, the borders between Buddhism and the older community religions were fluid. Buddhism respected other belief systems and worship of nature; spirits and gods could easily be accommodated within it (**plate 190**). As a result, distinct local religious forms developed which should be understood in their own right.

Photographers generally showed little interest in how Buddhism shaped everyday life in the hills (**plate 191**). But they were interested in temple architecture, monks and Buddha statues. The teak-built temple at Chitmaram was an old centre of pilgrimage (**plate 192**). The new temple at Rangamati was no more than a poor reflection of the old one, submerged in the Kaptai reservoir in 1960. It was a centre of pilgrimage and devotion, especially during the annual *punya* ceremony in December (**plate 193**).

In shrine architecture the Burmese style predominated (**plate 194**). Depending on the affluence of the community, the image of the Buddha could be of brass, alabaster or gilded wood (**plate 195**).

Village temples (khyong), usually built of bamboo and thatch, had a distinctive design (**plate 196**). They were local centres of sociability:

> 'In each village is seen a "khiong", or the house of religion. It is a bamboo structure ... generally built under the shade of some trees, with a clear space in front ... Inside, on a small platform of bamboo, stands an image of Gaudama, the last Boodh, made either of wood gilt over, or of alabaster ... Before it are placed offerings of flowers and rice ... By the side of the image of Boodh generally hangs

***Plate 192***. *Chitmaram temple. (Anderson, 1968-70)*

***Plate 193***. *Main Buddhist temple, Rangamati. (A. Mey, 1970)*

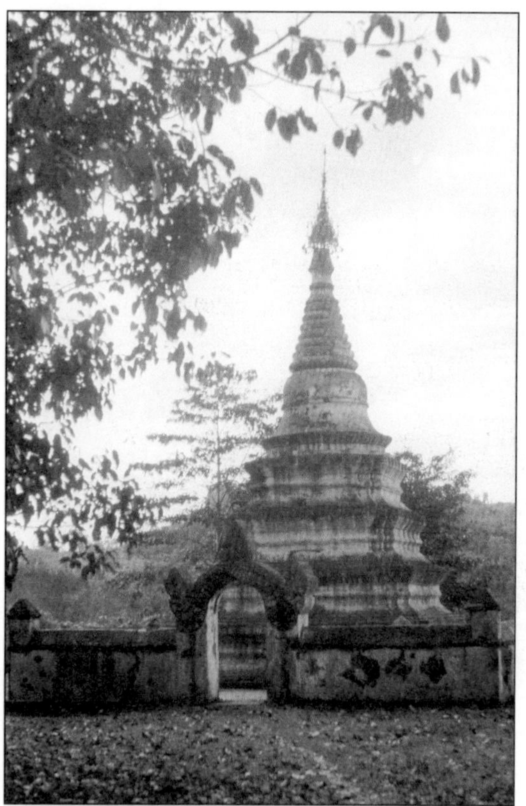

***Plate 194**. Buddhist shrine, Bandarban. (Lindsey, 1964)*

a small stand of bells, and morning and evening the villagers in twos and threes will ascend the small log of wood, cut into steps, by which the "khiong" is approached, remove their turbans, and on hands and knees reverently salute the semblance of their revered teacher, first ringing the bells to let him know that they are there ... The "khiong" is the great resort of all the bachelors of the village; it is there that all the talk and gossip goes on. At evening time, when the sun westers, and it grows cool, they assemble at the "khiong"; the lads and lasses play at "konyon" on the clear space below, while the elders sit above and peacefully chat, smoking their cigars' (Lewin, 1869, 39-40).

The village temple was the place where boys of eight or nine years old underwent their first religious rites. They would dress in the orange clothes of the monks, have their heads shaved, and take part in a ceremony of induction. Afterwards they would stay at the temple for seven days and then either return to normal life or choose to undergo training as a monk (**plate 197**).

The temple was also a centre of instruction. Here the village children learned how to read and write. Wooden blackboards were used for the purpose. **Plate 198** shows a Marma blackboard of the 1880s, on which the teacher would write with a soapstone pencil. The writing is in Burmese script.

For Buddhists in the Chittagong hills, the year was marked by a number of important rituals and festivals. The Mahamuni festival was one of the oldest and most significant. People would flock to the Mahamuni shrine once a year, arriving by villages, each community dressed in gala attire and

***Plate 195**. Brass Buddha, Mong chief's temple, Manikchhari. (Band, 1969)*

***Plate 196**. Village temple near Rangamati. (Konietzko collection, 1927)*

preceded by a drummer (Lewin, 1912, 220). The festival was a combination of worship, courtship and country fair:

> 'Around the shrine ran an outer gallery...and here day and night without intermission streamed the crowd of worshippers. Their devotions consisted apparently in placing before the image a small lighted lamp and then in pairs or fours linked arms and waist the young men and maidens went round and round ... playing on their hill pipes ... and singing songs in alternative strophe and antistrophe of male and female voices (Lewin letters, April 13, 1867) (**plate 199**).

The cremation of a venerated monk or a person of high rank required a sophisticated ritual. The coffin would be placed in a grandly ornamented funeral car made of bamboo and coloured paper, and willing hands would bring it to the site of the funeral pyre. Before the coffin was removed, four big ropes would be attached to the car and

***Plate 197**. Young Marma monk. (Seifert, 1963)*

**Plate 198**. *A blackboard used in a Marma temple. (Riebeck, 1885)*

**Plate 199**. *'Khyoungtha lad and his sweetheart dressed for the Mahamuni fair.' (Lewin, 1867)*

at a given signal the crowd would rush forward, seize the ropes and pull violently in opposite directions. This exciting tug-of-war was symbolic of the struggle of the evil spirits for the possession of the departing soul (**plate 200**; Hutchinson, 1909, 34).

The three chiefs of the Chittagong Hill Tracts, all Buddhists, had their duties towards the Sangha, the order of monks. They were bound to look after the well-being and reputation of the larger temples. In turn, the monks assisted at worldly functions such as the annual punya (see our chapter 'The Public Display of Power') and legitimised the power of the chiefs.

By doing good works and supporting the Buddhist faith the chiefs could gain merit. In **plate 201** we see Raja Maung Shwe Prue Chowdhury, the Bohmong chief, at a Buddhist ceremony in Bandarban in 1967. He is handing a portion of the Tripitaka (Pali scripture) to a monk.

***Plate 200***. *Decorated funeral car for a Buddhist abbot. (Barblan, 1959-61)*

***Plate 201***. *The Bohmong chief donating a portion of the Tripitaka to a monk. (Pak-Somachar, 1967)*

***Plate 202***. *'Entering the Chittagong Hills (Rev. Mr. Donald).' (Snehomoyi, n.d.)*

*Chapter 12*

# SPREADING THE GOSPEL

Christian missionaries had occasionally been active in the Chittagong Hills since the early nineteenth century, but it was not until the 1890s that:

> 'a [Baptist] substation was opened at Chandraghona and two Mugh evangelists stationed there. Many converts were from the Hill Tracts in spite of persecution from the Bohmong Raja ... In 1896 D.L. Donald took charge ... and [in 1899] Rangamati opened as a substation with an Assistant Missionary, Rev. P.N. Santh, in charge ... [Mr. Donald] refers to "the relief of turning from the hard and sterile field of Bengal to the breezy heights where honesty, truthfulness and merriment are not altogether unknown"' (*Ye Are My Witnesses*, 1942, 51; cf. Hutchinson, 1906, 84-86) (**plate 202**).

Soon Baptists were the most prominent group of Christian missionaries, although others (notably Roman Catholics) were not absent. Most missionaries were British.[1] Photography was an important skill for them: they used photographs to represent their work to co-religionists in Britain on whom they remained dependent for support, recruitment and donations. In 1903 George Hughes took charge of the Chittagong Hill Tracts mission. He was:

> 'greatly concerned about the lack of real faith among the Church members, and their idea that everything should be done for them and nothing required of them. He did his best to get the Church to realize its responsibility and undertake at least partial support of the evangelistic staff' (*Ye Are My Witnesses*, 1942, 52).[2]

Two themes stand out in the considerable body of Baptist missionary photography concerning the Chittagong Hill Tracts: spreading the Gospel, and contributing to health services in the area. In this chapter we deal with the former.

Foreign missionaries always worked with local helpers, as **plate 203** shows.

***Plate 203***. *'A Gospel Lesson by the Riverside in the Hill Tracts.' (Missionary Herald, 1912)*

One early local preacher was Sonaram Chakma, seen at work in **plate 204**. Half a century later, we see Aung Sau Khyang sitting behind the foreign missionary, Rev. Keith Skirrow, as they discuss a religious pamphlet with Buddhist monks (**plate 205**). The tape recorder, used to play Gospel recordings, was then a novel means of overcoming language barriers in missionary work.

In the winter months, missionaries and local preachers regularly went 'on tour,' preaching the Gospel in the villages of the Chittagong hills (**plate 206**).

***Plate 204***. *'Evangelist Sonaram Sen [Chakma] with a group at Rangamati,' about 1913. (Baptist Missionary Society)*

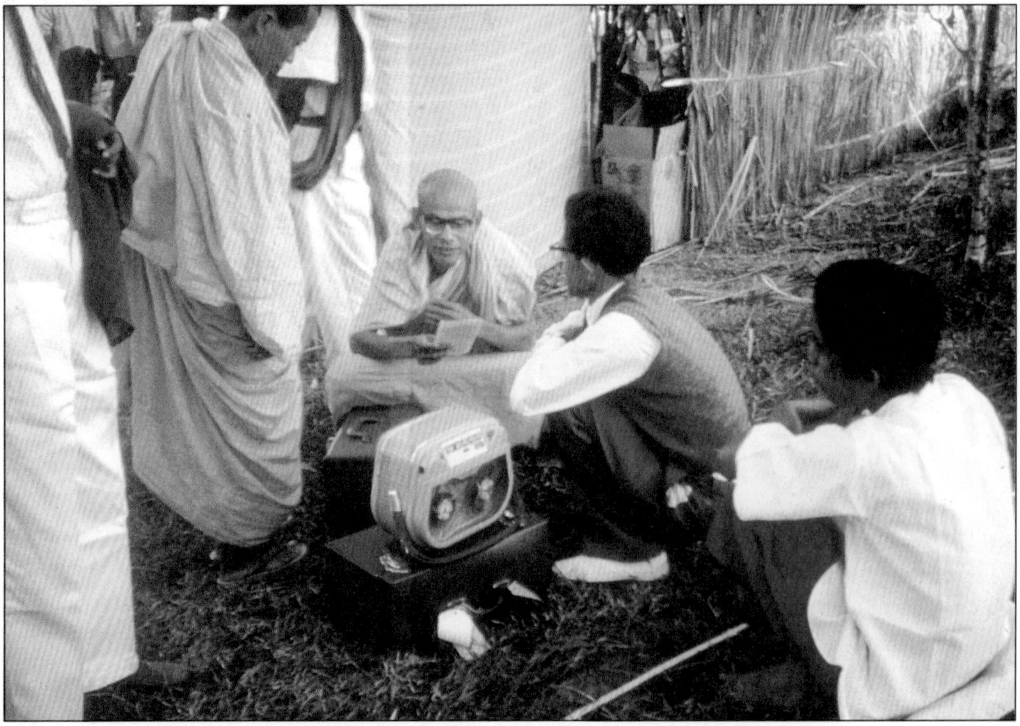

***Plate 205***. *Rev. Keith Skirrow and Aung Sau Khyang discussing a religious pamphlet with Buddhist monks. (Skirrow, 1964)*

***Plate 206***. *Aung Sau Khyang and Rev. Keith Skirrow setting out for a tour of Kaptai. (Skirrow, 1963)*

> 'We used to start at dusk,' reminisced Rev. Percy Jones in 1936, 'and travel in a canoe, rowed by the boys, to a convenient village. There we landed and fixed up the sheet in the middle of the street. The whole village turned out to see the pictures, and our Christian Endeavourers explained them' (Jones, 1936, 81; cf. Griffiths, 1927).

Doing this on bicycle could pose unexpected risks:

> 'One thing that surprised me in cycling was the number of snakes lying across the path. When one is walking they hear the footsteps and escape, but the cycle takes them by surprise ... Once I got one caught in my back wheel ... I only knew of it when Thoynsau shouted: "There's a snake in your back wheel." Not knowing the proper thing to do, I rode as hard as possible for awhile, and then suddenly jumped off. I found the snake so wound round the hub that it was quite a work to get it out' (Jones, 1936, 244; **plate 207**).

***Plate 207***. *Rev. F.W. Smith, Rangamati. (Smith, 1960)*

One of the initial problems for missionaries was a lack of written material in the local languages. They translated Gospel portions into Marma and Chakma, using the Roman script.

> 'Unfortunately both the Chackmas and the Mogs had a script of their own and try as we would they could not be made to learn the Roman script. So after a time we had to use their own scripts and Mr. Wenger made a translation which he had lithographed in the Chackma script which was widely accepted, and with the help of Thwainhlaphru I made a translation of the Gospel of John and also a small hymn book and cyclostyled it' (Teichmann, 1984, 21; **plate 208**).

Conversion to Christianity was symbolised by public baptism which was often photographed. **Plates 209-211** show local people joining the Baptist denomination.

The missionaries found that converts needed protection and constant instruction to keep them on the straight and narrow.

> 'When I arrived in ... 1911 the Christian community in the hill tracts was at a very low ebb,' wrote Teichmann, 'The newly baptised Christians had had very little constructive teaching in the essentials of Christianity ... we found that [the six local evangelists] did not really understand the message and much of what they taught was only a modification of Buddhism. Unfortunately the evangelists had been exempted from paying the Head-tax and this annoyed the Chiefs, who, instigated by the Buddhist priests, threatened reprisals. The result was that, like those in the parable, the Christians took fright and fell away and bore no fruit' (Teichmann, 1984, 12).

The combination of local and Christian styles can be seen in **plate 212**, showing Christians of a Tripura village in the Chittagong Hill Tracts, about 1962. They had brought in a *gayal* (semi-domesticated bull) which was to be sacrificed for a feast in honour of visiting missionaries.

***Plate 208****. A page of 'Prabhu Jishu Khrista: Tar Jibanar Kada' (1913), in Chakma script.*

***Plate 209****. 'Priya Babu baptizes in the Karnaphuli at Chandraghona, Ongu Chackma, who with his brother Shoblikya were eye patients & both desired baptism.' (Baptist Missionary Society, 1907)*

The sacrificing of gayals during ceremonial feasts was of central importance in some of the local religions of the Chittagong Hill Tracts (see our chapter 'Religions of the Hills').

Religious instruction was essential to keep the small flock together. Missionaries introduced schools, not only in Rangamati and Chandraghona, where they built hostels for students who came from far away (**plate 213**), but also in villages with a good number of converts. Teaching was done in Bengali (**plate 214**) and there was much emphasis on Bible stories, hymns, writing and sewing.

> 'Every morning we began with hymn-singing, and the girls learned to sing half-a-dozen hymns fairly tunefully, and certainly with understanding and enjoyment ... Then they heard a Bible story, always illustrated with pictures, and after that came reading' (Manson and Starke, 1935, 146; cf. Jones, 1936, 80).

***Plate 210**. 'Woman being baptised in Karnaphuli River.' (J. Bottoms, 1930s)*

***Plate 211**. Baptism by Dr Bottoms, Chandraghona. (D. Bottoms, 1959)*

**Plate 212**. *Christian Tripura with a gayal to be sacrificed in honour of visiting Baptist missionaries. (Smith, 1962)*

**Plate 213**. *'Lushai schoolboys' hostel, Rangamati,' about 1910. (Baptist Missionary Society)*

**Plate 214**. *'The Baptist Mission Primary School at Rangamati.' (Taylor, 1954)*

**Plate 215**. *Officers of the Chittagong Hill Tracts Baptist Union.*[3] *(Skirrow, 1963)*

Local Baptists were organised in the Chittagong Hill Tracts Baptist Union (**plate 215**). They had close links with other Baptist communities in eastern Bengal, especially in Barisal, Dhaka, Mymensingh and, before Partition, the Garo Hills and the Lushai Hills (**plate 216**).

Financial dependence on gifts from abroad remained acute. Photographs of school-children were favourites back in Britain. The number in the lower right-hand corner of **plate 217** indicates that this photograph was used for showing ('deputation') to Baptist congregations in Britain. The building of a new church was a major achievement and an activity of great symbolic significance (**plate 218**).

The missionaries often thought of themselves as pioneers who bore the hardships of life in the Chittagong hills with fortitude and good cheer.

> 'W.J.L. Wenger ... was a born pioneer and [in the 1930s] toured far up the valleys and across the hills in search of the wandering Chakmas. He and his wife made a house at Dighinala, two days' journey by cycle north of Rangamati, only to find, on arrival, that the Chakmas had moved on still further. This gives one a picture of the difficulties under which the work among these wild and ignorant people is still being carried out' (*Ye Are My Witnesses*, 1942, 54) (**plate 219**).

Pioneering of another kind was done by two women missionaries, Christine Manson (**plate 220**) and Muriel Starke (**plate 221**), who were 'specially appointed for Women's Work in the Chittagong Hill Tracts' in 1935. Despite some success with teaching young girls, they found working with women in Ultachori and Pablakhali villages difficult:

> 'Several of them came to the sewing class regularly, and listened to the Bible stories there, but one dare not affirm that they came for any purpose but the needlework. When a woman has for thirty, forty or more years lived a practically animal existence, is it surprising that she has no interest in the "things of God," and that the idea of a God Who loves her finds her unresponsive, as if she were listening to another language? We trust that it is worth while, that there is a soul to respond, but so far it is almost entirely a matter of faith and not sight' (Manson and Starke, 1935, 146-147) (**plate 222**).

Christian missionary work did not produce a large following among the inhabitants of the Chittagong hills. After 27 years in the area, one missionary wrote about the 'power of heathen surroundings':

> 'While steady progress was being made in the Station, both in our school work and the medical work of Dr. Teichmann, we had ever to bear in mind that it was the evangelisation of the Hill Tracts that was our real duty. With this end in view touring was carried on

***Plate 216**. Bhipendra Sarkar, a preacher from Barisal, at Rangamati. (Taylor, 1954)*

***Plate 217***. *'Rangamati girls return to school by launch from Chandraghona—1953.' (Manson, 1953)*

***Plate 218***. *'Opening of our new church,' Rangamati. (Skirrow, 1967)*

***Plate 219***. *Rev. F.W. and Mrs. L. Smith 'outside the house the Christians built for us at Ultachori (Maini Valley).' (Manson, 1958)*

every winter, but the story of these tours is a succession of bright hopes speedily dashed to the ground... multitudes would accept the Gospel message with enthusiasm, but throw it up again with the same ease a little later ... The tragedy was that while they belonged to us when they were little, most of them drifted farther and farther away as the years went by' (Jones, 1936, 166-167).

Very few Marma converted to Christianity. **Plate 223** shows a rare Marma Christian wedding. In 1968 Mra Shang Ching (fourth from the right) married Shwe Hla Phru, adopted son of Rev. and Mrs. Wenger. Other groups did, however, adopt Christianity in larger numbers. The religion became popular among e.g. Bawm and Lushai inhabitants of the Chittagong Hill Tracts (**plates 224** and **225**).

***Plate 220***. *'C. Manson with two children.' (Starke, 1940s)*

***Plate 221***. *'Children with M. Starke.' (Manson, about 1940)*

***Plate 222***. *'The Pablakhali house - 1941.' (Starke)*

***Plate 223***. *Wedding of Mra Shang Ching and Shwe Hla Phru.*
*(M.K. Maung collection, 1968)*

***Plate 224***. *The celebration of fifty years of Christianity in Munnuam, a Bawm village.*
*(A. Mey, 1968)*

***Plate 225***. *Wedding of Roman Catholic Lushai in Rangamati. (Skirrow, 1960s)*

**Plate 226**. *'The Rangamatti Dispensary and Temporary Wards,' 1904. (Baptist Missionary Society)*

**Plate 227**. *'Earth cutting Chandraghona,' 1907. The labourers employed to build the Chandraghona hospital were mostly Bengalis. (Baptist Missionary Society)*

**Plate 228**. *'Dispensary trench being made, May 1907. With umbrella Kio Zuo.' Kio Zuo, also spelled Kio Zwi, was a Marma evangelist at Chandraghona.*[1] *(Baptist Missionary Society)*

*Chapter 13*

# A HOSPITAL AT CHANDRAGHONA

In 1904 the Baptist Medical Mission began work in a dispensary in Rangamati (**plate 226**) but when the missionaries wanted to build a hospital there the plan was 'negatived by the Police Superintendent as he had planned to have a Government Hospital there. However, he offered a suitable site at Chandraghona.' This was welcomed:

> 'There are many interesting stations, but none, I fancy, will offer a more manifold field for usefulness and work than Chandraghona, touching as it does both the men of the hills and those of the plains' (Dr. Orissa Taylor (1907), quoted in Teichmann, 1984, 10).

The medical services offered by the missionaries soon attracted patients.

> 'Every morning patients gathered in the contre room,' writes Teichmann, 'and while

***Plate 229**. 'Skeleton of Dispensary Chandraghona, May 1907.' (Baptist Missionary Society)*

***Plate 230**. The hospital was opened in 1908, and gradually expanded in later years. The general view from a hill, with the Karnaphuli river in the background, was a favourite with photographers over the years. (Bottoms/Maslen collection, 1936)*

***Plate 231***. *'3 Tippera Patients, Rangamatti', 1905.' (Baptist Missionary Society)*

***Plate 232***. *'5 Hill Eye Patients, 1 Plains (Burma) Eye Patient, Chandraghona,' 1908. (Baptist Missionary Society)*

***Plate 233**. 'Group of Kala Azar Patients, Chandraghona,' about 1910.*
*(Baptist Missionary Society)*

***Plate 234****. 'A few of the houses on the Leper Hill.' (J. Bottoms, 1930s)*

***Plate 235****. Ongma (right) and friend in the leprosy colony. (D. Bottoms, 1959)*

the doctor was doing his rounds one of the compounders preached to them ... We did not make much headway, however, with evangelism as the people showed no desire to listen' (Teichmann, 1984, 17, 19).

Photographs of some of the earliest patients survive in the Medical Mission Log Book of the hospital.

The arrival of two lepers in 1913 prompted the creation of a leprosy colony (**plate 234**). The third patient to arrive shortly afterwards was Ongma, a Marma girl from the nearby village of Barogunia.

> 'As she had to leave the village, her father built a house outside the village and lived there with her until he heard of our small leprosy home. He brought her to us and asked us to look after her. She was only about thirteen years old. Her name was Ongma' (Teichmann, 1984, 33) (**plate 235**).

Few patients of the hospital wrote down their memories. An exception was Tridiv Roy of Rangamati.

> 'When I was about five I was taken to the Baptist Mission Hospital at Chandraghona in the Hill Tracts. They had opened a children's section in the hospital [the King George V Memorial Children's Ward, opened in 1937] and I was the first victim. My parents were reluctant at first but the missionary Doctor Teichmann prevailed upon them to let him take out my infected tonsils. I clung to Ayahbu [his maidservant], and one nurse not succeeding, two had to drag me away from her to get me into the operation theatre' (T. Roy, n.d.).

The hospital soon gained a reputation for the quality of its medical services. It also became an important training centre for medical staff. The hospital staff, small at first but growing steadily, was very diverse in terms of ethnic and regional background (**plate 236**).

***Plate 236**. Hospital staff, Chandraghona Baptist Mission Hospital, about 1910. From left to right: Syamcharan Chackma (compounder), Sadiv (Hindustani sweeper), Rajendra Lal Biswas (Doctor babu), Muckti Chackma (compounder). unidentified (dispenser?). (Baptist Missionary Society)*

It became a tradition at regular intervals to take photographs of members of staff and student nurses outside the hospital (**plates 237-239**). These pictures were always highly ordered, with individuals positioned in neat rows, looking composedly towards the camera. Such photographs later served as tools to recall a period of work or study spent together at the Chandraghona hospital.

The regular work of the staff was seldom photographed (**plate 240**) except for the operation theatre, which was a favourite with photographers through the years. **Plates 241-243** show operations in the 1920s and 1950s. The image of the medical team ministering to an anaesthetised patient symbolises the most lasting effect of missionary activity in the Chittagong Hill Tracts: the Chandraghona hospital outlived its colonial beginnings to become part of the health services of Pakistan and, later, Bangladesh.

***Plate 237***. *'The hospital staff outside the hospital, Feb. 1947.' The little girl, seated between her parents, is Jennifer Bottoms, daughter of the hospital's surgeon. (J. Bottoms)*

***Plate 238***. *Student nurses and student compounders. These students, flanking staff nurses Thwaingya Khyang and Sanga Lushai (seated 4th and 5th from the left), came from five Bengal districts. (Taylor, 1957)*

**Plate 239**. *Student nurses, Chandraghona hospital.*[2] *(Taylor, 1962)*

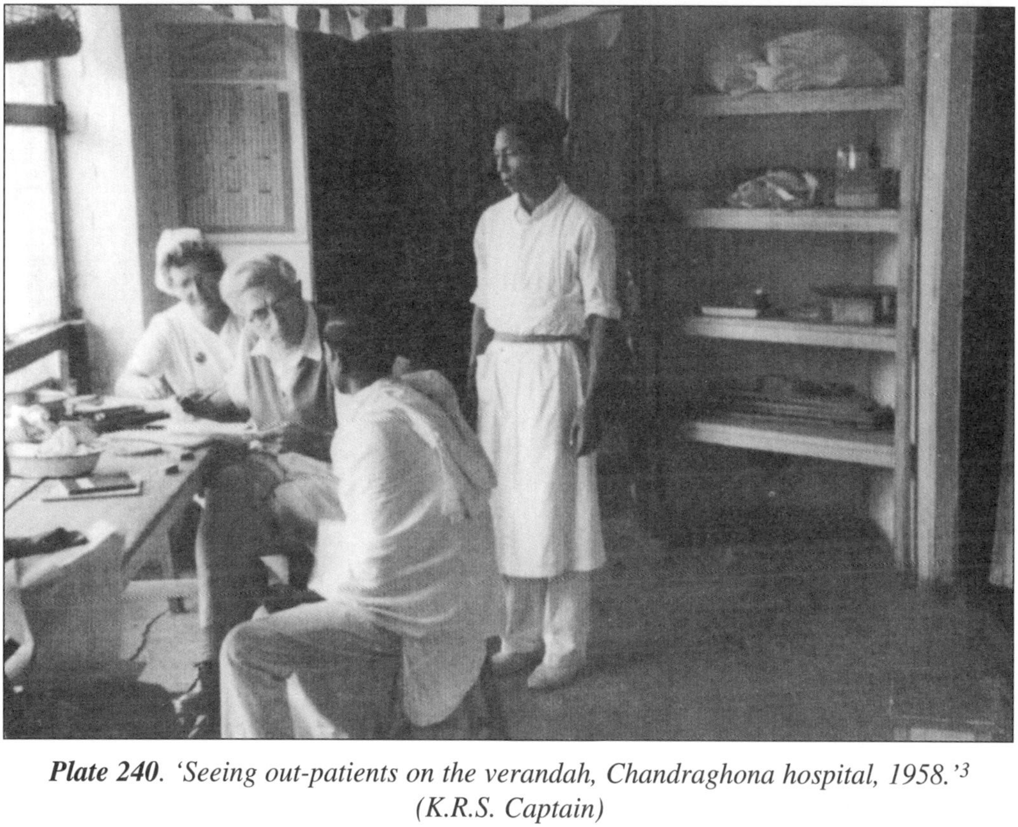

**Plate 240**. *'Seeing out-patients on the verandah, Chandraghona hospital, 1958.'*[3] *(K.R.S. Captain)*

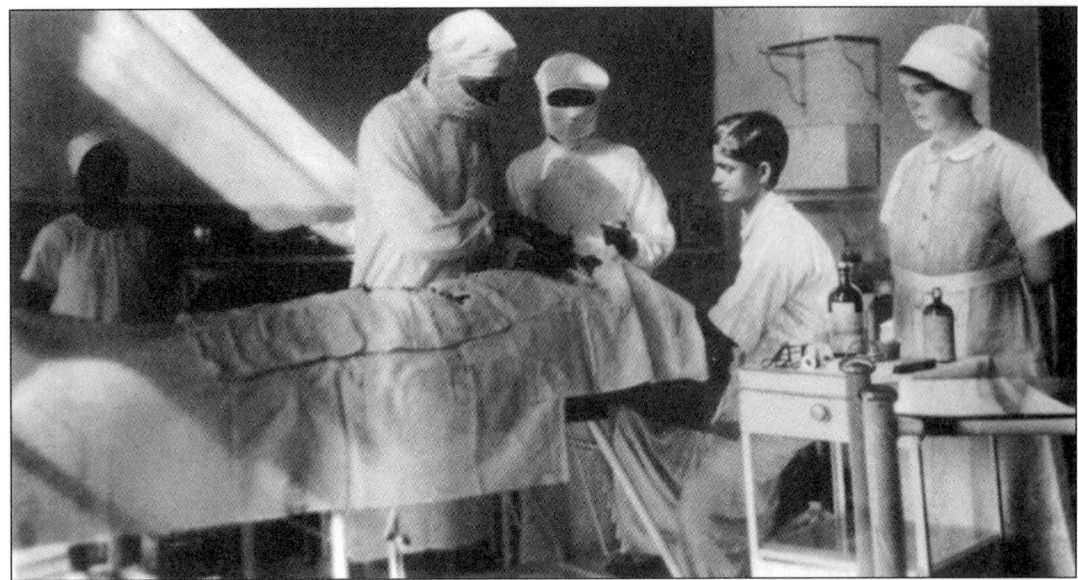

**Plate 241**. *'Dr. Teichmann assisted by Dr. Kedu Biswas at an operation for removal of piece of bone—Note: The Midday Sun'; 1920s. (Baptist Missionary Society)*

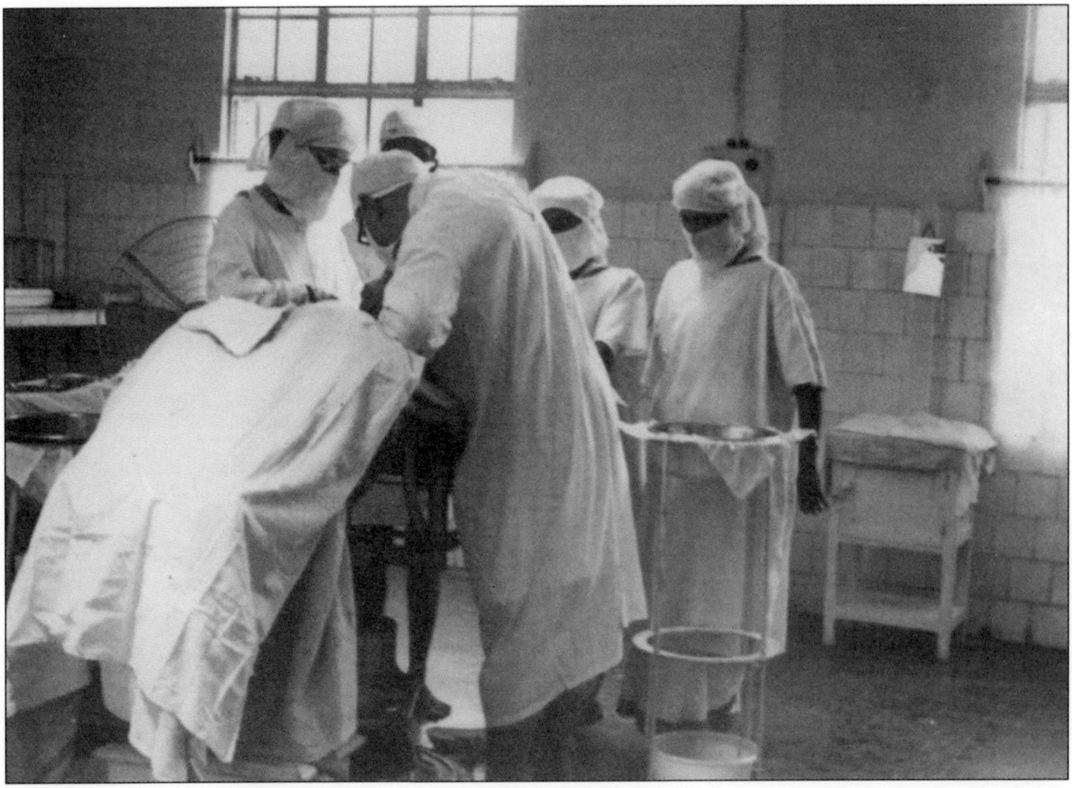

**Plate 242**. *'"Another op." Dr. J.W. Bottoms operating in Chandraghona hospital, c. 1956.' (Skirrow)*

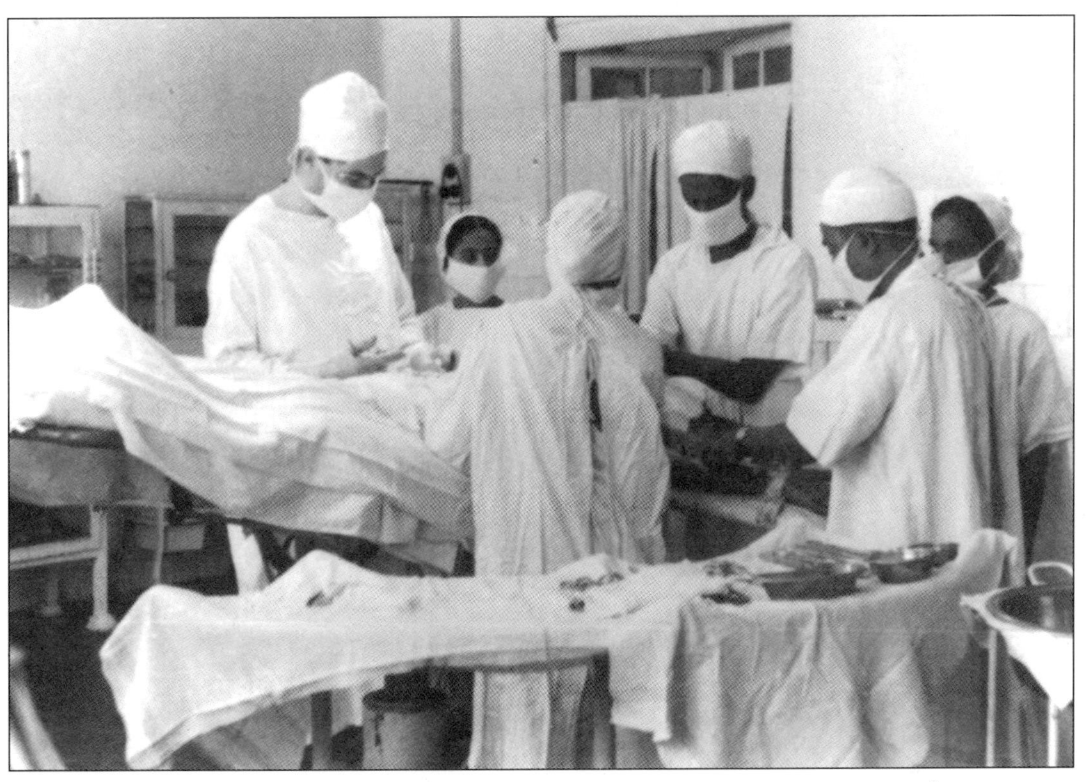

**Plate 243**. *'Operating Theatre.'*[4] *(Taylor collection, 1957)*

***Plate 244**. 'Site of the Paper Mill at Chandraghona in East Pakistan.' (Pakistan's Industries, 1953)*

***Plate 245**. 'Karnaphuli Paper Mill under construction.' (Taylor, 1953)*

***Plate 246**. Machinery being brought in by boat. (J. Bottoms, 1953)*

*Chapter 14*

# DEVELOPING THE HILLS

Right from its birth in 1947, the state of Pakistan presented itself as a development-oriented state. Its efforts to build a new nation, make the economy more market-oriented and 'integrate' minorities all dovetailed into what came to be known as development policy. It was therefore no coincidence that from the 1950s development emerged as an important theme in photographs of the Chittagong hills. The paucity of activities that could actually be identified as 'development' in the Chittagong Hill Tracts meant that two projects stood out.

## 14.1 The Karnaphuli Paper Mill.

In 1949 an Industrial Conference was held in Pakistan; it recommended the establishment of a pulp and paper factory in East Pakistan because:

> 'Pakistan has to import about 35,000 tons of paper every year—this when Pakistan possesses almost limitless quantities of fibrous raw material in the form of bamboos and grasses ...The site of the mill was selected at Chandraghona, 26 miles upstream from Chittagong ... keeping in view the accessability of the place from Chittagong port, and

***Plate 247**. 'Inside the Karnaphuli Paper Mill.' (J. Bottoms, 1950s)*

***Plate 248***. *Paper Mill, Chandraghona. (D. Bottoms, 1959)*

***Plate 249***. *The new manager (centre) doing the rounds. (Meier collection, 1955-61)*

***Plate 250***. *New housing scheme for mill labourers. (Meier collection, 1955-61)*

***Plate 251***. *Studying on the school verandah. (Meier collection, 1955-61)*

> nearness to the sources of raw material and water' ('On the Bank,' 1952, 66).

The Karnaphuli Paper Mill became the first large-scale development project in the Chittagong Hill Tracts. In 1951,

> 'hills began to be levelled, deep ravines and crevices filled, thick and dense forests cleared to make way for the birth of a giant industrial unit—one of the biggest paper mills in the East' (*Pakistan Moves*, 1956, 2) (**plates 244** and **245**).

The mill was given the right for 99 years to extract its raw material from forest areas along two distant tributaries of the Karnaphuli river. In the dry season, some 2,000 contract labourers were employed in these forests to cut down and transport bamboo and wood. Machinery was brought up by river (**plate 246**) and thousands of mill-hands from the plains settled in Chandraghona when the mill came into production in 1953 (**plate 247**).

The paper mill became a source of national pride and was described in glowing terms.

> 'Today the site presents an exhilarating spectacle of the happy blending of nature's seductive beauty with the impressive workmanship of human effort. The lush and green forests of the Hill Tracts and the placid and serene waters of the river lend a touch of romance to the project' (Pakistan Moves, 1956, 2) (**plate 248**).

Soon, however, this idyll was shattered. In 1954 the Bihari manager and nine others got killed in a violent clash. As a result the Pakistan Industrial Development Corporation (PIDC) decided to employ foreign experts as managers of the mill and make the area a protected zone under the jurisdiction of the mill manager who was given armed Pakhtun (Pathan) security men. With the new manager, a Swiss named Hans Meier, came a new style of management, including daily rounds through all sections of the mill (**plate 249**), a housing scheme for staff (**plate 250**), a school (**plate 251**) and some attempts to reduce the severe pollution of the Karnaphuli river caused by the mill's effluents (cf. Chowdhury, 1957).

***Plate 252***. *The President of Pakistan, Ayub Khan, on a visit to the Paper Mill. (Meier collection, about 1959)*

In the late 1950s and 1960s the Karnaphuli Paper Mill became one of the industrial show-pieces of East Pakistan. High government officials were frequent visitors and foreign state guests were also taken to see it (**plates 252-254**). As an important symbol of Pakistan's economic development, the mill celebrated 'state events' such as Pakistan's Liberation Day with due ceremony (**plate 255**).

***Plate 253****. A visit by Nawab Malik Amir Mohammed, Khan of Kalabagh and President of the Pakistan Industrial Development Corporation (PIDC). (Meier collection, about 1959)*

***Plate 254****. 'Visitors from Saudi Arabia.' (Meier collection, about 1959)*

***Plate 255***. *'Liberation Day.' (Meier collection, about 1959)*

In his memoirs, the manager of the paper mill recalled his reception:

> 'The Chief Engineer, who during the interregnum had acted as General Manager, was very unhappy [with my arrival]. For a Lancashireman who once told me: "We Britishers colonised almost the whole world," it must have been almost an affront that I, a Swiss, had been appointed. (Perhaps his attitude had been the cause of this.) In short, the "Number One" usually rides in Jeep No. 1 and lives in Bungalow No. 1, but this number was already in use. I recognised immediately how embarrassed the staff were... My decision: let me have Jeep No. 11. After all, eleven consists of two ones. Upon this, the bungalow was also designated as 11 ... and the Volkswagen which I got later also took 11 as its number' (Meier, 1996, 9). **(plate 256)**

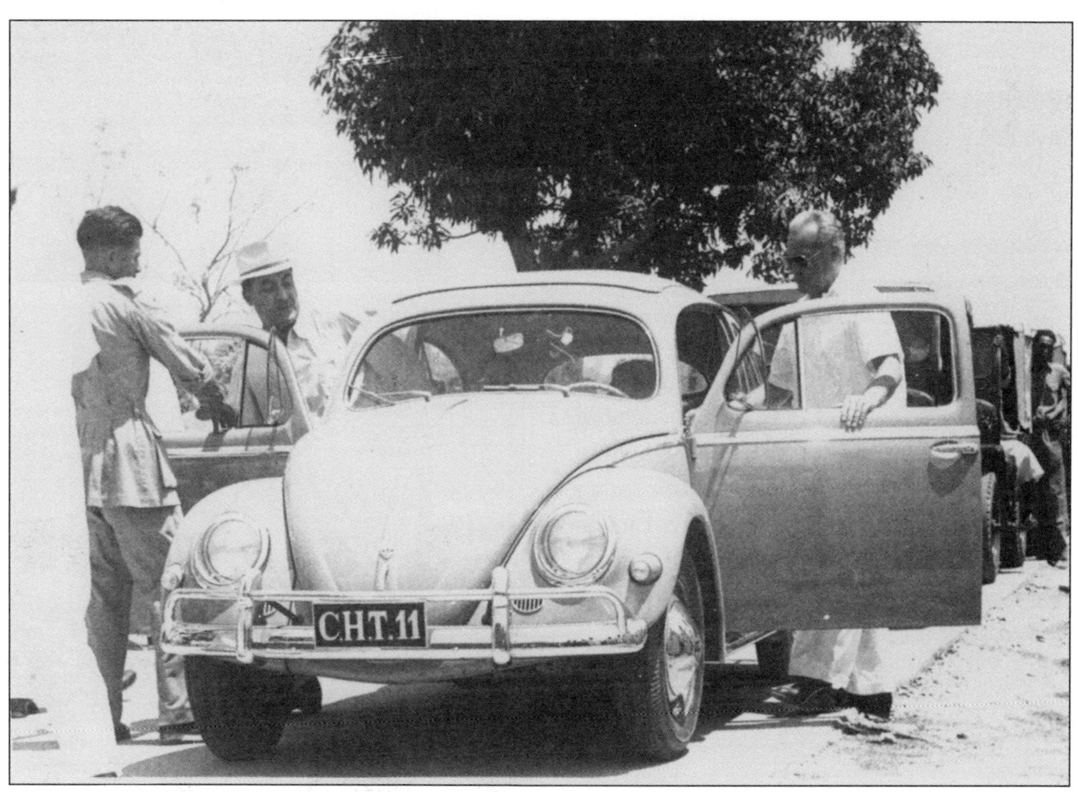


***Plate 256****. The manager's Volkswagen. (Meier collection, 1958)*

***Plate 257***. *Karnaphuli Rayon & Chemicals Factory, Chandraghona, 1966.*

Between 1959 and 1964 the PIDC gradually transferred the management and ownership of the paper mill to the Dawood Corporation. In 1966 this corporation set up the Karnaphuli Rayon & Chemicals Ltd. in Chandraghona; in a brochure the new factory presented itself proudly as a picture of modernity and development (**plate 257**).

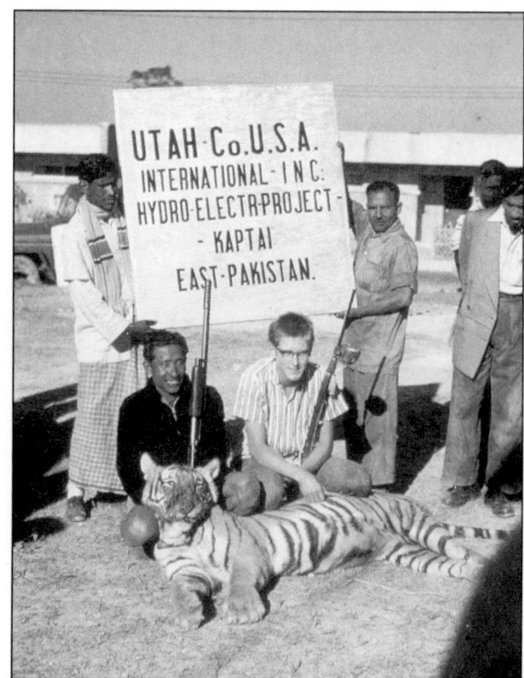


***Plate 258***. *The UTAH Company at Kaptai. (Barblan, 1959)*

## 14.2 The Kaptai Hydroelectric Project

Begun slightly later than the paper mill, the hydroelectric project developed into the pre-eminent symbol of state-driven development in the Chittagong Hill Tracts. A hydroelectric dam had been proposed as early as 1906 at one of the four places where there are rapids in the Karnaphuli river. The rapids at Barkal were recommended. But it was not till 1951 that the plan was put into operation, and by that time the partition of India and Pakistan had made it impossible to build a dam at Barkal: this would have created a reservoir extending well into Indian territory. It was decided to build the hydroelectric complex at Kaptai, a village on the Karnaphuli between Rangamati and Chandraghona. The work, carried out largely by a U.S. construction company employing largely non-local labour, involved engineer-ing feats that had never been seen before in the Chittagong hills (**plates 258-263**).

***Plate 259***. *Constructing the dam. (Barblan, 1959)*

When the first phase of the project was completed (**plate 264**) and the power-house officially opened (**plate 265**), it provided an image of development that many residents of Kaptai and their visitors found irresistible; the Kaptai spillway became a much photographed landmark (**plate 266**).

The Pakistan government was proud of its achievement and the Kaptai hydroelectric project became a show-piece. Much was written about the project and it was shown to foreign state guests as a symbol of Pakistan's development (**plates 267** and **268**).

The village of Kaptai, until the mid-1950s a hill village like any other, was transformed; it became a development enclave—a small town with modern amenities such as electricity and comfortable bungalows for hundreds of expatriate experts, a large school and an elegant mosque for new settlers (**plates 269-271**).

***Plates 260*** *and* ***261***. *Building and levelling, Kaptai project. (Barblan, 1959-60)*

***Plate 262***. *Bengali labourers unloading stone, Kaptai. (Barblan, 1959)*

***Plate 263***. *Welding together a penstock. (Barblan, 1960)*

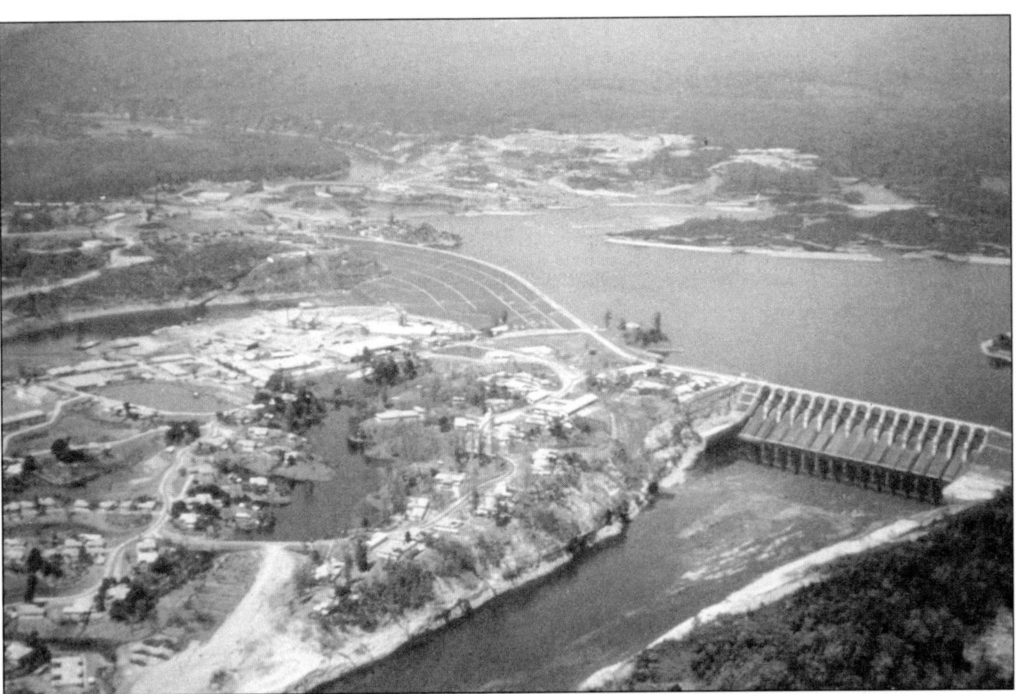

***Plate 264**. Aerial view, Kaptai town and dam. (Sandercock, 1964-65)*

***Plate 265**. President Ayub Khan at the official opening of the Kaptai power house. (Bientjes, 1963)*

***Plate 266***. *Spillway at Kaptai. (Bientjes, 1962)*

***Plate 267***. *General Ne Win, president of Burma, visits Kaptai. (Recter, 1965)*

***Plate 268***. *At Kaptai, dancers and officials are waiting for the arrival of a Turkish delegation. On the arch is written: 'We support the Turkish position on Cyprus.' (Sigl, 1965-69)*

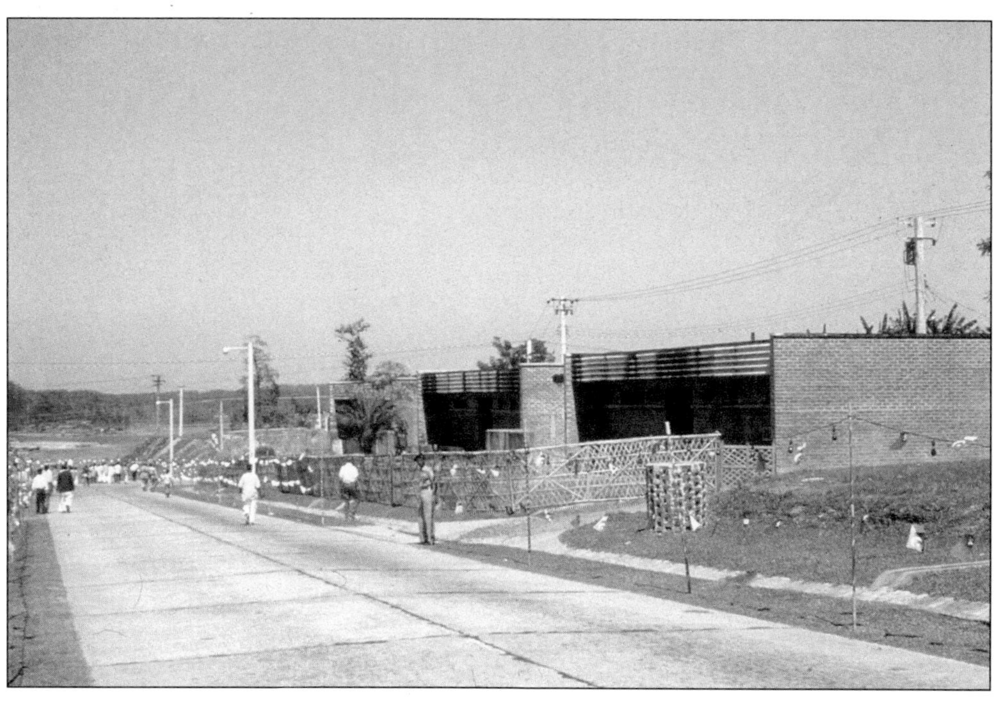

***Plate 269***. *View of expatriates' bungalows in Kaptai. (Recter, 1965)*

***Plate 270***. *Kaptai school. (Sigl, 1965-69)*

***Plate 271***. *Id celebration at Kaptai mosque. (Barblan, 1959-61)*

The Kaptai dam was widely celebrated as a triumph of modernity.

> 'Emerging in Kaptai, [the traveller] suddenly faces the harsh light of 20th century engineering. Sweeping majestically before him is a clean-lined, 100 million dollar hydro-electric dam, 2,200 feet across the broad expanse of the Karnaphuli river ... Rising beyond the dense elephant-infested hills, the river meanders through the valley and courses down the plain to the Bay of Bengal ... The dam was constructed to tame this turbulent river, control flooding and provide round-the-year irrigation to the farmers in the valley ... High voltage transmission wires, stringing from the crest of the hills down to the trackless horizon below, carry 80,000 KW of electricity generated at the nearby Karnaphuli Power House to feed the main grid going down to the provincial capital of Dacca and its twin city of Narayanganj, light homes and turn the wheels of industry ... Backing the dam is a reservoir ... giving access to the roadless jungles with their rare animals, birds and plants. The lake itself, in idyllic setting, has been turned into a holiday resort ... And yet so close to the comforts and conveniences of the 20th century clings the ancient mystic East' (Ali, 1971, 12).

The Kaptai dam created an upstream reservoir of 650 square kilometers, flooding some 40 percent of the most productive valley land of the Chittagong Hill Tracts.

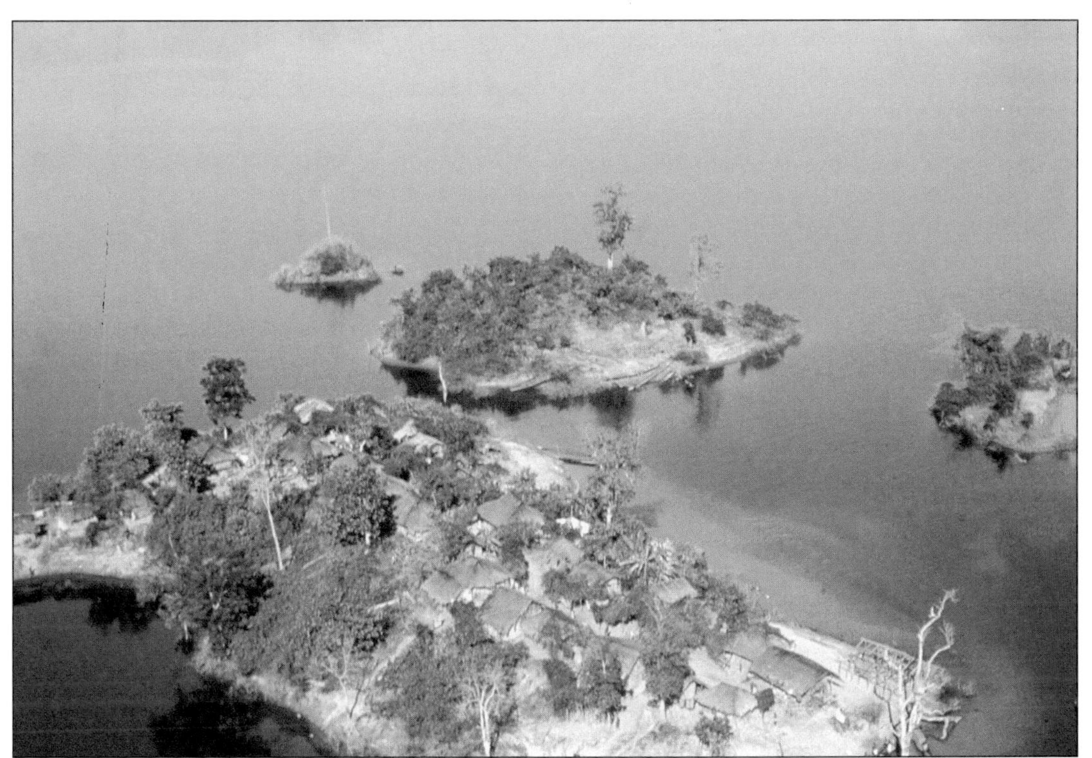

***Plate 272**. Refugee huts on a hill-top island in Kaptai lake. (Recter, 1965)*

It submerged many villages and forests, dislocated more than one-quarter of the region's total population and caused enormous environmental damage (Forestal Report, 1966; Johnson and Ahmad, 1957) (**plate 272**). Some hill people felt that the decision to locate the dam at Kaptai had been politically motivated because it would result in the dispersal and weakening of a large and vocal population (T. Roy, n.d.). The economic, social, environmental and, eventually, political costs of the Kaptai project would prove to be enormous. This made the project the pre-eminent symbol of the ill effects of authoritarian, top-down 'development' in East Pakistan:

> 'It was called a multi-purpose dam, for it was supposed to provide not only electricity, but flood control in the plains of Chittagong and irrigation facilities. As it turned out, every year since the dam was built there have been floods in the very region it was supposed to save, with unfailing regularity. As for irrigation, by its very coming into existence it submerged most of the cultivable lands and there was hardly anything left to irrigate ... there were two benefits besides the generation of electricity—improvement of navigation, though rates of siltation have been more rapid in the upper reaches of the [reservoir] than expected, and fishery. Needless to say, despite oft-repeated and grandiose government plans and promises, not a single tribal village has been electrified —though electricity found its way into towns, as well as villages in the plains districts' (T. Roy, n.d.).

Most of those who were uprooted by the reservoir were completely unprepared; they remember the sudden flooding of their homesteads and land, the panic of their flight, and the breaking up of families and communities as the *Boro Porong* (Great Exodus). The social trauma caused by the Kaptai project was deep and lasting. In the words of Shilabrata Tangchangya:

> 'I still hear the booming sounds of the dam gate closing that continued throughout the whole night. By the morning, the water had reached our door-steps. We set free our cows and goats, hens and ducks, and then began the rush with the affected people to take their rice, paddy, furniture and whatever else possible to the nearby hills ... Though every possible belonging was taken to the hill top, many still went to their houses to spend the night. But many of them had to rush out of their houses at dead of night when the swelling water touched them while they slept' (H. Chakma et al., 1995, 26).

Although some cultivators were resettled in erstwhile reserved forests (**plate 273**), the great majority was not 'rehabilitated' at all, and had to fend for themselves. The most prominent evacuee, the Chakma chief, refused the amount offered to defray the expense of moving house:

> 'I told the government that they paid more money to their *peons* and *chaprassis* [low-paid office orderlies] when they were transferred from one station to another ... what the provincial government did ... was grotesque and monstrously iniquitous ... We had no guns so we wept in silence, in humiliation and anger' (T. Roy, n.d.).

Nripati Ranjan Tripura used to live in Kellamura village:

> 'Our village was also devoured. We first took shelter on an adjacent hill. The hill was not affected by the inundation in the first year. The water came up to the base of the hill and stopped. During that time it looked like an island. But gradually, in the following months, the sides of the hill began to erode as the waves hit them. It completely went under water in the second year. We had no choice but to move ...' (H. Chakma et al., 1995, 26-27).

Many ordinary hill people were forced to seek refuge in other parts of the Chittagong hills. A group of scientists from the Asiatic Society of Pakistan, on 'expedition' in the southern hills in 1965, came across several settlements of development refugees, east of Ruma:

> 'We passed through the Murung [Mru] para ... It was a "mixed" para as we could see some Tipra families. The Murung Karbari told us that these helpless families came from lower Karnaphuli, meaning the "affected" people of the Kaptai lake area, and were looking for a suitable place to stay. He tried to help and so allowed them to settle here.' In another newly-settled village, in the Rainkhyong Forest Reserve, the Tipra headman 'was rather good in speaking broken Bengali. He started talking about his misfortune, etc., because he came, we were told, from the Kaptai area. He was a rich man, and boasted of once seeing and actually shaking hands with "Raja Ayub Khan"' (Husain, 1967, 136, 138).

Concerned about the destruction of the Rainkhyong Forest Reserve by these new settlers, the scientists reported the settlement to the authorities. They were pleased to learn shortly afterwards that:

> 'the para which existed on the shore of the [Rainkhyong] Lake for the previous five years was no more there. The authority had given them extreme punishment, which meant burning down the para. They and all other intruders had been completely ousted from the Reserve or nearly so ... That was the happiest news I heard for sometime ...We take this opportunity to congratulate our Forest Deptt. for this action which saved a beautiful forest and an extremely valuable fauna ... The intruders always claimed that they were from the area affected by the Kaptai Dam. This was a very weak point for the Government' (Husain, 1967, 164).

People dislocated by the Kaptai dam certainly destroyed forest land in their search for cultivable land but this destruction was much smaller than the momentous environmental damage done directly by the Kaptai lake (see chapter on 'Images of Nature and Destruction').

Tens of thousands of those who were displaced by the Kaptai project could not find a new niche in the Chittagong hills and had to seek refuge in India and Burma. The Indian government settled most of these development refugees in the state of Arunachal Pradesh in the 1960s, and they and their descendents are still there.

***Plate 273***. *'New Chakma settlement, Kasalong Rehabilitation Area.' (Sopher, 1962)*

## 14.3 The Surveyors are Coming

Although the Chandraghona paper mill and the Kaptai hydroelectric project were the first and most visible signs of 'development,' the 1960s saw many other activities. They were a period of prospecting and surveying all over the Chittagong hills, and the surveyors, Westerners armed with cameras, documented this. In the early 1960s, a survey of the Sangu and Matamuhuri rivers was carried out with a view to building a dam across these two rivers and establishing new hydroelectric projects there. **Plates 274** and **275** show something of the conditions under which the Sangu survey was carried out. The proposed hydroelectric projects themselves never materialised (cf. Husain, 1967, 164-165).

A much larger affair were the Forestry Surveys and the Soil and Land Use Survey, generally known as the Forestal survey (after the Canadian forestry and engineering firm which carried it out in 1964-65).

> 'The primary purpose of this soil and land use survey [was] to provide maps and reports on the land use, land classification and land capability of all land outside the Reserved Forests in the Chittagong Hill Tracts District [and] to recommend how this information can be integrated into a comprehensive development of the physical and human resources of the Project Area' (Forestal Report, I, 3).

The survey was funded lavishly, and had 'base camps' in different parts of the region. Forestal staff moved about in an oft-photographed helicopter; they took almost all aerial photographs included in this book (**plates 276-278**).

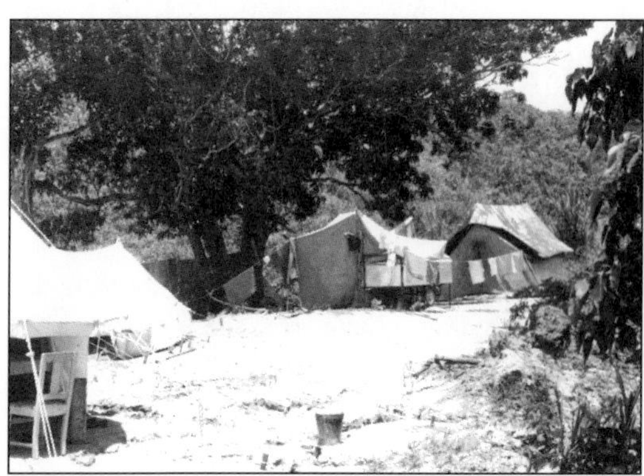

***Plates 274** and **275**. 'Sangu Survey.' (Laurence, about 1963)*

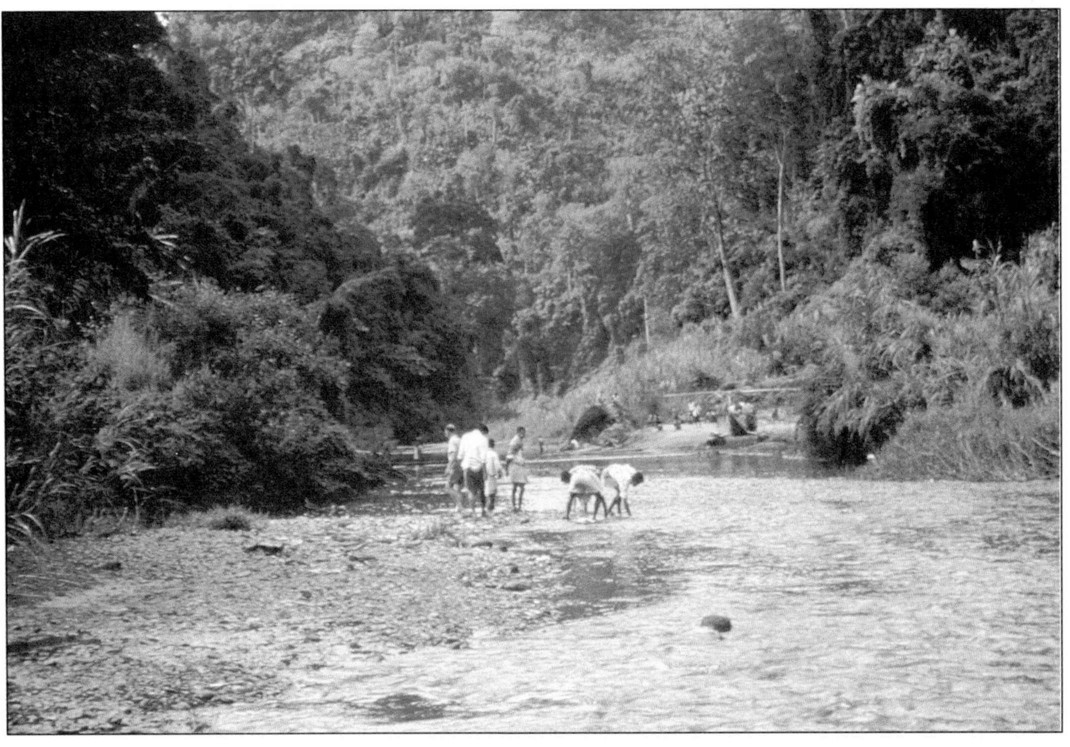

***Plate 276***. *Surveying fish in a tributary of the Rainkhyong river. (Lindsey, 1964)*

***Plate 277**. Forestal Survey signboard. (Recter, 1965)*

***Plate 278**. Dick Recter, agricultural engineer, in front of Forestal base camp at Khagrachhari. (Recter collection, 1965)*

Both the helicopter and the Forestal speedboat were frequently photographed (**plate 279**). Other important means of transport were Landrovers, but these were useless in many parts of the Chittagong hills because of the lack of roads and the very steep terrain. Surveying in the hills had to depend heavily on river and air transport. **Plates 280** and **281** illustrate some aspects of the work of the surveyors: observing a young rubber plantation at Rangamati and a Canadian forest expert studying logs in a reserved forest.

The 1960s also saw prospecting for oil in the Chittagong Hill Tracts. **Plate 282** shows Forestal staff visiting a Russian geologist (in shorts) who was working for the Russian-supported Oil & Gas Development Corporation, near Rangamati in 1965.

Although social services were slow to develop in the Chittagong hills, population control was a growing concern of the developmental state. Family planning centres were established but their effectiveness was low (**plate 283**).

***Plate 279**. Forestal field staff pose in front of the speedboat at Baradam. (Recter, 1965)*

***Plate 280***. *Rubber plantation near Rangamati. (Recter, 1965)*

***Plate 281***. *Forest expert W.J. Welsh inspecting logs in the Kasalong Reserved Forest. (Bientjes, 1963)*

**Plate 282**. *Visiting the Russian geologists' camp. (Recter, 1965)*

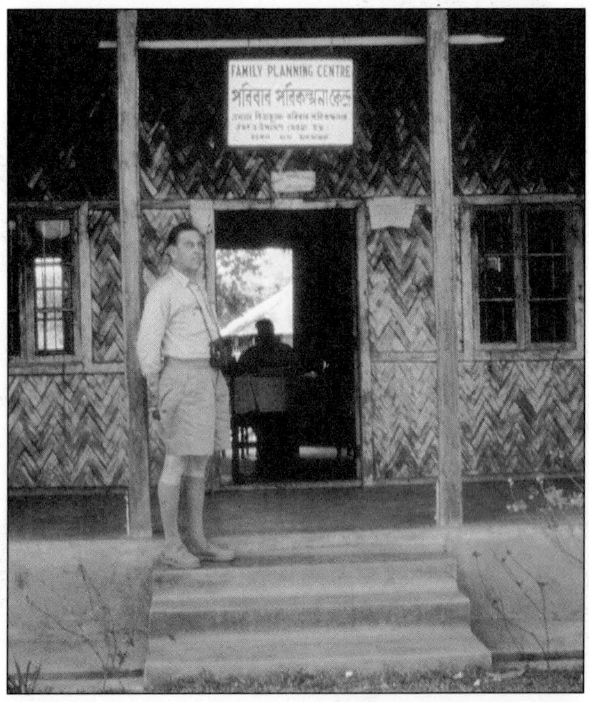


**Plate 283**. *Surveyor Stan Weston posing on the steps of the family planning centre in Barkal in the eastern Chittagong Hill Tracts. The signboard announced: 'Here you can get free family planning products and advice.' (Recter, 1965)*

## 14.4 Tourism

When Pakistani officials and entrepreneurs thought of the development potential of the Chittagong Hill Tracts, tourism was high on their agenda. The selling of the Chittagong Hill Tracts and their inhabitants focussed on the themes of natural beauty, exotic people and unchanging tradition. A tourist leaflet of the 1960s put it like this:

> 'Towering clouds—those magnificent clouds seen only in tropical skies—are reflected in the still waters of the rivers and lakes, over which float sampans and long rafts of roped bamboo. Primitive grandeur mingles with the exotic in these hill ranges and dense green forests which with sylvan pools present a fascinating panorama. The tribal life in the hill tracts contrasts sharply with that in the settled areas. The tribal folk lead a life of extreme simplicity earning little for modern ways and content with their few needs ... They dwell as did their ancestors in centuries past, untouched by time and progress ... Physically they are a short-statured but well proportioned race. Their features are distinctly Asiatic with high cheekbones, small almond eyes and jet-black hair. The menfolk are mostly beardless. The women are generally pretty and possess good figures. The usual male dress consists of a loin cloth while the women wear the sarong. These slender, bronze-hued people form a picture sque race' (Pakistan, 1968, 2-3).

The hill people were pictured as 'peace-loving, friendly and extremely hospitable,' 'jovial and carefree by nature,' and welcoming strangers to their 'communal festivities.' The state smiled on selected elements of the cultures of the hill people. These could play a role in the development of tourism. Folkloristic dance and 'tribal' handicrafts became the symbols of a carefree and unspoilt hill lifestyle which could attract tourists. 'Merely lazing in the dappled shade to watch the tribal girls dance' was the foremost attraction of the Chittagong Hill Tracts and leaflets routinely contained photographs captioned 'a dancing tribal girl,' 'a tribal damsel,' or 'a tribal belle' (e.g. Bangladesh—Chittagong Hill Tracts, 1974).

The second selling point was the Kaptai reservoir. In an advertisement of 1967, the Department of Tourism addressed the national elite and its escapist fantasies of freedom and relaxation (**plate 284**).

*Rediscovering Pakistan*

# THiS LAND THAT i LOVE...

## Speed-boating on Kaptai Lake

Who was this that whizzed past us
on the **Kaptai Lake?**
Surely, I remember him
from McLeod Road in Karachi.
A banker probably...
or a businessman!
Like me, he has left his cares behind.

After a strenuous speed-boating holiday,
he will return relaxed
to the strenuous work that awaits him
—until the next holiday.

Where shall we meet again?
—at **Mangla** perhaps!
Or, who knows, on **Kaptai** again...
this *256 sq. mile man-made lake!*

# Know your country!

DEPARTMENT OF TOURISM, GOVERNMENT OF PAKISTAN

On a promotional calendar, the Department described 'the biggest man-made lake in the Subcontinent' as providing 'excellent cruising by Motor Launches and Speedboats.' It also invested in tourism infrastructure, including houseboats and canoes (**plates 285** and **286**).

But folklore and natural beauty were not enough to make the Chittagong hills an important tourist destination. While the tourism authorities promised a Shangri-La, other government departments were far less welcoming to tourists, especially foreign ones. Those wishing to see more of the hills than Rangamati and Kaptai were warned that 'prior permission from government is required.' In reality, the Chittagong hills have been largely off-limits for outsiders since British times. As a result, tourism remained stunted. Its development was a failure. The chittagong hills never attracted many international travellers; they were more often the aim of local holiday-makers, Bengalis as well as foreigners.

Most of these went up to Rangamati and the Kaptai lake for boating, fishing, or water-skiing. Some did get permission to go beyond, and could stay in the resthouses which the government kept for its officials on tour (**plate 287**).

***Plate 285***. *Tourist Department houseboat on Kaptai lake. (Rashid, 1969)*

***Plate 286***. *Department of Tourism calendar, 1970. (Van Tellingen collection)*

***Plate 287***. *On a trek through the Chittagong hills. (Seifert, 1963)*

## 14.5 Development and the Local People

The state elite of Pakistan saw the Chittagong hills as a useful part of the country because it had exploitable natural resources. When they thought of the area, they thought of timber, bamboo, hydroelectric power, rubber and oil. But what about the local population? By and large, the hill people were not considered a useful resource. The exploitation of the natural resources of the Chittagong hills was not entrusted to them but to foreigners, West Pakistanis and Bengalis. Moreover, hill agriculture was seen as a nuisance, a harmful practice which interfered with forestry and plantations. Hill people were in the way of development projects, such as the Kaptai dam, and had to be removed. In short, the people of the hills were seen as a liability, except in tourism. They did not provide a large tax income to the state and were considered to be still too 'uncivilised' to partake of development. Some observers considered them good material for a future wage labour force in forestry and industry:

> 'With a leavening of civilisation these robust, healthy and courageous people may one day provide a fine manpower' (Kermani, 1953, 48; cf. Chittagong Hill Tracts Commission, 1991, 76) (**plate 288**).

But many others were less sanguine. They felt that the Chittagong Hill Tracts could not be developed properly without replacing jhum cultivation with intensive permanent agriculture. It was only a step from here to the idea that hill people should be replaced on their own land by wet-rice cultivators from the plains. That idea linked up with another: that the hills were 'empty' in comparison with the heavily populated plains. Although this view was sharply criticised in various reports of the 1960s, it continues to live a life of its own. In 1967, the East Pakistan Agricultural Development Corporation stated unequivocally:

'This leads to the startling conclusion that at present (1967) about 190,000 acres are being cultivated by about 475,000 persons, which means a density of 1,600 persons per square mile of cultivated land. The emptiness of the Hill Tracts is, therefore, a myth. As far as its developed resources are concerned, the Hill Tracts is as constrained as the most thickly populated [plains] District' (*Master-Plan*, 1967, 19).

Most officials would cast hill people in an anti-development role: too backward to join the national 'mainstream,' too attached to harmful hill agriculture, too often in the way of progress. Such assumptions fed a development model which excluded hill people, not only from positions of authority and policy-making, but even as beneficiaries of new employment, e.g. in the building and staffing of the paper mill and the Kaptai project. 'Development' was a bundle of activities carried out in the hills and legitimised rhetorically as beneficial to the hills, but largely without participation, let alone leadership, by hill people.

This pattern was to have dire consequences. The notion that the Chittagong hills were too precious to be left to their original inhabitants led to authoritarian interventions, first in the form of infrastructure projects, then in that of state-sponsored transmigration of settlers from the plains and eviction of hill people, and finally to military occupation. By the late 1970s, the hostility between the (military) authorities in charge of development and the local people had become complete. Occasionally, the authorities' anger and frustration would boil over, most infamously in the case of two high-ranking military officers who declared in a public meeting in Panchhari in 1979:

'We want only the land, and not the people of the Chittagong Hill Tracts' ('We want the land,' 1983, 21).[1]

Ultimately, then, in the Chittagong Hill Tracts it was a case of 'development for the people,' without the people.

***Plate 288***. *Day labourer on his way to work. (Wahlquist, 1977)*

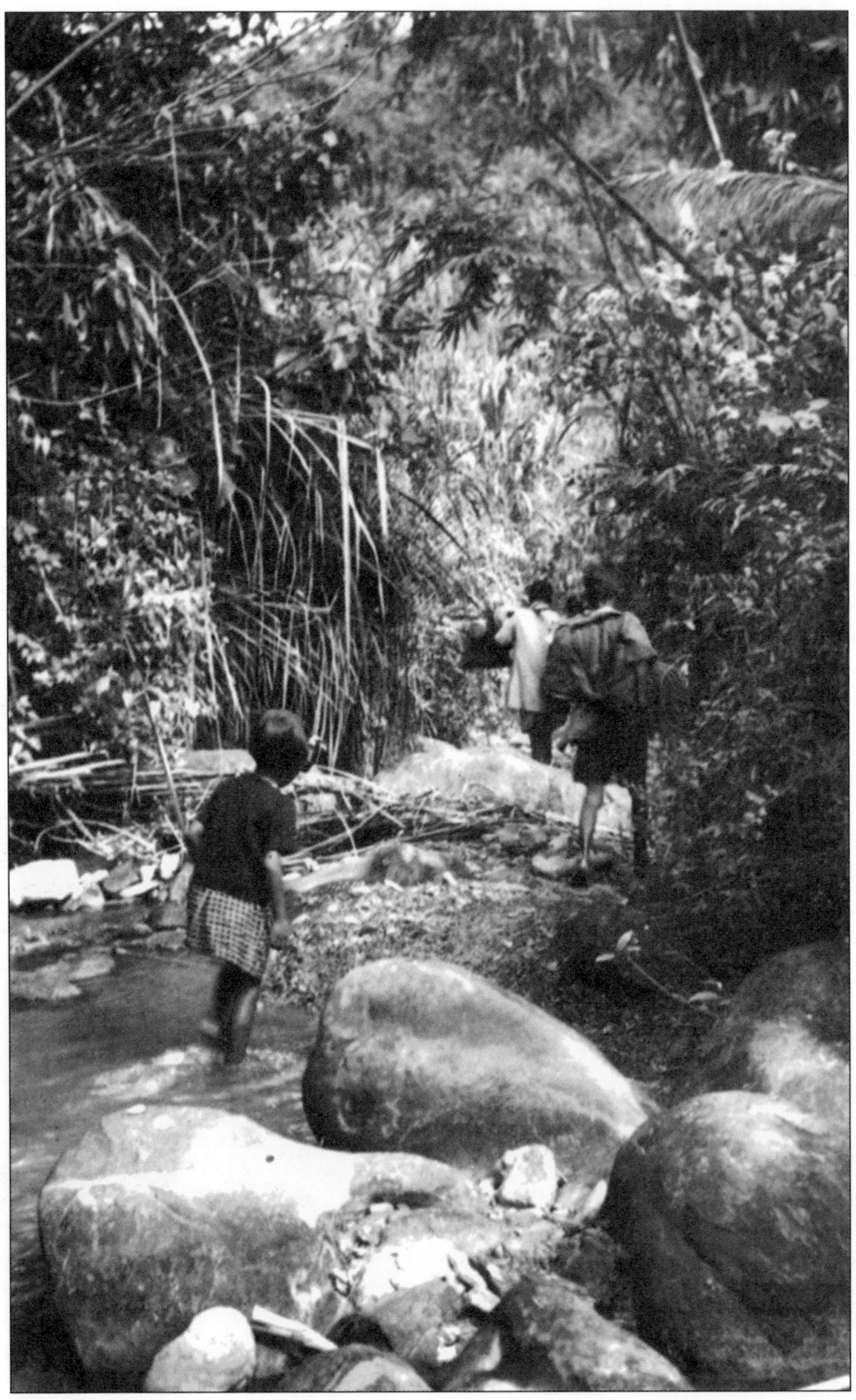

***Plate 289**. 'Melani in the Shilchhora.' (Starke, 1940s)*

*Chapter 15*

# GETTING AROUND

Most of the written material on the Chittagong Hill Tracts presents the local people as isolated, stagnant, timeless, changeless and traditional—waiting patiently for benevolent outsiders to bestow the dynamics of modernity upon them. This presumed stagnation does not, however, imply a lack of motion. The hill people are also seen as 'nomadic,' moving regularly within the district in search of new sites to practise swidden cultivation.

This image has given rise to much misinformed debate in which tradition is associated with being nomadic and modernity with being settled. The debate is misinformed because the history of the Chittagong hills has never been one of stagnant tradition but of constant transformation, renewal from within and interaction with the world beyond the hills. And although shifting cultivation does require regular rotation of fields, this is neither a sign of traditionalism nor does it require cultivators to be nomadic, i.e. leave their homes.

The photographic record bears this out. It shows the hill people to have been settled in permanent villages and towns and it testifies to the importance of their continual interaction with the outside world. It also demonstrates the almost complete neglect of the area's infrastructure by successive governments until the 1960s. Railways were never constructed, and even roads were considered too expensive:

> 'The extreme hilliness of the district and its intersection by numberless small streams and the sandy nature of the soil render the construction of cart roads extremely difficult and in cost prohibitive' (Hutchinson, 1909, 66)

'Wheel traffic is impossible in the Hill Tracts,' wrote Hutchinson (1906, 46), adding, 'Till recently the rivers provided the sole means of communication between the different parts of the district, but at the present time four first-class bridle-paths exist.' Till the late 1950s the situation remained the same: there were no paved roads at all in the district: the Chittagong-Rangamati road was paved in the plains but turned into a bridle track just before reaching the hills. In the mid-1950s the road to Kaptai, the development showcase, became 'one of the finest' in East Pakistan (Ishaq, 1971, 142; cf. Ahmad, 1958, 248, 340). By 1964 it was still the only paved road and there were not even 100 miles of unpaved roads in the entire 5,000-square-mile district. Consequently, most traffic was on foot and used either footpaths or the beds of rivulets (**plate 289**) and what Lewin had described in the 1860s remained true up to the 1960s: 'The favorite path throughout the district is the sandy bed of a stream, as it offers coolness for the feet and shade from the umbrageous canopy of jungle overhead' (Lewin, 1869, 7).

Except for elephants, there were no pack animals in the hills and people carried heavy loads in large baskets over long distances (**plate 290**).

Wherever possible, the larger rivers were used for travel and transport. These were generally shallow and navigable for sizeable boats only up to the hills (**plate 291**). Officials used the government launch 'Swallow' and

***Plate 290***. *Villagers entering Rangamati on market day. (Smith, 1940s)*

***Plate 291***. *Construction materials for the new hospital at Chandraghona were brought up in barges, 1908. (Baptist Missionary Society)*

***Plate 292**. 'Our boat getting through "rapid" on way to Lushai.' (Manson, 1941)*

generations of missionaries at Chandraghona the missionary launch 'Asha.'

Small dugouts could go further upstream and were 'in universal use on all the rivers of the district and provide[d] the principal means of transport' (Hutchinson, 1906, 44). The Karnaphuli river acted as the main thoroughfare to the Lushai hills to the east. Boats could be pulled over the smaller rapids (**plate 292**) but this was impossible at the larger rapids near Barkal.

J. Herbert Lorrain, missionary in the Lushai hills, documented the journey in 1904 in a series of photographs. At Barkal, 'there are some very fine rapids about two miles in length. During the Lushai Expedition of 1888-89 a light tramway was constructed along the right bank for the conveyance of stores' (Hutchinson, 1906, 8). The Lorrains used this facility: men pushed trolleys loaded with goods and passengers up the rapids (**plates 293-295**; cf. R.A. Lorrain, 1988, 38-39).

Further upstream more rapids were encountered. **Plate 296** was taken halfway up the Utanchatra Rapids between Barkal and Demagiri (Tlabung), which now marks the border between Bangladesh and India.

***Plate 293***. *'Getting our baggage ashore at Barkal in order to have it carried up the "Rapids" on the trollies provided for the purpose,' 1904. (Baptist Missionary Society)*

***Plate 294***. *'The baggage has been carried up the steep bank & is now on the trolley ready to be pushed by the black Santal coolies to the head of the Rapids 1¼ miles off ... The Babu in charge of the line brought out chairs & stools for us to sit on, & also gave me a bunch of bananas as a present', 1904. (Baptist Missionary Society)*

***Plate 295**. 'Herbert & Mabel trolleying up the Barkal Rapids–the Baggage is on the goods trolley just behind. Our Lushai boy Junga is standing behind us. The men at the sides are Santal coolies who push the trolley along at a rattling pace with their feet while they sit on the back of the conveyance,' 1904. (Baptist Missionary Society)*

***Plate 296**. 'Our boatmen are taking a rest on a tiny grass grown island in the middle of the foaming torrent. The second man from the left is a Santali; the rest are Maghs. Some of the men wade up the shallow parts of the rapid hauling at the rope while two of them remain on the boat to keep it in the deeper channels & prevent it from turning broadside to the waves,' 1913. (Baptist Missionary Society)*

***Plate 297***. *'On Sangu river.' (Laurence, about 1963)*

As there were no bridges across the rivers, dugouts were essential for ferrying people across (**plate 297**).

Dugouts were made locally as were sampans and a multitude of other country boats which were used on the hill rivers to transport goods and people (**plates 298-299**).

***Plate 298***. *Making a dugout at Shishok Mukh. (Bientjes, 1963)*

***Plate 299***. *Country boat on the Karnaphuli river. (Lindsey, 1964)*

***Plate 300**. Ferrying a jeep across the Karnaphuli river. (Taylor, 1957)*

***Plate 301**. Bus crossing the Karnaphuli river. (Taylor, 1957)*

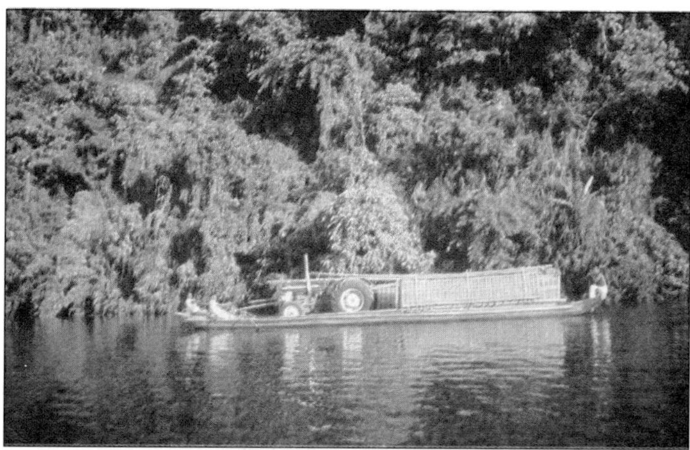

**Plate 302**. *'"How to transport your tractor!" near Pablakhali village.' (Band, 1970)*

**Plate 303**. *Kaptai landing. (Lindsey, 1964)*

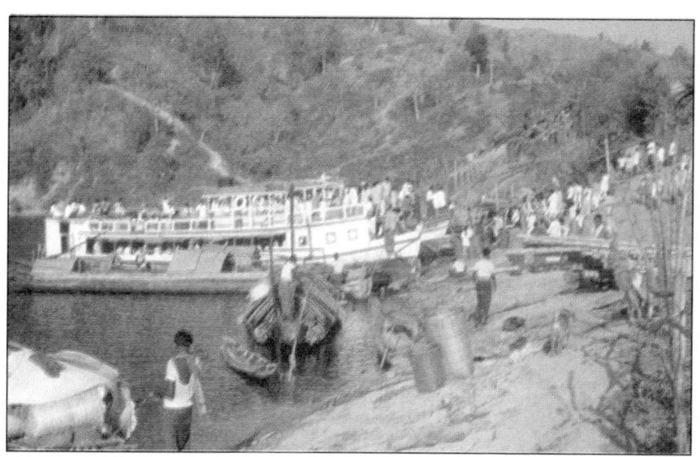

**Plate 304**. *Public service launch in the Kaptai area. (Welsh, 1963)*

***Plate 305***. *Country boat being lifted, Karnaphuli river in the background. (Anderson, 1968-70)*

After the Kaptai road was paved, motor vehicles began to appear. By 1967 there were 27 private cars, 31 buses, 101 jeeps, 9 auto rickshaws and 188 trucks in the district. When these had to cross the Karnaphuli river, a double ferry was used (**plates 300** and **301**); a tractor could fit onto a small country boat (**plate 302**).

The creation of the Kaptai reservoir made it possible for larger boats, ferries and motor launches to move much more easily in the northern and central parts of the Chittagong hills. Along the shores of the new lake landings developed (**plates 303** and **304**), and regular launch services began to operate far into the interior.

The Kaptai lake greatly facilitated the movement of people and goods but the dam at Kaptai also hampered transport and traffic. No locks had been made there for boats and rafts to pass through. And yet, many boats had to pass the dam. Moreover, it was of crucial importance that the paper mill at Chandraghona, down the river, get its regular supply of raw material—bamboo. To make this possible, boats, bundles of bamboo and logs were lifted out of the reservoir and into the river about 50 metres lower (**plates 305** and **306**).

As a result of road-building, motorised wheel traffic became possible in the hills from the late 1950s. Bus services were set up and auto rickshaws became a fixture of life in Kaptai (**plates 307-309**). Meanwhile, the most well-heeled denizens of the Chittagong Hill Tracts in the 1960s, the Forestal engineers, used their helicopter to get around (**plate 310**).

***Plate 306***. *Boat lift, river side. (Barblan, 1959-1961)*

**Plate 307**. *'En route to Rangamati ... per mile [Rs.]-/1/-.' (Sopher, 1959)*

**Plate 308**. *'Public bus disaster on Chittagong-Kaptai road.' (Taylor, 1962)*

***Plate 309***. *'Kaptai taxi.' (Lindsey, 1964)*

***Plate 310***. *Helicopter and crowd at Bandarban. (Lindsey, 1964)*

## 15.1 Moving goods

In the early years of colonial rule, there were only a few markets in the Chittagong hills.

> 'There are four bazars or markets in the hills, to which the hill people resort to barter their produce for such articles of daily consumption as salt, spices, dried fish, and the like, which are only procurable from the plains. These bazars are situated at Kassalong, Rangamuttee, and Chandragoona, on the Kurnafoolee, and at Bundrabun, on the River Sungoo ... The population of the hills also resort to such of the markets of the plain as may be within a day's journey from their homes, along the border of the Chittagong District' (Lewin, 1869, 7).

Soon after the Chittagong hills were incorporated into British India and the fear of raids from the Lushai hills had decreased, traders from the plains became prominent.

> 'The trade of the Hill Tracts is principally in the hands of Chittagonian Bengalis, who convey their goods from place to place by means of boats and rafts ... The principal trade centres of the district are Chandraghona, Rainkhyong, Rangamati, Shubalong, Kasalong, Bandarban, and Ajodhiya. These centres are very busy places during the winter months, and their respective river-ghats (landing-places) are crowded with varieties of boats and bamboo and timber rafts, while on the banks are stacks of grass, piles of baskets full of cotton, and heaps of paddy or rice. These have all been brought in by the hillmen to be taken away by the Bengali trader in return for the cash advances he has made earlier during the cultivating season or in exchange for goods brought from Chittagong for the purpose of barter' (Hutchinson, 1906, 44-45).

Seventy years later, itinerant Bengali traders were still crucially important in getting the harvest to market. The cultivators took care of the arduous first stage. The produce had to be packed in baskets or bags and carried to a road or river. Miniature bamboo rafts were floated down small rivers to a collection point. There Bengali traders would transfer the produce to larger boats or trucks (**plate 311-313**).

The visual record of retail activities in the Chittagong Hill Tracts during the colonial period is not very extensive. In view of the fact that most camera owners in the hills resided in market towns, they have left us remarkably little visual information on everyday commercial activities. Two images from the 1930s give an impression of market activities (**plates 314** and **315**). **Plate 316** shows the main shopping area of Bandarban, the southern hills' most important town, in the 1960s.

It was in the towns, and especially in commercial activities, that the small settled Bengali population came into its own. Most Bengalis in the Chittagong Hill Tracts were temporary visitors or short-term residents. They were agricultural labourers who came up from the plains for ploughing and harvesting in the hill valleys, boatmen who were vital for transporting goods to and from the hills, fishermen, and government officials who were stationed there for a while. But some Bengali tradesmen and shopkeepers had long been permanent residents in the hill towns, and such families were considered locals. During the Pakistan period, new traders, also from West Pakistan, joined them (**plates 317-321**).

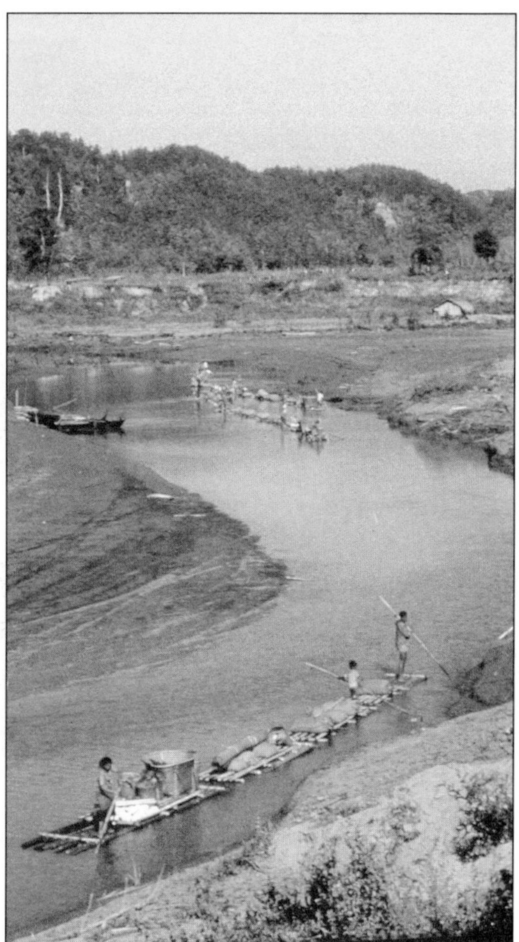

***Plate 312***. *Rafts with jhum harvest (Rainkhyong khal). (Wahlquist, 1977)*

***Plate 311***. *Transporting grain (Luichongpara). (Wahlquist, 1977)*

***Plate 313***. *Bengalis taking the harvest downstream. (Wahlquist, 1977)*

***Plate 314***. *'Boats assembled on bazaar day, Ramgarh.' (Baptist Missionary Society, 1930s)*

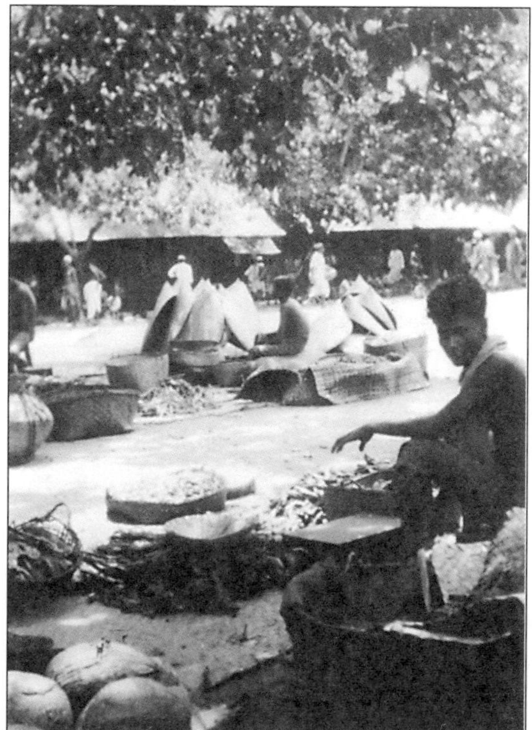

**Plate 315**. *'Fish market, Rangamati.' (Starke, 1930s)*

**Plate 316**. *Bandarban bazar. (Laurence, about 1962)*

***Plate 317***. *'Bazar stall at Mainimukh.' (Welsh, 1963)*

***Plate 318***. *Hindu widows selling fish. (Sandercock, 1964-65)*

***Plate 319***. *The more established tradesmen had brick-built shops; Café Hawai in downtown Kaptai promised 'good arrangements for eating and staying.' (Lindsey, 1964)*

***Plate 320***. *A Chakma woman at a permanent shop selling brightly-coloured yarn. (Sandercock, 1964-65)*

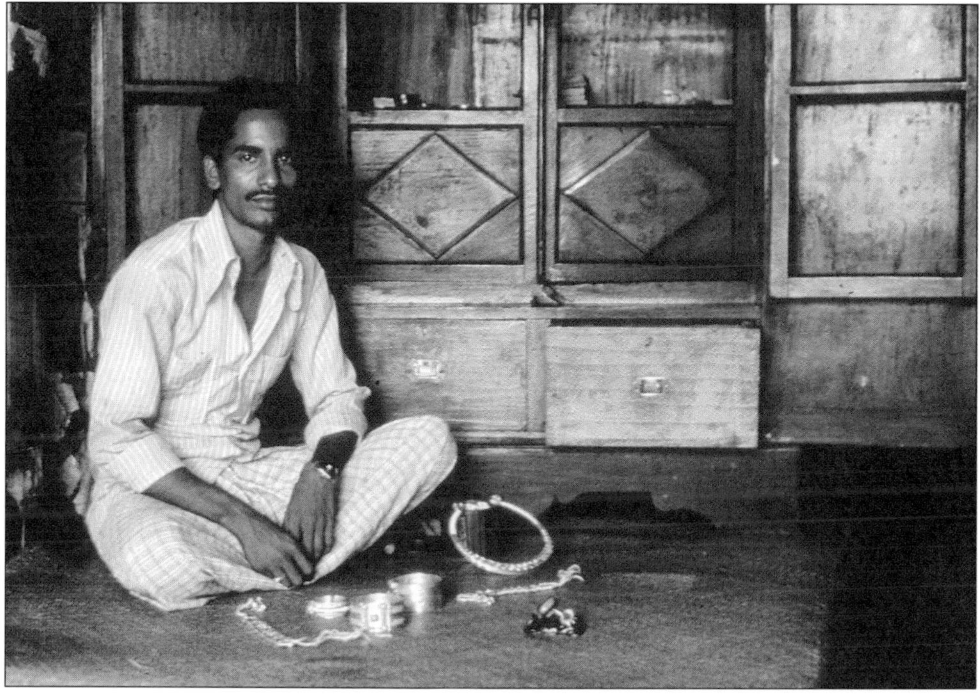

***Plate 321***. *A Bengali jeweller and moneylender exhibits 'tribal' jewellery, Rangamati. (Wahlquist, 1977)*

***Plate 322***. *Riding the Mong chief's elephant. (Lübker collection, 1957-58)*

***Plate 323***. *On the elephant. Götz (Peter) Penz from Chandraghona, on the trunk, is being photographed by his brother Wolfhart. (Lübker, 1957-58)*

*Chapter 16*

# THE THRILL OF FREEDOM

Visitors have associated the Chittagong Hill Tracts with emotions varying from a sense of being exiled to a feeling of being transposed into heaven. The hills served, and still serve to some extent, as the backdrop to various fantasies. To travellers, tourists, scholars, administrators and businessmen, the hills could be a malaria hole, a paradise lost, a wild and exotic place, a place to 'stay back,' or a dirty, hateful place inhabited by uncivilised and detested savages.

With few exceptions, colonial administrators considered their stay in the hills an exile from the good life, a hardship posting. To them it was a chore—they did their work and were grateful when they were eventually given a posting in a more civilised part of the colony. To Christian missionaries the hills were a pasture on which to tend and augment their flock. To traders the hills were a happy hunting ground and to tourists a picturesque playground.

In the 1950s and 1960s, Western businessmen, technical experts and other professionals from Chittagong town would come up to the hills to spend a weekend. They came to enjoy the 'free' life among people who fitted in with, and did not contradict, their image of 'primitives.' Most came away with romantic memories; one of them said: 'Everyone who entered the hills came out changed.'

## 16.1 Adventure

The photographic record reflects some of the fantasies and emotions that the Chittagong Hill Tracts elicited. Many Westerners perceived the hills as wild and exciting, an untamed region which had to be conquered rather than merely traversed. Travelling in the hills offered a special thrill because roads were few and far between, overland travel was very difficult, and rivers were the main channels of communication.

Even for H.E. Kauffmann, a seasoned anthropologist who had worked in the Naga hills in Northeast India and knew all about mountainous terrain, travelling in the Chittagong hills had a connotation of adventure. In 1955, while travelling up the Sangu river, he noted in his diary: 'Once more we raise the flags of Pakistan and Germany on tall bamboos, and off we are towards new adventures' (Kauffmann, December 20, 1955).

One way of travelling was on elephant. Earlier only high government officials had kept elephants as symbols of their own authority. In 1867, T.H. Lewin wrote proudly to his mother: 'Govt. have given me 9 elephants' (Lewin letters, October 20, 1867). Apart from the government, only rich persons such as chiefs could afford the cost of keeping elephants. In Manikchhari, the Mong chief used to keep one, and during the 1950s and 1960s he entertained many visitors by offering them a ride (**plates 322** and **323**).

The same sense of adventure comes across in the account of a photo-journalist, Harald Lechenperg:

> 'So I headed for the last two aims of my trip: ... Murangs [Mru] and tigers. Let me explain. In India I searched in vain for so-called primitive jungle tribes. I knew that they

***Plate 324***. *On expedition in the Chittagong hills. (Seifert, 1963)*

> existed in East Pakistan, near the Burmese border. One of these tribes was called Murang, and I have met the happiest people there' (Lechenperg, 1962, 1248).

They were the happiest people, he explained, because they 'wanted to stick to their own easy and totally uncivilised happiness.' He met his tigers later on, in the Sunderbans, and shot one. It was indeed the adventure he had imagined: wild people, 'lovely nude Murang girls,' and wild animals.

## 16.2 The Explorer's Advance

Where nature and people were considered to be wild, they had to be met in adequate fashion. Consequently, trips became expeditions. Local people were hired to carry the luggage and act as guides. Outfits were always similar, patterned on the dress code of the colonial explorer and adventurer: strong boots or mountain shoes, shorts, white or khaki shirt, pith helmet, bush knife and rifle (**plate 324**). This costume was chosen deliberately, it carried a message of white superiority:

> 'We go to the fair in full war-paint, i.e. with pith helmet, bush-shirt and gun. Romjan [Kauffmann's servant] thinks that people will say: "The Saheb comes to the Mela with a rifle carrier; he is a Boro Saheb, a big man"' (Kauffmann, December 13, 1955).

Other symbols of power were also used. **Plate 325** shows the power relations which underlay hill explorations. A white man with a sun hat stands in the middle of a group, resting his arms on the shoulders of his Bengali travel companions, and the 'natives' squat in front of them. But also notice the theme of imitation: one of the Westerners squats and 'socialises with the natives.' Westerners would engage more in such socialising, on their own terms, as they felt further away from civilisation. This temporary reversal of conventional power relations was crucial to the appeal of the hills and the 'freedom' they offered these visitors.

For many, the dream of Western man conquering the world had survived decolonisation. That dream would later be exploited and marketed successfully by mass tourism but in the 1950s and 1960s would-be explorers were neither heroes of colonialism nor travellers on a package tour. Their photographs show the adventure of free-lance exploration. In the Chittagong hills their advance was relentless; where

***Plate 325***. *Visitors and locals posing for a snapshot. (Seifert, 1963)*

roads gave out they crossed rivers and hired local boats to reach their goal (**plate 326**).

## 16.3 Meeting 'Primitive People'

Being with the people of the Chittagong hills was like entering another world. Visitors often described it as an intensely personal experience. For example, the anthropologist Kauffmann observed a ceremony at a Mru village and noted:

> 'And these tones [of small mouth organs] in a strict, measured rhythm are overpowering. Supported by the deep u-u-u of the gigantic pipes, they hammer their way unrelentingly into the ear. One cannot hear a word, all are touched by ecstasy and the heady rice wine does the rest. Now the young girls get up and join hands. They form a compact row of twelve or fifteen, exactly according to size—the 10 to 12-year-old ones on the far side. And they dance backwards, their faces towards the slow-moving mouth-organ players: right leg

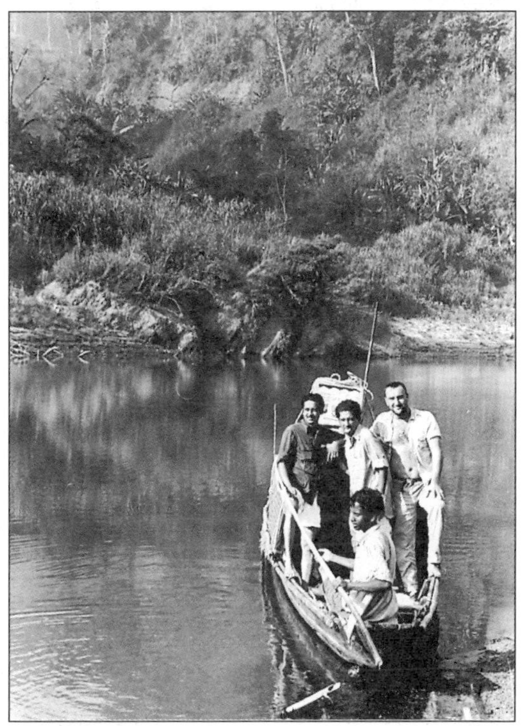

***Plate 326***. *Crossing a river. (Seifert, 1963)*

> back, bending slightly at the knee, then the left leg, again bending slightly at the knee, then repeating the movement starting from the left—and so on, for hours. Right in front of the seemingly detached players, a row of girls dances, a steaming chain of hot young bodies. In the light of torches and fire their brown thighs and legs shine as if chiselled, their rich silver or mock-silver ornaments glitter on their waists and arms, and some have put coloured paper rosettes in their hair' (Kauffmann, March 21, 1956).

Years later Claus-Dieter Brauns took a photograph which illustrates Kauffmann's text (**plate 327**).

Kauffmann continued:

> 'They wear their prettiest skirts with beautiful coloured embroidery on the back and now, during the feast, they have also covered the upper part of their bodies with a dark cloth. But now and then a marvellously shaped, solid breast flashes out, a provocative fruit of love for the eyes of the playing men. "Komola," orange, is what Bengalis euphorically call girls and, really, these are the finest specimens which would drive 99 out of 100 European women green with envy ... I also squat down and stare at this strange and wild sight, carried away by the soul-stirring pounding of the melody, by the dance of these Children of Nature in the flaring glow of the fire. Oh, I think, it has been well worth coming here from so far for this one night; this is still the real, authentic life, this is still very close to the primal stage of mankind' (Kauffmann, March 21, 1956).

Here, man reduced to his mere outline symbolises freedom: there is nothing that separates him from Nature (**plates 328** and **329**).

In their search for the primitive, Westerners employed other strategies as well. One was inversion. Westerners would occasionally highlight the primitive by turning notions

***Plate 327**. Mru girls dancing. (Brauns, 1970)*

***Plate 328****. Mru villagers. (Brauns, 1969)*

of order upside down. For example, whereas normally a Westerner or his driver would drive a jeep, in the jungle 'savage' women were put behind the steering wheel (**plate 330**). The special appeal, even fascination, of such a composition lay in the contrast between the sex appeal of the women's half-nude bodies and the cold, functional, yet enormously powerful machine with its own erotic message.

In similar vein, the dominance of Westerners over natives was turned upside down. Under 'normal' circumstances, superior knowledge allowed Westerners to dominate both nature and 'less civilised' people. In the hills and the jungle, however, 'natives' were the experts, and Westerners had to defer to them. This is brought out in photographs showing Westerners imitating 'natives' and associating with them with some sympathy (**plate 331**). The body language of squatting and standing up was turned upside down, with the more powerful men squatting and the women standing (**plate 332**). This also allowed the physical attractions of the women to be as visible as possible. How women felt about this can be seen clearly. Two of the men look straight into the camera but all the women look firmly in another direction. Obviously, they feel awkward and do not wish to have anything to do with this kind of 'presentation.' This was a common reaction of women in the Chittagong Hill Tracts who were photographed in this way.

***Plate 329***. *Mru girls at festive dance. (Brauns, 1970)*

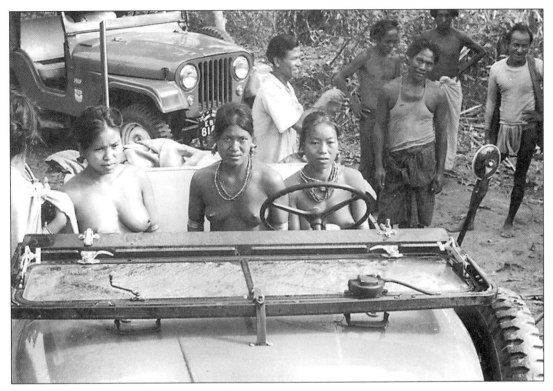

***Plate 330**. Mru women in a jeep. (Seifert, 1963)*

***Plate 331**. Visitors and locals. (Seifert, 1963)*

***Plate 332**. Posed Mru group. (Seifert, 1963)*

***Plate 333****. Mru with Bengali and Western visitors. (Seifert, 1963)*

## 16.4 The Ambiguities of 'Going Native'

In their search for the primitive, visitors to the hills also followed a second strategy: going native. For quite a number of them, being in the hills was an invitation temporarily to do away with 'civilisation.' There was a clear distinction in their mind between themselves, Bengalis and primitives. Whereas civilised people, both Western and Bengali, were fully clothed, it was the hallmark of the primitive natives to dress scantily. In the jungle, however, Westerners felt free to unwind, remove their shirts and leave part of the body uncovered. Bengalis, however, remained fully clad; to them, going native held no particular attraction (**plate 333**).

Going native involved imitating the hill people. Thus the local custom of (almost) nude bathing was imitated by Westerners whose rules of modesty normally forbade public nudity. Here, away from civilisation, they could let go (**plates 334** and **335**). Western women played at carrying, somewhat uncomfortably, baskets in the local way (**plate 336**). Playing the mouth organ, the task of Mru men, became fun when imitated by Western visitors (**plate 337**). Imitation helped them to break out of their social restrictions, to experience for a fleeting moment a freedom that they yearned for. Going native transposed them to a world without restrictive conventions, a fantasy which was willed into existence in the Chittagong hills.

***Plate 334***. *Mru bathing in a gorge. (Brauns, 1970)*

***Plate 335***. *Western visitors bathing in the nude. (Seifert, 1963)*

***Plate 336***. *Western and Mru women. (Seifert, 1963)*

***Plate 337***. *Playing the mouth organ. (Seifert, 1963)*

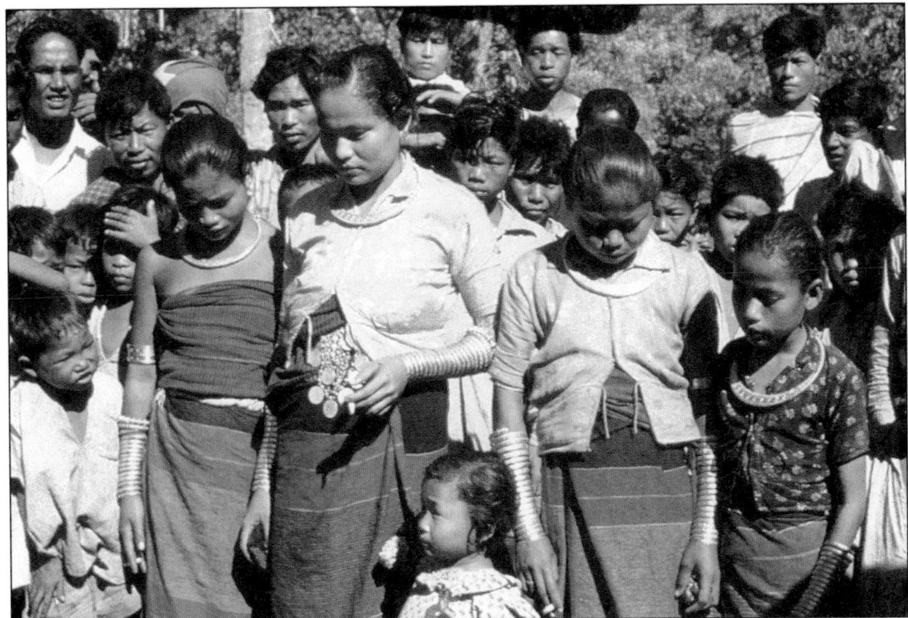

***Plate 338**. 'Belaichhari, Chakma women.' (Bientjes, 1961)*

But going 'native' was also a receding mirage. When Western visitors created their fantasies in front of a camera, they could not help but fall short of their aim. Their photographs often breathed an atmosphere of embarrassment, reluctance and social distance (**plate 338**; cf. our chapter 'Portraits').

The wildness of the Chittagong hills could attract as well as repel. The adventure of temporary inversion and imitation certainly provided a thrill. But under different circumstances, wildness was seen as a threat. In 1866 T.H. Lewin wrote to his mother from the Koladan river, deep in the jungle of northern Arakan: 'I don't know what it is or rather what there is in this wild jungle life to deaden the intellect but I am unable to settle down to anything' (Lewin letters, January 15, 1866).

And only two days after Kauffmann had attended the Mru feast (see section on 'meeting "primitive people"' above) and celebrated their 'real, authentic life,' he portrayed their 'wildness' in much darker colours. Stating that 'the White Man will never get accustomed here, everything remains foreign to him forever' (Kauffmann, March 10, 1956), he noted,

> 'never before did I become so conscious of the fact that all these people, be they Marma or Bengali, do not really live (according to our active understanding of that term) but simply vegetate like animals. They are ignorant, they do not know anything, and they do not take interest in anything. They—and especially the women—are altogether passive. They just drag themselves along without any specific aim, without even entertaining a hope or nourishing a wish. They are not happy but neither, despite their poverty, really unhappy.'

He substantiates this conviction with a lengthy discussion of a particular woman, concluding:

> 'this woman knows only 2 things: how to nourish herself and how to breed. Willing and dull as an animal, she endures the man every night, an automatic reaction' (Kauffmann, March 23, 1956).

***Plate 339**. Chimbuk—John Cohen (tea buyer), Charles Richardson-Bryant (tea broker), George Band (Shell geologist) and two local men with Shell Land Rover. (Taylor, 1968)*

***Plate 340**. 'Chimbuk—The village band and dancers, who are nearly hidden on the left, as are the smaller pipes—all being photographed.' (Taylor, 1968)*

## 16.5 Holidaying in the hills

Not all Westerners in East Pakistan (and later Bangladesh) went in for this type of adventure. For those living in Chittagong, Chimbuk hill in the Mru hills, only a few hours' drive, became a popular weekend destination. Chimbuk developed from a simple hilltop into a budding hill station. Kauffmann gives an account of such a trip in the mid-1950s.

> 'Breakfast is not quite over when Padre Rodrigues and Mr. Wildfeuer arrive in the Jeep ... The two of them are about to drive to Chimbuk, on the "new road" which has cost 16 lakh (Rs. 1,600,000) to construct. Without thinking twice I ask whether they have a vacant seat. Yes! And Ronjan [Kauffmann's servant] can come along to carry the gun and camera, and heat up the tinned food of the well-equipped Padre ... The "road" is still only "jeepable"; the first part has many wooden bridges with steep ramps and often the road becomes so narrow because of landslides that we can only just get through. The rocking and jolting is extremely unpleasant and the driver, who does an excellent job, often suddenly applies the brake to drive cautiously through holes, dents and ditches. All along the road, to the left and right, we see the large black patches of swidden fields, cleared in the last few days. The ash lies a foot high and promises to be excellent fertiliser. Some fields are almost completely levelled, cleared of any growth, but in others there are many stumps, half-burned logs and even some surviving trees ... The second half of the road climbs continually and soon we reach the ridge of a hill range and have a view of the country. Deep down the Sangu meanders, and Taratha village is on a terrace on its left bank. Then we see on the other side, high on the summit of the westernmost range, the Chimbuk bungalow ... At our final destination we are welcomed in flowery language by the road sub-overseer, a Bengali who has long worked in Burma. The Padre and Mr. W. at once descend the steep slope to the Mru village of Thümbru-Karbari-Para ... In the village, which consists of only a few houses, I find them sitting on the verandah of a small house on stilts which bears no resemblance to a Mru house. This is the guesthouse. Mr. W. is already drinking tea which makes him sweat even more. He goes off on a photo safari and I pounce upon the sacrificial posts, which I had spotted immediately, and become ethnographically immersed ... To quench my burning thirst, I want to take a quick swig of rice beer in one of the houses. Sangrao [the chowkidar at the guesthouse] guides me and I call Mr. W. and the Padre to join me because they have never seen this before ... the house owner, unwashed and with unkempt hair but exceptionally friendly, spreads out a blanket and we have to sit down on it ... Mr. W. is sitting down shaking his head in consternation: so much dirt, such primitivism! I laugh and say, "This is our daily bread," bending over one tube after another, wiping them lightly and tasting the rice beer ... Mr. W. cannot be moved to have a try, he shudders too much at the sight of the tubes from which so many dirty mouths have drunk.'

Eventually they return to the bungalow:

> 'It is situated magnificently on the ridge, allowing for a panoramic view of the lower foothills and the plain, all the way to the sea which fades away in the haze. Ronjan has heated up the Padre's tins in water and we eat a kind of Lyon sausages, asparagus and carrots with genuine bread which I have not seen for a long time. We hurry down to the vehicle ... Off at 16.00 hours and at Bandarban by 18.00 hours' (Kauffmann, April 8, 1956).

By the late 1960s, travelling in the hills, at least to such 'developed' hill stations, had lost its aura of adventure. Jeeps had given way to more comfortable Landrovers, expedition dress was no longer considered necessary, and casual wear was now deemed appropriate. But the power relations as reflected in the photographs are still intact: Westerners portray themselves in higher positions and are identified by name; Mru people, on the other hand, are not identified as individuals (**plate 339**).

In those years, one could just call the rest house on Chimbuk hill, order roast chicken or whatever was available, and perhaps a Mru group to make music and dance. 'If a dance is requested, the Mru of Chimbuk are likely to comply for a fee. Their hearts are generally not in it' (Rashid, 1969, 73) (**plate 340**).

# *Chapter 17*
# LIFESTYLES

During the colonial period, the district elite consisted chiefly of British administrators and missionaries, and prominent local families, with Bengali officials in supporting roles. After Partition, the latter, and (West–) Pakistani colleagues rose to the highest positions in the bureaucracy, and Westerners moved into new positions as development personnel. The lifestyles of these groups differed markedly.

## 17.1 Westerners: Remaining 'Civilised'

In the early days of colonial rule in the Chittagong Hill Tracts, British officials adapted to local styles when they toured the district. In a letter home in 1875, the Commissioner of Chittagong wrote:

> 'You may imagine that the people are a very pleasant contrast to those of India generally when I tell you that nearly all the officers who have been stationed in the Hill Tracts like to go about in the District & live in the houses of the natives eating their food and sleeping in their houses, and even adopting their style of dress and habits. Both Mr. Power & Lieutt Gordon when they go out in the District (and they do this for more than 6 months in the year) wear a waistcloth (made of silk), a coat & nothing else—not even shoes or socks. Not only do they do this but they eat with their fingers & in every other respect live with the natives as if belonging to them. You must not think that Mr. Power & Lt. Gordon are [a] rough sort of men, they are quite the reverse, both of them being of very good families & very fond of civilized society; it is simply the attractive character of the people that makes all who come in contact with them conform to their ways. Captn Lewin who was Power's predecessor adopted the same habits & so does everyone who lives in the Hill Tracts. I need hardly say that once your feet get hardened it is far more pleasant to be without shoes & socks than to have them on. You can then cross streams and ascend steep hills with[out] difficulty or delay and a wash when you reach your resting place puts you all right & clean' (Kisch Papers, June 9, 1875).

The social distance between local population and early colonial administrators was smaller than in the plains of Bengal (see also our chapter 'Innocence and Charm'). The Commissioner of Chittagong, on a visit to the Chittagong hills, experienced his first 'native dinner,' and described it colourfully in one of his letters:

> 'On Sunday we all (i.e. Power, Gordon, Showers & myself) went to dinner at a Magh's house. Power and Gordon like native dinners very much & I was very anxious to see what one was like. When we went into the house we were welcomed by the host & his wife & sisters & other relatives & then sat down on pillows which were ranged along one side of the room. In front of each pillow was a wooden stand to hold a dish & behind this stand was a salt cellar & glasses. All these were placed on a clean white cloth on the floor. The natives do not eat at the same time as their guests but wait upon them & have their own meal afterwards. About as soon as we were comfortably seated a large dish of boiled rice was placed in front of each of us on the wooden stand mentioned above & between each two of us was placed another dish containing about twelve round brass or silver (some of each kind) cups. In each of these cups were different kinds of food: fish done in different ways, fowls, cutlets &

vegetables. Our host & his relatives then took out from each of these cups a small portion of its contents & placed it round the edge of our dishes of rice, so that each of us had a dish of rice with meat, fish & vegetables forming a circular rim outside it. Power, Flowers & Gordon are quite accustomed to eating with their fingers & did so on this occasion but I made use of a spoon & fork. Both before and after dinner we washed our hands & this all natives do' (Kisch Papers, June 16, 1875).

Soon, however, British administrators and missionaries no longer felt the need to adapt to local styles. Instead, they maintained a lifestyle that was self-consciously Western. Their leisure time centred round the verandah and the garden, outdoor sports and parties. For Europeans in the Chittagong hills, the verandah stood for an idyll: it afforded an opportunity to imagine oneself in touch with the surrounding nature while keeping all the amenities of civilisation close at hand. Whether it was Christmas at the Kodala Tea Estate in 1939 (**plate 341**), or life on the verandah in Chandraghona in the 1950s (**plates 342** and **343**), dress and food were emphatically Western, and servants never far away.

Servants were crucial in maintaining this lifestyle, even in the relatively modest households of missionaries.

> 'Early breakfast over, I went across to the school for classes or study, and Mrs. Jones began her housework. With the number of servants there are in India, it is surprising how much work there is to be done. To begin with, it is quite a business looking after the servants themselves. One is the water carrier ... Then there is the sweeper ... there was a washerman to wash the clothes ... Another servant was the cook ... In the morning we were much too busy to take [the children out for a walk], so one of the boys had to be used for this, as we had a horror of ayahs ... They generally came home to the big breakfast at nine o'clock, bursting with accounts of what they had seen. This meal consisted of porridge, followed by an egg dish, or something made up from last night's dinner, with fruit, or the remains of last night's pudding' (Jones, 1936, 141-142).

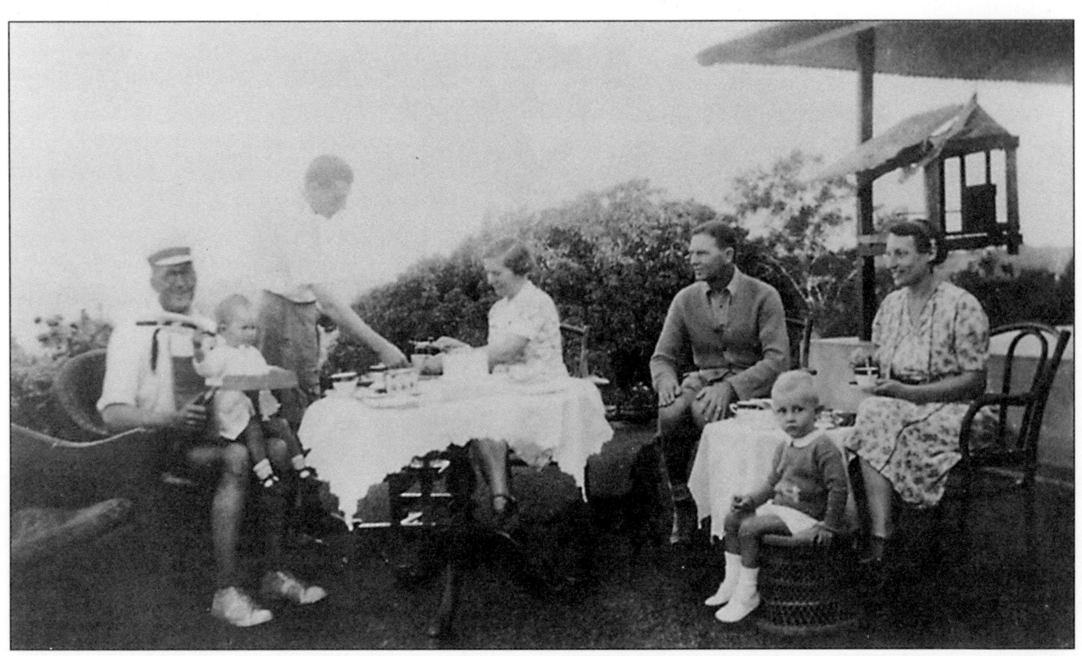

***Plate 341***. *'Boxing day at Kodala.'*[1] *(Bottoms/ Maslen collection, 1939)*

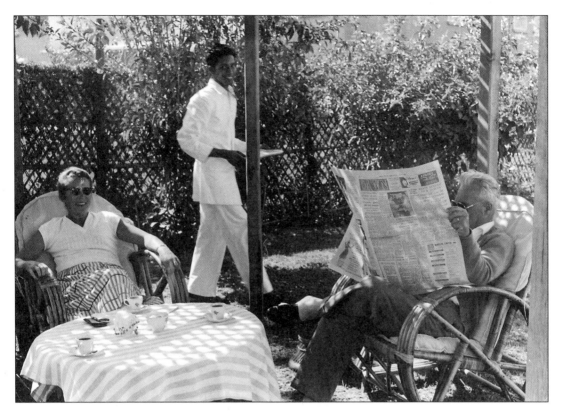

***Plate 342***. *The manager of the Karnaphuli Paper Mill and his wife with their servant on the verandah in Chandraghona. (Meier collection, about 1957)*

***Plate 343***. *Mrs. Bottoms, wife of the surgeon at Chandraghona, having tea with a friend. (Bottoms/Maslen collection, about 1950)*

***Plate 344***. *'Donald [Bottoms] with one of my house "boys" in our garden,' Chandraghona. (J. Bottoms, 1937)*

The verandah or garden often acted as a background to photographs of the children with their toys, playmates and servants (**plates 344-346**).

After the creation of the Kaptai lake, new leisure activities became available for children as well as adults. Boating, waterskiing and swimming became favourite pastimes which were often photographed (**plates 347** and **348**).

Various commercial companies in Chittagong town and in the Chittagong Hill Tracts kept houseboats on the lake. Their employees and their families would socialise and relax there during weekends and holidays (**plate 349**).

In the development enclaves of Kaptai and Chandraghona, Western-style parties were important as lifestyle markers, and they were much photographed (**plates 350** and **351**).

***Plate 345***. *'Timothy Smith being greeted by his new friends Melani (big girl) and Koruna in the garden in Rangamati.' (Smith, 1949)*

***Plate 346***. *'David, Mark and Andrew [Flowers] on the verandah of the bungalow,' Chandraghona Mission Hospital. (Flowers, 1962)*

***Plate 347***. *Waterskiing, Lake Kaptai. (Seyfried, 1960s)*

***Plate 348***. *Regatta on Lake Kaptai. (Seyfried, 1960s)*

**Plate 349**. *The 'Cowrie,' the Shell Company's houseboat, flying the flags of Pakistan and the Netherlands. (Van Tellingen, 1969)*

**Plate 350**. *Party at Kaptai. (Meier, 1955-61)*

***Plate 351***. *Party at Chandraghona. (Meier, 1955-61)*

***Plate 352**. The children of Chakma chief Raja Bhuban Mohan Roy, photographed in the garden of the Rangamati rajbari.[2] (Chakma Raja collection, about 1922)*

***Plate 353***. *Studio portrait showing Utpalaksha Roy, son of the Chakma chief, with his cousin Anil Roy and two small nieces. (Chakma Raja collection, about 1930)*

## 17.2 Prominent Local Families: Stylish Modernity

By the early decades of the twentieth-century, prominent Chakma families in the Chittagong Hill Tracts had adopted the dress styles of the upper classes of Bengal. This colonial style combined local elements (e.g. the sari and the dhoti) with European jackets, neckties and shoes. When the younger members of the Roy family of Rangamati presented themselves to the camera for a formal portrait, they exemplified the trend (**plates 352-354**).

Another example of the colonial dress style is provided by a group portrait of students and teachers of the Government High English School in Rangamati. This lone secondary school in the district, established in 1890, moulded successive generations of the local elite. Several politicians who wished to abolish the undemocratic system of chiefly administration, e.g. Kamini Mohan Dewan (**plate 355**) and Sneha Kumar Chakma (**plate 356**), were students here.

In the more recent formal portraits of prominent Chakma families, women continued to wear the sari but the men no longer used the dhoti which had come to be seen as a Hindu garment after the creation of Pakistan; instead, they donned Western-style pants and shirts, signalling both communal neutrality and modernity (**plates 357-359**).

***Plate 354***. *Utpalaksha Roy with his cousin Anil Roy (Chakma Raja collection, about 1930)*

*Plate 355. Kamini Mohan Dewan (born 1890). (Chakma Raja collection)*

**Plate 356**. *Rangamati Government High English School, 1929. Among the students are Sneha Kumar Chakma (standing third from right) and Bigna Binashan Khisa (sitting on the far right), both born in 1914. (Dipak and Gautam Chakma collection, 1929)*

***Plate 357***. *Renuka Dewan and her husband Manjulaksha Roy (note embroidered Chakma Raj crest on his blazer), Rangamati. (Talukdar collection, about 1940)*

*Plate 358. The family of Hemanta Talukdar, a magistrate. (Chakma Raja collection, about 1965)*

***Plate 359***. *The family of Saradendu Chakma, an official. (Saradendu S. Chakma collection, 1960s)*

***Plate 360**. 'Another son of Bohmong & wife,' Bandarban. (Mills, 1926)*

Whereas Chakma families appear to have preferred Bengali-style clothes for formal occasions and Chakma-style ones for less formal ones, notable Marma families were seen to alternate between styles. In **plates 360** and **361**, the Bohmong family follow Burmese examples.

When the Kong Hla Aung family had their picture taken in a studio in Chittagong in 1948, they dressed as Bengalis but a picture taken 19 years later shows the men in neutral 'Western' style, the mother in Marma dress, and the daughter in sari. In two other family portraits of this period, the women wear Marma dress (**plates 362-365**).

***Plate 361**. 'Bohmong's family,' Bandarban. (Mills, 1926)*

***Plates 362** and **363**. The first photograph, taken in a Chittagong studio in 1948, shows Kong Hla Aung, his wife Nong Thui and their 5-year-old daughter Mee Shwe Hpru. In the second one (1967), they are joined by son-in-law Mong Sathowai Chowdhury. (M.S. Choudhury/Mee Shwe Hpru collection)*

***Plate 364***. *An informal portrait shows the Mong chief's family in front of the old Manikchhari rajbari.*[3] *(Chakma Raja collection, 1964)*

***Plate 365***. *Members of a prominent Marma family had their photograph taken in a studio in Chittagong.*[4] *(M.K. Maung/Ching Kwai Hpru collection, 1973)*

***Plate 366***. *Raja Tridiv Roy married Arati Dewan of Barkal on the day of his investiture (2 March 1953); here they pose in front of the old rajbari at Rangamati. (Chakma Raja collection)*

***Plate 367****. In this photograph taken in Chandraghona in 1962 we see newlyweds Keith and Edna Skirrow with (from left to right): Mary Taylor, Shwe Hla Maung, Dr Alan Taylor, Janet Taylor and Sue LeQuesne. (Flowers, 1962)*

In many ways the two sections of the Chittagong Hill Tracts elite—British and local—continued to live separate lives. The differences in lifestyle are summed up well in the wedding pictures of two couples, the Roys of Rangamati and the Skirrows of Chandraghona (**plates 366** and **367**).

## 17.3 The National Elite: Far from the Madding Crowd

After Partition, the Chittagong Hill Tracts came to play a role in the leisure activities and escapist fantasies of the budding national elite of Pakistan. Kaptai lake, in particular, was profiled as a 'beauty spot' where one could unwind. Not only was tourism encouraged but the lake, and the 'tribal beauties' supposedly inhabiting its slopes, figured frequently as picturesque elements in popular films geared at a national audience (**plate 368**).

## 17.4 Coming Together

The lives of the various sections of the elite in the Chittagong Hill Tracts may have been very different, but they did touch each other, not only in work situations but also in leisure activities. Outdoor sports in particular brought them together. Soccer games were popular, and they were promoted by the authorities. Two soccer cups were named after deputy commissioners (Hands, Hume), and two others after the Bohmong and Chakma chiefs. One of the most important soccer games of the year was the one between the Rangamati and Kaptai teams (**plates 369-70**).

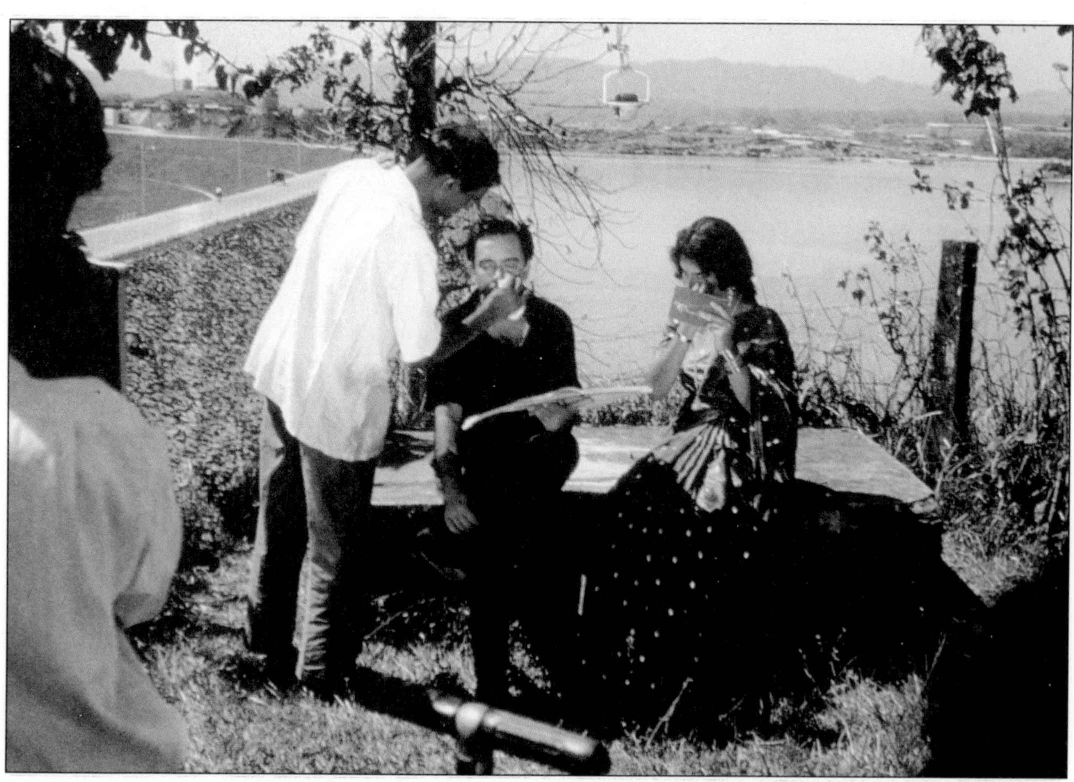

***Plate 368***. *'Film production, Kaptai.' (Recter, 1965)*

**Plate 369**. *'Rangamati vs. Kaptai, 1955– Parade Ground,' Rangamati. The Deputy Commissioner of the Chittagong Hill Tracts, L.H. Niblett, and his daughter June, are watching the game, surrounded by high officials from Rangamati and Kaptai.*[5] *(Chakma Raja collection)*

**Plate 370**. *'Pipes, Parade Ground, 1955.' The police band is seen playing bagpipes under the shishu trees whose dead branches, sticking out of Lake Kaptai, would later become a familiar site. (Chakma Raja collection)*

**Plate 371**. *Kaptai soccer team. (Chakma Raja collection, 1958)*

**Plate 372**. *Raja Tridiv Roy with the Hume soccer cup. (Chakma Raja collection, about 1956)*

**Plate 373**. *A soccer match at the Baptist Missionary Hospital, Chandraghona. (Flowers, 1960s)*

***Plate 374***. *School champions being honoured. (Meier, 1955-61)*

Outdoor sports competitions and hunting were two other activities which were part of the overlapping lifestyles of different sections of the elite. Competitions were organised regularly by the high school and the paper mill at Chandraghona, and hunting was part of the 'manly' adventures that the Chittagong Hill Tracts offered to visitors and locals alike (**plates 371-379**).

***Plate 375***. *The manager of the Chandraghona paper mill, Hans Meier, being garlanded. (Meier collection, 1955-61)*

***Plate 376***. *The staff of the Kodala Tea Estate posing with a deer shot during their annual outing in the hills. (Stevens, early 1950s)*

***Plate 377***. *Hunt organised by the Chakma chief for the Deputy Commissioner, Mr. F. Afzal Agha, Barkal. (Chakma Raja collection, 1957)*

***Plate 378**. Raja Tridiv Roy posing with a tiger which he had shot near Barkal.*
*(Chakma Raja collection, 1957)*

***Plate 379***. *A deer being carried off after a hunting trip. (Sigl, 1965-69)*

## Chapter 18

# ENCOUNTERS

**Plate 380**. *'Study in contrast.' (Sandercock, 1964-65)*

Many visitors who took pictures in the Chittagong Hill Tracts visualised it as a place where two 'worlds' met. They often focussed on contrasts, encounters and mergers.

**Plate 381**. *'Mong Raja, Manikchhari, in front of Okinagan helicopter.' (Recter, 1965)*

Most common are photographs in which power-engined machinery (e.g. a jeep, or a speedboat) was used as a Western counterpoint to the 'bamboo technology' and local cultures of the hills. In photographs of the 1960s, the foremost emblem of modernity, development and disjunction was a Canadian helicopter which was vital for the extensive surveying work then going on. In a photograph actually captioned 'study in contrast,' F.K. Sandercock portrayed a working elephant and young next to the helicopter at Kaptai. Similarly, the helicopter figured as a coveted symbol of modernity when the Mong chief and his family posed for the camera in Manikchhari (**plates 380** and **381**).

In similar vein the meeting and, in a way, clashing of two contrasting worlds is depicted in **plate 382**; what was a venerated image for many was to others a charming backdrop for a family photograph.

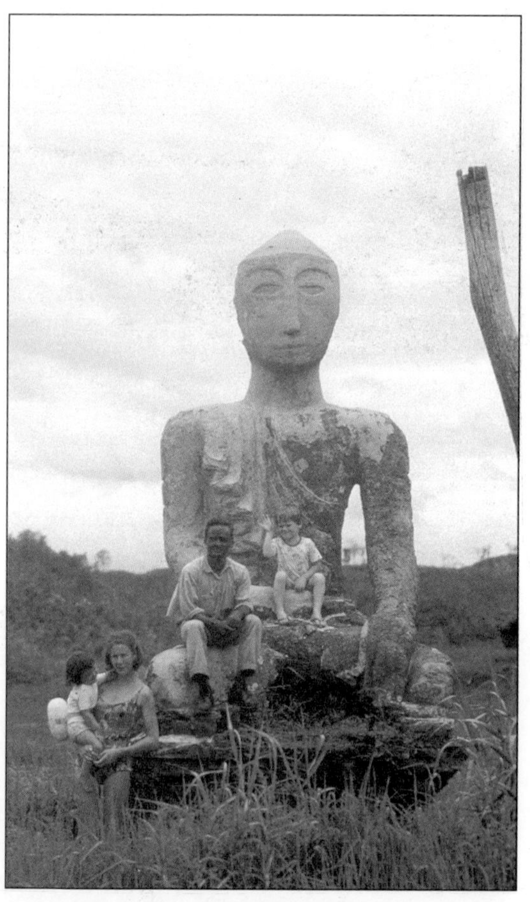

***Plate 382**. 'The Kaptai Buddha (submerged when lake is high), with my family and Sharif, boat driver.' (Band, 1968)*

***Plate 383**. Policeman Nogendro Karbari and Bengali friend. (Krishna Khisa (Karbari) collection, 1940s)*

Rather more complicated encounters can be seen in **plates 383** and **384**. The first shows Nogendro Karbari, a Chakma, with his Bengali friend and colleague; they both served the colonial state as police officers. In the second we see Shwe Hla Phru, adopted son of a British Baptist missionary family, with his uncle, a Buddhist monk, and Rev Keith Skirrow, a British missionary.

Finally, **plate 385** symbolises the encounter between bamboo and iron, hills and plains, minority and majority, and local and visitor.

***Plate 384***. *'Shwe Hla Phru, his uncle the monk, and Rev. Keith Skirrow.' (Skirrow, 1967)*

***Plate 385***. *Observing the other. (Seifert, 1963)*

# Chapter 19
# PORTRAITS

One way of grouping photographs of the Chittagong Hill Tracts is by considering the relationship between the photographer and her or his subject, and the audience for which the photograph was intended.

Much has been written about how Westerners have used the camera to represent non-Westerners to Western audiences; many photographs in this book belong to that category. But in the Chittagong Hill Tracts, as elsewhere, local inhabitants also used the camera for their own purposes: to represent themselves to themselves, or to represent themselves to outsiders. Again, many examples can be found in this book.

Facile assumptions about Westerners producing merely 'Orientalist' photographs which reflected and reinforced their dominant position, their distance from local culture, and their need to construct an exotic 'other,' simply do not hold up. Focusing on the relationship between the people on either side of the camera, and on the audience for which a photograph was meant, brings out a more complex reality. In this chapter we explore this for one particular type of photograph, the portrait of one or more individuals.

***Plate 386**. 'Gopi the fair. A Khumi lass.' (Lewin, 1867)*

## 19.1 The Earliest Photographs: Personal Mementoes

T.H. Lewin made the first photographic portraits of people in the Chittagong hills. As we have seen, his relationship with them was full of ambiguity and contradiction. He was a colonial administrator who, as the first Deputy Commissioner of the Chittagong Hill Tracts, was committed to establishing British rule in a newly conquered region. But he was also unusually attracted to the local people, their lifestyle and their languages; at times he toyed with the idea of permanently settling down among them. Over time he became very knowledgeable about social life in the hills; he also became intimately acquainted with many individuals, and he wrote about them in his books (Lewin, 1869, 1873, 1912; cf. Whitehead, 1992).

This complex relationship is reflected in his portraits which were created as personal mementoes rather than with a specific group of viewers in mind. Remarkable for a man who wrote so much about the Chittagong hills, he never used these photographs in his publications.[1] Published here for the first time, they show a rare sensitivity to individual dignity (**plates 386-390**; see also **plate 416**).

***Plate 387***. *'Sonarutton & his wife, Chittagong Hill Tracts.' Sonarutton was Lewin's bearer. (Lewin, 1867; cf Lewin, 1912, 239)*

***Plate 388***. *'Looshai captive woman after 15 years.' Lewin met this Lushai woman who had been captured by Shendoos during a raid and had spent 15 years with them before being able to return to her own people. (Lewin, about 1866)*

***Plate 389****. 'Pankho Kookie.' (Lewin, 1867)*

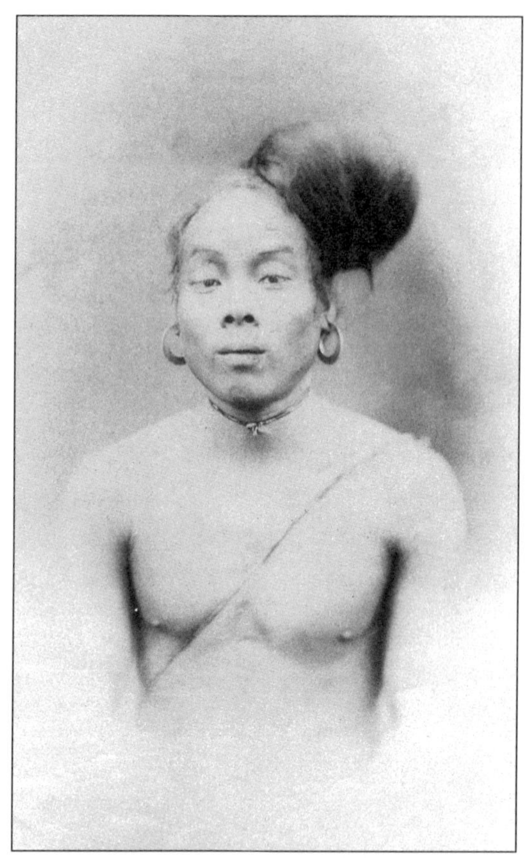

***Plate 390****. 'Young man of Mro or Mrung tribe.' (Lewin, 1867)*

## 19.2. The Family Album Portrait: Images of Respect

Most people in the Chittagong hills did not have access to cameras till quite late but some families kept collections of photographs—in albums, trunks or boxes—for family use. These photographs were often portraits, although the cameras available to them usually did not allow for close-ups. Many of these portraits were images of respect or remembrance.

When amateur photographers in the Chittagong Hill Tracts trained their lenses respectfully at the oldest members of their families or communities, remarkable portraits could be the result (**plates 391-395**).

***Plate 391**. Sadness and resignation are reflected in the face of the mother of Kamini Mohan Dewan, in her late eighties, as she sits on the kitchen verandah of Kamini's house in old Rangamati after the sraddh (death ceremony) for Kamini's wife in 1953. Next to her are her daughter and niece. (T. Roy, 1953)*

**Plate 392**. *It is with a composed gaze that Chin Hla, a 70-year-old cultivator and banana wholesaler of Taitongpara village, Rajasthali, poses for his son. (M.K. Maung, 1963)*

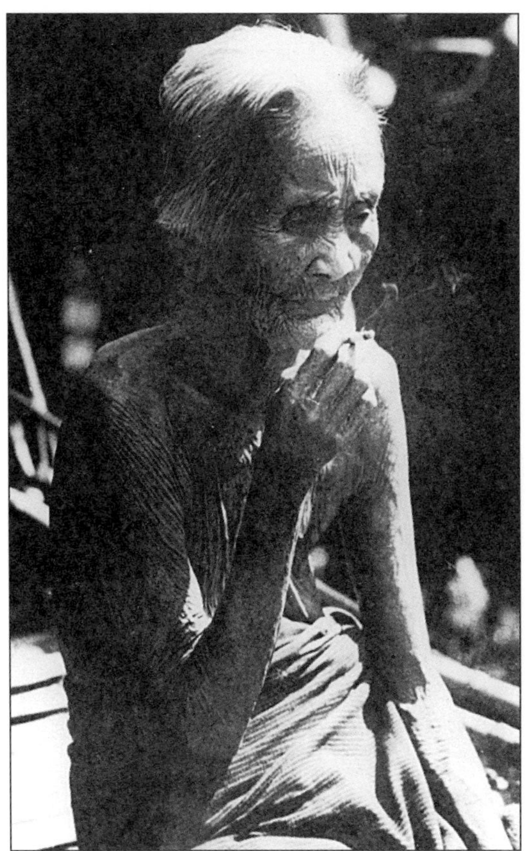

**Plate 393**. *Chakma woman said to be over 100 years old, Rangapani village. (Devasish Dewan, 1976)*

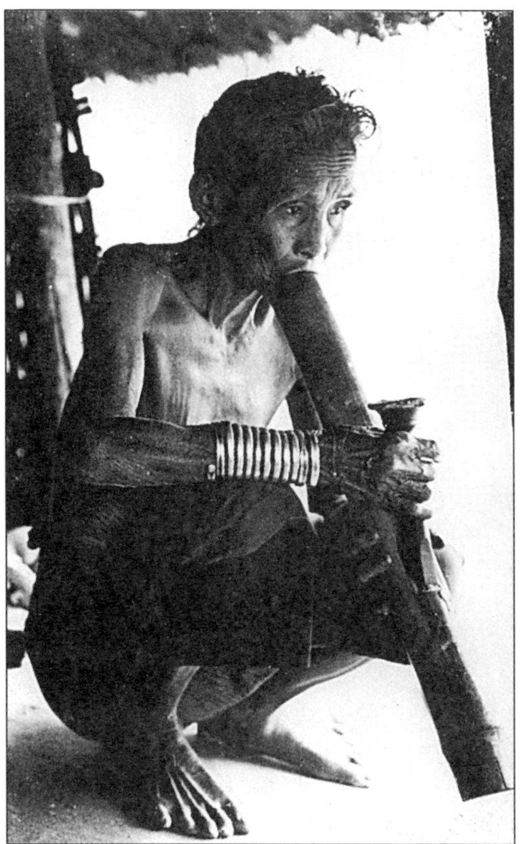

**Plate 394**. *Chakma woman smoking a bamboo pipe, Rangapani village. (Devashish Dewan, 1977)*

**Plate 395**. *The ultimate and most intimate portrait of respect and remembrance is that of a deceased parent. Here we see the body of the father of Saradendu Sekhar Chakma, surrounded by his family and a priest. (Saradendu S. Chakma collection, 1960s)*

## 19.3 The Family Album Portrait: Images of Growing Up

Family collections also contain many pictures of children, usually as members of family groups, but occasionally alone. An example is a three-generation picture (**plate 396**) showing Hla Han Maung with his mother and paternal grandmother. Another example is the studio portrait of Maung Chin Nu, a self-possessed schoolboy dressed in his very best clothes (**plate 397**).

**Plate 398** is a family album picture with a difference. Two decades after the photograph was made, these boys would emerge as leaders of the armed insurgency in the Chittagong hills. **Plate 399** shows another genre; students sometimes had their photograph taken in a professional studio.

A remarkable image of growing up, and the passing of time, is provided by the combination of two photographs. In 1937, Rev. W.J.L. Wenger took a picture of his adopted baby son Shwe Hla Phru in the arms of Dr Teichmann. A generation later, in a striking mirror image, Shwe Hla Phru is holding up his own son Ba Ching. These images also indicate that the line between locals and outsiders, or Westerners and non-Westerners, was sometimes more blurred than is commonly recognised (**plates 400** and **401**).

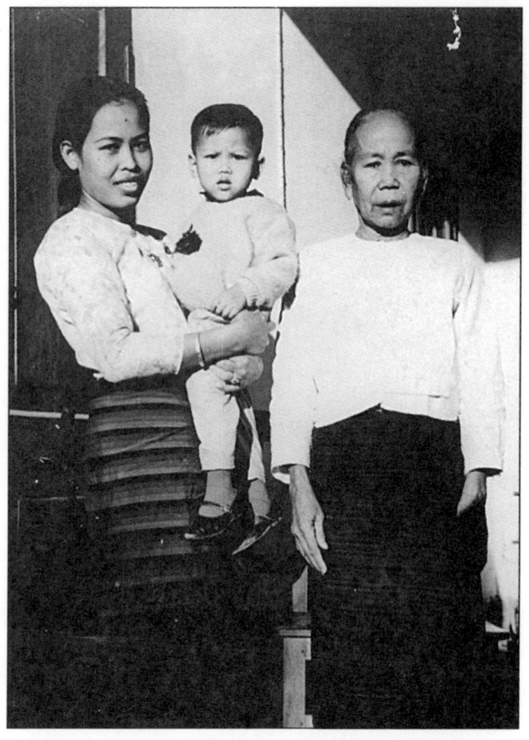

***Plate 396***. *Hla Han Maung with mother and grandmother.*[2] *(Tripura, 1968)*

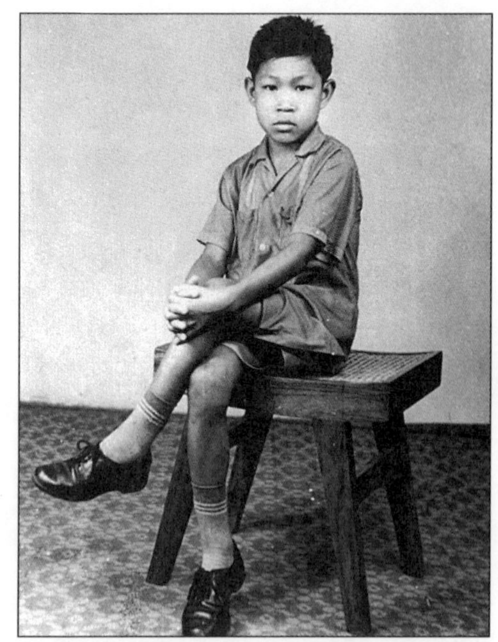

***Plate 397***. *Maung Chin Nu. (M.K. Maung/Ching Kwai Hpru collection, 1968)*

**Plate 398**. *The three sons of Chitto Kishore Larma. From the left: Subhendu, Manabendra Narayan and Jyotirindra Buddhapriya (Shantu) Larma.*[3] *(Pankajini Larma collection, 1953)*

***Plate 399***. *Sailendra Narayan Dewan as an engineering student in Dhaka. (Sailendra N. Dewan collection, 1952)*

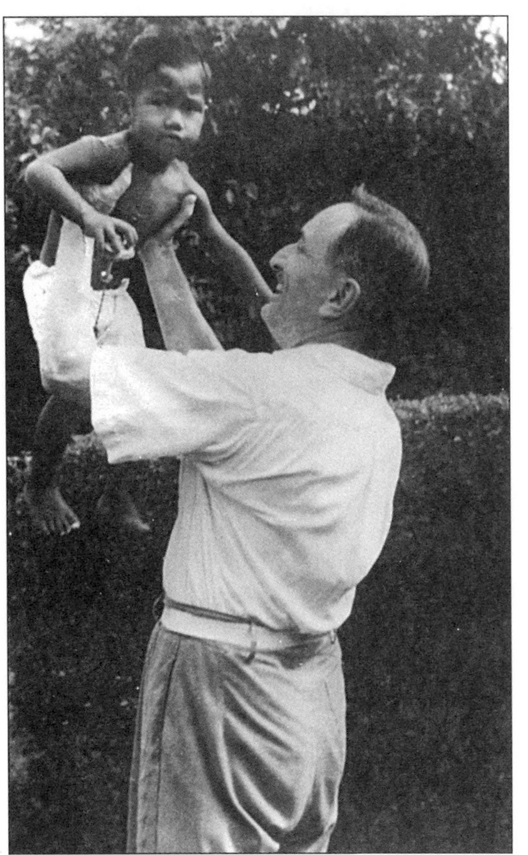

***Plate 400***. *'Shwe Hla Phru and Doctor Teichmann.' (W.J.L. Wenger, 1937)*

***Plate 401***. *'Shwe Hla Phru and Ba Ching.' (Leslie Wenger collection, 1971)*

## 19.4 Missionaries' Collections: Images of Dignity

Missionaries had family albums as well; they took photographs for private use as well as for their constituency in Britain. It is not always easy to distinguish between the two, and some photographs may have been taken with both uses in mind. Missionaries in the Chittagong Hill Tracts took many photographs of local co-workers and co-religionists which show them as dignified and modern, looking confidently and smilingly into the camera. An early example of the genre, from the Baptist Missionary Society Medical Logbook, depicts an orderly at the new mission hospital and his son against the zigzag pattern of a bamboo wall (**plate 402**).

***Plate 402***. *'Shamcharan & his baby, Chandraghona 1907.' (Baptist Missionary Society)*

In another portrait, Tilak Chandra Chakma, an 'educated Christian Chakma headman' from Lower Betchhari, leans casually on a bamboo fence as he looks confidently at the photographer (**plate 403**).

In what is as much a portrait of Staff Nurse Thwaingya as of the two objects he holds in his hands ('in his right hand a 13½oz stone taken out of a bladder, in his left hand an orange'), the atmosphere is one of photographer (Edna Skirrow) and her subject sharing an amusing moment as professionals (**plate 404**).

Whereas these photographs were mostly for private use, images of children were also used extensively in presentations ('deputations') in Britain. Children were a favourite topic for Christine Manson, a missionary who left behind a notable photographic record. In her studies she brought out the individuality of village girls as no other photographer of that period did (**plates 405** and **406**).

**Plate 403**. *Tilak Chandra Chakma (Tilak Headman), Rangamati. (Taylor, 1954)*

**Plate 404**. *Staff nurse Thwaingya, Chandraghona. (Skirrow, 1958)*

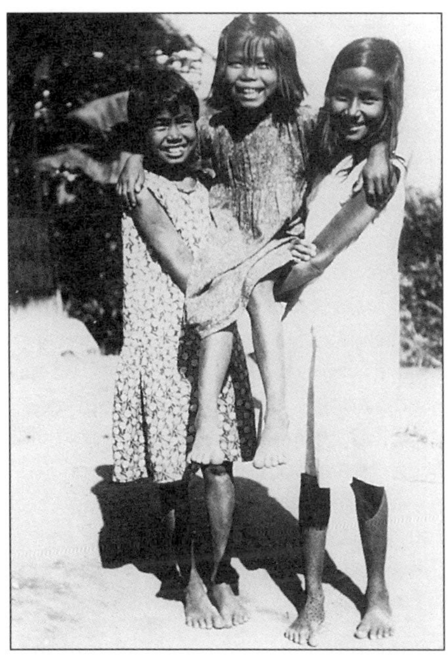

**Plate 405**. *'Girls at Toimidong, Rangamati, 1936.' (Manson, 1936)*

**Plate 406**. *'Kolabunia, 1948.' (Manson, 1948)*

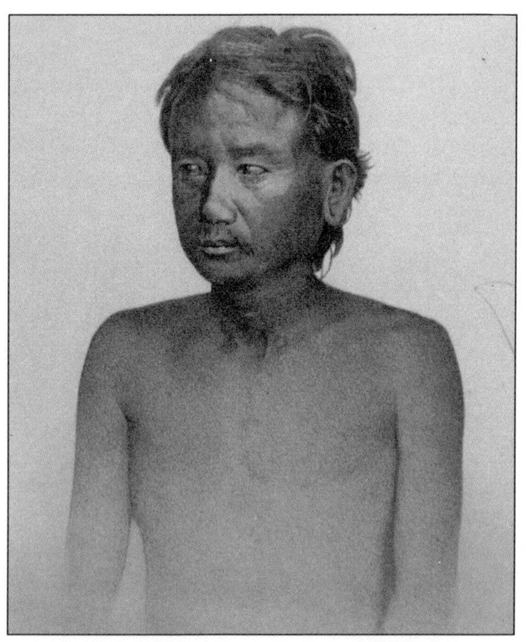

***Plate 407**. 'A Mug,' about 1870. (Simpson, in Dalton, 1872)*

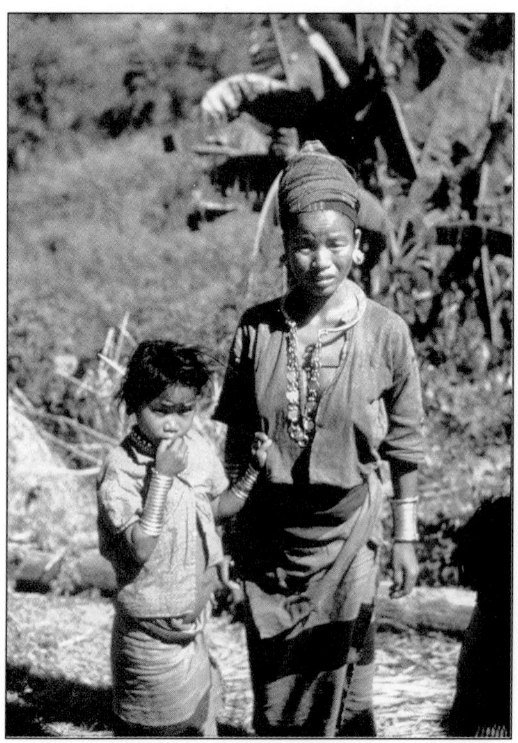

***Plate 408**. Woman and child on Ghagra road. (Barblan, about 1959)*

## 19.5 The 'Tribal' Portrait: Images of Embarrassment

The element of empathy and mutual trust is often lacking in photographs which portray individuals as anonymous 'tribal types.' A classic example is the portrait of 'A Mug,' whose identity as an individual and as a member of an ethnic group remains unknown. One author guesses that he may be a Barua (Bengali Buddhist) and in another book he is tentatively identified as a Marma.4 Looking supremely ill at ease in front of the camera, he survives as a naked specimen of some ill-defined social category (**plate 407**).

Suspicion, embarrassment and trepidation are palpable in a genre of photographs, resulting from chance meetings, which were portraits of 'tribal finery' rather than of the individuals displaying it (**plates 408-411**).

In **plate 409**, for example, it is the vacant gaze of an unidentified young Bawm man which is most striking. The photograph, published in the American National Geographic Magazine in 1955, was accompanied by a text which stressed that this individual should be considered as representing an exotic group:

> 'This Bunjoogie [=Bawm] tribesman, pictured while on a shopping trip to the bazaars of Rangamati, comes from a tribe once regarded as the fiercest in Bengal. His red headband and carefully tended topknot used to be regarded as symbols of luck in head-taking expeditions. Pierced and stretched ear lobes carry ivory disks that have been handed down from father to son. An expert could glance at the copper comb and beaded necklace and name the tribe' (Shor and Shor, 1955, 415).

***Plate 409***. *'Son of Head-hunters Lives at Peace.' (Shor and Shor, 1955)*

***Plate 410***. *Suspicion and obedient awkwardness: a Mru man looks into the lens of a European visitor. (Seifert, 1963)*

***Plate 411***. *'Sak women with the characteristic, large earrings.' (Brauns, 1969)*

In all these cases outsiders represented people from the Chittagong Hill Tracts to outsiders. But these outsiders (both photographers and audiences) were not necessarily Westerners. Increasingly 'tribal' portraits were created by, a catered to, Pakistanis and Bengalis. Popular images from the early 1960s (**plates 412** and **413**) show that the hallmarks of this genre—anonymity and awkwardness—remained intact.

***Plate 412***. *'A young Murung [Mru] smoking home-grown tobacco.' (Rajput, 1963)*

***Plate 413***. *'A Tippera girl dressed in all the finery for the jungle Bazaar.' (Rajput, 1965)*

**Plate 414** is one of the most-published photographs from the Chittagong Hill Tracts. It shows an annoyed young man. In his article 'A Trek in the Hills of Chittagong,' A.B. Rajput (who had taken the trek with an unidentified photographer), captioned it 'A Chakma dancer in typical festive dress and headgear.' In a later publication, however, the caption read 'A Pankhu dancer in festive dress and headgear' (Rajput, 1965). This Pangkhua-Chakma confusion was continued by Abdus Sattar, a writer on 'tribal culture,' who used the photograph in several publications which became widely distributed in Bangladesh.[5]

The photograph reached the status of the archetypal 'tribal' portrait from the Chittagong Hill Tracts when it served as model for a painting on the gate to the Folk Festival and Exhibition (**plate 415**).

***Plate 414***. *Member of a Pangkhua dance troupe. (Rajput, 1962)*

***Plate 415***. *Detail of the gateway to the Folk Festival and Exhibition, 1969. (Sigl, 1969)*

# Chapter 20

# CONCLUSION: WHAT COUNTS AS HISTORY?

In the Introduction, we described the Chittagong Hill Tracts as an out-of-the-way, unusual and little known district of Bangladesh. The idea behind this book was to take a serious look at its photographic record and to demonstrate how useful photographs can be in constructing long-term historical accounts of the area. The stories suggested by the material in this book are, however, of much wider than local interest. They show us that there is more to the history of the people living in Bangladesh than the two state-centred, nationalist narratives which have dominated the scene for so long. These narratives, which we have dubbed 'The Struggle for Bengali Nationhood' and 'The Emancipation of the Muslim,' have covered up a multitude of alternative histories. It is high time to explore these alternatives, especially those based on gender, class and ethnic identity.

## 20.1 What Counts as History?

History-writing in Bangladesh is fed largely by a dominant ideology, nationalism, which comes in two variants. The importance of past events, personalities and movements is measured against the yardstick of either Bengali nationhood or Muslim emancipation. This has led to a much too restricted notion of what is important in Bangladesh history. Historians have usually given prominence to the doings of a small group of persons whom they considered to be the agents of Bangladesh history. At the same time, they have paid very little attention to the doings of large groups of other inhabitants whose role has been constructed as that of mere followers, onlookers, or outsiders. Historians who concern themselves with the activities of politicians, administrators, military men, university students and intellectuals—mostly male, mostly located in Dhaka—are considered to deal with the general history of the country, whereas researchers who write about 'ordinary people' (women, peasants, labourers, minorities) are seen as 'specialists.'

The nation has come to be a favoured subject of history-writing all over the world. Many historians accept nationalism as a 'naturalised' ideology which needs no legitimation. And yet, it is necessary to ask two sets of questions. First, what makes the nation a legitimate subject of history? Should it frame the way historians study a society? In what ways is it more important than other subjects? How can it be studied together with other subjects, e.g. social orders, religious groups, economic networks, linguistic communities?

Second, should the nation be studied from a nationalist point of view? Is it not a task of historians to distance themselves from their subject of study in order to analyse it better? It would seem extremely important to reconsider the assumption that the nation is a culturally uniform unit. As a result, the nationalist genre of writing 'history in the singular' can be replaced by a style of history-writing which explores multiple narratives of the past.

Such questions are especially relevant in Bangladesh, with its two rival versions of nationalist history-writing. It is essential to carry out careful empirical studies of the changing meanings of 'nation' and 'nation state' during the British, Pakistan and Bangladesh periods. How did nationalist thinking come about? How, when, and to what extent did it become influential in different social groups? How can its permutations be explained? So far, historians have built their accounts far too simplistically on the experiences of the narrow group of 'historical agents' mentioned above. Looking at other groups suggests different patterns and periodicities. Most of all, it allows us to step back from the binary opposites on which nationalist thought thrives. When we read about nationalism in Bangladesh, it is usually in dichotomies such as British/Bengali and later Pakistani/Bengali, colonial/indigenous, Muslim/Hindu. Such dichotomies hide important complexities of class, gender, region, language and religion which were never dichotomous.

## 20.2 The Chittagong Hill Tracts and Bangladesh History

Studying the history of the Chittagong Hill Tracts provides an excellent opportunity to rethink nationalist biases. A first question relates to the construction of a Bengali national identity. There is a whole literature exploring certain aspects and historical connections: the impact of British colonial rule; a growing familiarity of elite Bengalis with Western nationalist thought; the (re)discovery and revaluation of Bengal's cultural past; the celebration of the Bengali linguistic community, particularly vis-à-vis English and Urdu; and the struggle to establish nationalist institutions in the public domain.

But this literature also reveals remarkable silences. The *category of 'Bengali'* is rarely questioned. Who considered themselves and others as Bengalis? What were the boundaries of Bengali identity, how were these maintained, and how did they change over time? How was Bengali nationalist identity shaped vis-à-vis other identities, especially those of people who were considered to be within the category but who refused to join? Particularly relevant here are groups who were sometimes considered to speak 'lower' forms of the Bengali language but who insisted on a separate linguistic identity. Examples are the Oriyas and Assamese, who successfully established separate linguistic states in India, as well as the Chakma and, to a certain extent, Sylhetis and Chittagonians in Bangladesh. In Bangladesh, language became a potent symbol of nationalist aspirations. History-writing generally assumes that the removal of English and then Urdu as linguistic threats made Bengali an uncontested symbol of the nation. The recent history of the Chittagong Hill Tracts shows this to have been a serious misrepresentation.

A second nationalist bias has been *scapegoating*. The people of the Chittagong Hill Tracts are often blamed for not having contributed sufficiently to the nationalist struggle, first for Pakistan and then for Bangladesh. To what extent they actually did contribute is still a hotly debated empirical question. The nationalist bias in the discussion lies in the assumption that they committed a sin against the nation, that they betrayed the high ideal. But it is entirely legitimate to ask what Pakistani and then Bengali/Bangladeshi nationalism actually had to offer to them. The nationalist narratives promised liberation for Muslims in Pakistan, and liberation for Bengalis in Bangladesh. Couched in the modernist language of citizens' rights and obligations, these narratives did not allow for citizenship *and* cultural/religious difference: it was the nation which excluded the people of the Chittagong hills, not the people of the Chittagong hills who failed to 'join the mainstream.' Being neither

Muslims nor Bengalis, they were denied full citizenship in both Pakistani and Bengali/ Bangladeshi nationalism.

The Chittagong Hill Tracts provide an example of what exclusion from a nation may entail. As such, it is not only illustrative of other groups which were more or less completely excluded from the nation in Pakistan/Bangladesh (e.g. women, peasants, non-Muslims, non-Bengalis) but also of similar groups excluded from nations worldwide. We have seen that nationalism represented the Chittagong Hill Tracts as the pre-social, the non-rational, the tribal. Thought to be passive, docile, and backward, the people of the Chittagong hills had to be led by the nationalist elite and its concerns. The emancipation of the hill people could be brought about by absolute government, and the civilising mission of the leaders of the nation allowed them to use any means to achieve that goal in the Chittagong Hill Tracts, even bringing peace and progress by violent forms of disruption. Such developments point to the violence built into the making of all nation states, and the struggles for cultural rights, regional autonomy, and democracy spawned by it. Struggles for the right to citizenship as well as cultural difference are a common phenomenon in today's world, and each state will have to find its own way of accommodating these. But if dominant groups do not accept that nationalist exclusion is a root cause, such struggles will be misunderstood.

A third nationalist bias has been the *representation* of the Chittagong Hill Tracts and their inhabitants. Dominant representations have stressed the binary opposites of both nationalist and developmentalist discourse, and have used markers such as 'tribal,' 'primitive' and 'backward' to deny the people of the Chittagong hills a 'modern' voice. In reaction, writers and politicians from the Chittagong hills as well as outsiders writing about the area have increasingly adopted indigenist positions which echo the same oppositional thinking. The 'indigenous' is represented as an internally unified category in opposition to an equally monolithic nation from which it is excluded. In this way, a new nation-of-intent, known to many as the *Jumma* nation, was created. Adherents of this indigenist view concentrate on the new nation and its suffering, celebrate its emancipation, and seek to inscribe the *Jumma* nation in world history. In the process they accept the categorisation underlying the category 'tribal' while seeking to reverse opposites like primitive and civilised, and searching for the authentic core of the new-found nation.

We think historians should not adopt this new nationalist perspective but rather stand back and look at the ways in which social identities in the Chittagong hills have been shaped by continual negotiations across the nationalist divide. The accepted category of 'tribal' is an empty one, used in historical and political narratives to divide, marginalise and disempower. The role of the people of the Chittagong Hill Tracts in constituting modernity in the wider society of British India, Pakistan and Bangladesh has so far remained unacknowledged. The idea of recovering, through history, the 'pure,' authentic core of the Chittagong hills is self-defeating; the area and its inhabitants have become what they are through a long series of experiences and transformations in the pre-colonial, British, Pakistan and Bangladesh periods.

What is equally important is that study of the Chittagong Hill Tracts opens up an opportunity to disestablish nationalist historiography in yet another way. It was, of course, never ordained that the Chittagong hills would end up as part of the territory of a colony called British India, or successive states called Pakistan and Bangladesh. A history which seems marginal and peripheral if looked at from the capitals of Calcutta, Islamabad, Delhi, Dhaka or Rangoon, looks very different if seen from Rangamati or Bandarban.[1] The Chittagong hills, which remain at the margins of nationalist consciousness in Bangladesh, are in fact part of an enormous mountainous region which separates the valleys of the Brahmaputra, Irrawaddy, Mekong and Yangze, and connects South, Southeast and East Asia. In the past, state power came to be located in these lowlands, and historical narratives have followed the lowland-oriented nationalisms which became dominant in Bangladesh, India, Burma, Thailand, China and Vietnam. In each, the mountain area was seen as peripheral, a marginal area that had to be integrated, dominated and developed from the lowland. As a result, history-writing on the mountain region became fragmented, lowland-oriented and disjointed. The history of the mountain region became a *'Triangle of Ignorance,'* considered to be more of antiquarian and anthropological than of modern historical interest. A reintegration of that history requires historians to overcome the nationalist ideologies to which they have so long been subservient.

## 20.3 Threatened Memories

But how to go about this? What is the historical evidence which can guide us in such explorations? One of the legacies of colonialism in Bangladesh is an enormous body of state records, and most history-writing continues to rely heavily upon this gold mine. Other sources of historical information have not been preserved with the same care, although certain national institutions (e.g. the Bangla Academy and the Asiatic Society of Bangladesh) and private organisations and individuals have made an effort. But none of these have been particularly effective in preserving material relating to alternative voices in Bangladesh's history. This could be demonstrated for women's history, labour history, regional histories, or the histories of non-Bengali groups in the country. The history of the Chittagong Hill Tracts is just one case in point.

Historians are well aware that current power relations always determine why certain material is deemed important enough to be preserved for posterity and other material is neglected or destroyed. A society's archives are never just there; they have been carefully constructed and selected. In any society, it is extremely important for the dominant classes to legitimise their position by referring to history, and to make sure that their version of history is preserved and accepted. The history that is preserved in archives, museums and libraries tends to be the history of the political victors, the official memory, in which the non-dominant appear as passive, docile and consenting. Rules for inclusion of material, and the perceived authority of historical records, may change when new groups rise to dominance.

But non-dominant groups are not always passive, docile and consenting. The revolt in the Chittagong Hill Tracts from the 1970s is a good example. That revolt and the widespread counter-insurgency measures it occasioned force us to rethink questions of power and representation. How have marginalised and subordinated groups been represented in Bangladesh history? How do they want to represent themselves? To what extent are their memories and historical imagination threatened by the clamour of nation-building?

Preserving the history of the Chittagong Hill Tracts was never a priority in British India, Pakistan or Bangladesh. As a result, most of it is rapidly fading into darkness. This book has briefly lit up a few pockets but much has remained unilluminated.

Why is the history of the Chittagong Hill Tracts fading into darkness? First, the source material on the basis of which to construct historical accounts of the Chittagong hills has always been limited. Local society produced relatively little written material. This was a result of very low rates of literacy (even by 1961 only 3 per cent of the women and 20 per cent of the men could read or write) and the existence of only a minute elite with an interest in producing and preserving written material. Moreover, the system of administration in the Chittagong hills differed from that in the rest of Bangladesh. It was based partly on indirect rule and decentralisation, and mitigated against the development of a district-level bureaucracy which might have left behind detailed accounts of local society.

Non-written sources of historical information are also relatively scarce. There are few old buildings and objects because the chief building material, bamboo, is perishable; textiles were rarely preserved for generations; and precious metal ornaments would be recast to make them fit new fashions. The rich oral traditions of the hill people have not been preserved in a systematic manner, although composers and singers of ballads (e.g. the Chakma *gengkhuli*) could still provide important historical information. Photographs appear to be the most readily accessible non-written source on the history of the Chittagong Hill Tracts but, as we have seen, much of the photographic record has already been lost.

Second, the Chittagong Hill Tracts became a marginal district in one of the poorest states of the world. Clearly, the keeping of historical records had a very low priority. The district record rooms built up during the colonial period went into decline all over East Pakistan/Bangladesh, and the state records on the Chittagong Hill Tracts suffered extensive neglect and destruction. Non-state material on local history was never collected systematically; and other depositories which could have preserved material relating to the broad sweep of local history never came into existence.

And third, normal life in the Chittagong Hill Tracts was continually disrupted. Large numbers of inhabitants were dislocated as a result of successive interventions. The Kaptai dam (1960) forced one-quarter of the population to move house, the Bangladesh War of Independence (1971) impelled people to leave their homes and go into hiding, and from the mid-1970s guerrilla warfare and militarisation led to serious dislocations as people had to seek refuge in India, were herded into 'cluster villages,' were displaced by army posts or settlers from the plains, or saw their houses go up in flames. Official depositories of land records were also destroyed on purpose in the struggle over land control in the hills between locals and immigrant plainsmen.

## 20.4 Hidden Images and Realities

Why should the preservation of this material concern us? What is the importance of the social memory embedded in photographs and texts of the Chittagong hills? First of all, this material is of obvious relevance to the inhabitants of the Chittagong Hill Tracts themselves; it provides them with an anchor in time, points of identification and self-esteem, and an antidote to the political and historiographical marginalisation to which they have been subjected for over a century. To the extent that photographic images were made by hill people themselves, or under their instructions (as in a photo studio), they can be taken to reflect their historical imaginations and presentations of self..

So far, such (re)presentations have hardly been taken into account in history-writing. A history of the Chittagong Hill Tracts which is dominated by neither colonial nor nationalist imagery has to rely largely on self-representation to order the past, give meaning to the present and prepare for the future.

But these images and texts are also of much wider national and international importance because of the troubled and bloody recent history of the Chittagong Hill Tracts. The social memory contained in them is needed to understand why political crisis, militarisation and human rights abuses overwhelmed the area from the 1970s, how these developments impinged on local identities, and how realistic visions of the future can be shaped. This cannot be done successfully without detailed documentation.

As in any situation of warfare, different sides in the conflict in the Chittagong Hill Tracts have created mutually incompatible accounts of local history.[2] Few of these accounts were grounded solidly in historical evidence and many of them constitute wilful myth-making, disinformation and political propaganda fabricated to sway public opinion. There is a great need for more reliable accounts of how the people of the Chittagong hills came to be in the unenviable position that they found themselves in during the last quarter of the twentieth century. Such accounts can only be based on historical evidence.

Collecting such information and making it publicly available is one way of giving voice to ideas, perspectives, and interests of ordinary people who have been marginalised or silenced. It allows the construction of more grounded and less partisan accounts of the history of the Chittagong Hill Tracts.

We have chosen to concentrate on visual material because we felt it was rarer, more scattered and less accessible than written material. This proved to be true. It was only owing to the support of many helpful people that we were able over several years to locate photographs in private collections as far-flung as Bandarban, Dhaka, Vancouver, Buenos Aires and Stockholm.

The images tell stories which could not have been constructed from texts. They have added new insights into the realities of life in the Chittagong hills between the 1860s and the 1970s. But they also point the way to new interpretations of the history of Bangladesh and the wider region. In particular, they may help us break out of the shackles of nationalist history-writing and begin contributing to a more integrated understanding of historical developments in the highlands connecting South, Southeast and East Asia.

# Notes

## Introduction

1 The linguistic map of the Chittagong hills is extraordinarily complex. Most languages spoken here belong to the large language family known to linguists as Sino-Tibetan. The classification of languages within this family is contested and many individual languages are still very inadequately (or not at all) described in the scholarly literature. According to one classification (Shafer, 1955), Sino-Tibetan languages in the Chittagong hills belong to the Burmic division (Mru, Khumi, Lushai, Pangkhua, Bawm, Sak, Khyeng, Marma) and the Baric division (Kok-Borok (Tripura, Riang/Brong)). The other major language family in the Chittagong hills is the Indo-European family, represented by Chakma, Taungchengya and Bengali. A small group of Santali-speakers represents the Munda family of languages (Shapiro and Schiffman, 1983; Brauns and Löffler, 248).

2 There are now some books of photographs on particular episodes, such as the War of Independence, 1971 (e.g. *Bangla Name Desh*, 1972; *Dhaka* 1971, 1988; Ahmad, 1996), or the movement for the restoration of democracy (1982-1990; Muhammed, 1993). There are also books of contem-porary photographs on Bangladesh as a whole (e.g. Ahmed and Islam, 1976) or on special themes (e.g. Bølstad and Jansen, 1992; Hossain, 1992; Chandan, 1994; Warren and Ison, n.d.).

3 The division has become more distinct over time. In 1798, Francis Buchanan found hill people practising shifting cultivation on higher lands in Chittagong district, and even on Maheshkhali island in the Bay of Bengal (Van Schendel (ed.), 1992). The colonial government's decisions—to prohibit shifting cultivation in Chittagong district and to curb Bengali access to and activities in the Chittagong Hill Tracts—contributed greatly to the spatial separation of hill people and Bengalis. Shifting cultivators had to move to the Chittagong Hill Tracts. The Chakma chiefs, who were also large landlords (zamindars) in the plains, gradually moved their main establishment from Rangunia (in Chittagong district) to Rangamati (in the Chittagong Hill Tracts).

4 See Chittagong Hill Tracts Commission, 1991-1997; Bhaumik et al., 1997.

5 See e.g. Worswick and Embree (eds.), 1976; Worswick (ed.), 1980; Gutman, 1982; Desmond, 1982; Allen, 1979; Allen and Dwivedi, 1984; Beaton, 1945-46; Edwards, 1992; Pinney, 1997.

6 Unlike the Nagas of Northeast India, who 'came to exemplify an exotic society,' the Andaman Islanders, or the Bhutanese aristocracy, the inhabitants of the Chittagong Hill Tracts were not extensively studied or photographed by colonial travellers and anthropologists. Nor were collections of cultural artefacts from the Chittagong Hill Tracts deposited in colonial museums or research institutes. The only surviving historical collection consists of the remnants of the one gathered by Riebeck, a dealer in ethnographic objects. Cf. Jacobs et al., 1990; Edwards (ed.), 1992; Aris, 1994; Riebeck, 1885.

7 For a list of private and public collections, see the Acknowledgements.

8 Please contact us:

C/o Centre for Asian Studies Amsterdam (CASA),
University of Amsterdam,
Oude Hoogstraat 24,
1012 CE Amsterdam, The Netherlands.

## 1. Photographic Obsessions

1 Throughout this book we use quotation marks in captions whenever we reproduce the caption which was provided with the original photograph. Translations of quotations and captions into English are by the authors.

## 3. Creating a Colonial Aristocracy

1 For details of the administrative changes, see Bengal, 1929.

## 4. How to Be a Raja

1 This photograph is a good example of European classicism in the presentation of the human body. The classical tradition favoured an anatomical asymmetry resulting from placing the body's weight on one leg, leaving the other free to 'roam' (Kramer, 1989).

2 Sitting (from left to right): Romoni Mohan Roy, Kyaw Zen Prue, Bhuban Mohan Roy (Chakma chief from 1897 to 1935), Sir Lancelot Hare, Cho Hla Prue (Bohmong chief from 1902 to 1916), Ne Phru Sain (Mong chief from 1893 to 1936), Sain Kyaw Zen, a *dewan*. Standing (from left to right): some unidentified *dewans* and *roazas*, Roaza Hnee of Sara-O Mouza (standing to the left of seated Chakma chief), aide-de-camp, officer, military secretary, R.H.S. Hutchinson (Deputy Commissioner of the Chittagong Hill Tracts), private secretary to Lt.-Governor, private doctor to Lt.-Governor, Trilochan Dewan.

## 5. The Public Display of Power

1 In the spelling of local words we have been eclectic because for many no orthography has been established. *Punya* is a case in point. This spelling follows the standard Bengali/Sanskritic system of transliteration. Pronunciation in Bengali is *punna*, in Chittagonian Bengali and Chakma *phunna*. We could have chosen any of these forms. Since this is a word connected closely with kingship, we have retained the standard form. For words in other languages of the Chittagong Hill Tracts (e.g. Mru and Marma) we have followed the available literature. Names present another major problem of transliteration because of lack of rules, sketchy knowledge of most languages of the region, dialect variation within languages, and persons' individual preference for a specific rendering of their name in Roman script (which could change over their lifetime). We have tried to stay closest to personal preferences, when known, and have reproduced names as given in original captions, when available.

## 7. Pakistan and the Chiefs

1 In the Constitution of Pakistan (1956), the Chittagong Hill Tracts were declared a Wholly Excluded Area, as they had been under the Government of India Act of 1935, and were administered by the central authorities. In a new constitution in 1962, the Chittagong Hill Tracts were made a Tribal Area but not put under direct central administration. The Regulation of 1900 remained in force.

## 8. Innocence and Charm

1 1 = Marma sun and rain hat; 2 = Lushai basket for carrying cotton; 3 = Lushai basket for storing clothes; 4 = Kyoung-tha fish trap; 5 = Shindu basket; 6 = Mru seed basket; 7 = Marma fish basket; 8 = Grass band for carrying baskets on the back (Bawm); 9 = Vegetable basket (Mru); 10 = Sharpened bone used by Marma bamboo weavers; 11 = Bamboo hook, used as support by Lushai and Bawm in carrying big baskets (Riebeck, 1885, Illustration 14).

2 1 & 3 = Cloths used for carrying babies (Khumi); 2 & 7 = Marma woman's turban; 4 & 5 = Marma breast cloth; 6 = Goat's-hair ear insignia for headmen (Shindu); 8 = Marma boy's loincloth; 9 = Border of a Ka-khyen cloth (mountain areas of Burma); 10 = Lushai woman's loincloth worn underneath long robe; 11 & 12 = Khumi man's bag (front and back); 13 = Khumi woman's breast cloth; 14 = Khumi man's loincloth.

## 9. Bodies and Costumes

1 'The [first Lushai] expedition [of 1870-71] penetrated as far as the village of Lalbura, the son of Volonel (sic), a noted chief of the Howlong tribe, who dwelt in the northern Lushai Hills. The tribes tendered their submission and the columns were withdrawn. Lord Roberts named the famous white Arab charger that carried him so well between 1877 and 1896 "Volonel," after the great Kuki Chief. This noble steed, by the special permission of Her late Majesty Queen Victoria, was decorated with the Kabul Medal with four clasps, and the Kabul-Kandahar Star' (Hutchinson, 1906, 6).

## 11. Religions of the Hills

1 Although in the past researchers have studied these religions and made photographs, these photographs were not always available to us. As a result, our coverage has had to be rather restricted.

## 12. Spreading the Gospel

1 This chapter deals with British missionaries and their local followers. Missionary work in the Chittagong hills was also done by others, notably Christianised Mizo (Lushai) who became active among the Bawm in the 1920s and eventually

converted most of them (see Spielmann, 1966). We have not found any photographic evidence of Lushai missionary work.

2 This attitude hampered the spread of Christianity among groups who expected missionaries to behave as big chiefs whose duty it was to give rather than to receive (see section on feasts in our chapter 'Religions of the Hills'). According to some accounts, Christianity initially proved most attractive to poorer kinship groups. In this way they could, among other things, escape the onerous task of giving expensive cattle feasts; the richer kinship groups converted later, partly in an attempt to re-establish their dominance over their erstwhile followers (see Spielmann, 1966).

3 From left to right: Shwe Hla Maung, Tilak Chandra Chakma, Alan Taylor, Dhiren.

## 13. A Hospital in Chandraghona

1 The umbrella, and old symbol of high status and power in the Chittagong hills, gradually took on new connotations of education and modernity. In the words of R.H. Sneyd Hutchinson:

> 'With our occupation of the country and the spread of civilisation the love of novelty has asserted itself, and the noble savage Chieftain may be seen wending his way over the mountains wearing a battered white Ellwood's sun-hat, a filthy flannel shirt, a pair of old dress trousers, ammunition boots well down at the heel, with a flaring "Como" silk rug (a present from the Political Officer) thrown across his shoulders, and the ubiquitous eight-anna bazaar umbrella held over his head. Ichabod! Ichabod!!' (Hutchinson, 1906, 133)

In this picture the old and new meanings seem to merge as Kio Zuo supervises the workmen.

2 From left to right: Sephalika Chakraborti (from Barisal), Renuka Mondol (from Khulna), Shandhya Tudu (from Rajshahi) and Kusumika Chakma (from Chittagong).

3 Seeing out-patients on the verandah, 1958. From left to right: Nurse Enid Toseland (later Skirrow), unidentified patient, Dr. J.W. Bottoms, unidentified nurse.

4 Left to right: Dr. Alan Taylor (surgeon), Madhabi Baker (student nurse), Wong Shang Ching (theatre sister), Ananta Mali (threatre porter/sweeper); Ranjit Karmakar (compounder); Supriti Das (student nurse), 1950s.

## 14. Developing the Hills

1 'On 26 May 1979, Brigadier Hannan and Lt.Col. Salam declared in a public meeting at Panchari: "We want only the land, and not the people of the Chittagong Hill Tracts." Mr. Ali Haider Khan, the Deputy Commissioner of the CHT, and Mr. Abdul Awal, the former Commissioner of Chittagong Division, warned the tribal leaders several times by saying that they could be extinct in the next five years' ('We want the land,' 1983, 21). Compare this attitude to that of the Head of the colonial Forest Department who, in the 1870s, 'calmly proposed that the whole Mugh and Chakma population should be removed from their native hills! He did not say where they were to go to. He merely said, in the true departmental spirit, "These people destroy the trees, therefore let them be sent away"' (Beames, 1984, 282; quoted in chapter 'The Colonial Overlords').

## 17. Lifestyles

1 'L. to R.: Woodford (Murphy's bro' in law) & Peggy, JWB [J.W. Bottoms], Mrs M. [Murphy], Pat Murphy [the tea planter], H.N., Mummie [Mrs. Jill E. Bottoms].'

2 From left to right: Dibya(laksha), Kubalay/ Kubalaksha, Birupaksha, Nihar Bala, Shushuma Bala, Manju(laksha), Koko(nadaksha), Nalinaksha, Kimtala, Utpal(aksha).

3 From left, Rajib Roy, his wife Unika (Juthika), Shwe Ching Hpru, Maung Hpru Sain, Ching Hpru Sain, Nihar Bala.

4 From left: Thein Han Maung, a maidservant, Ma Aung with her daughter on her lap, her younger brother Maung Kyo Maung (M.K. Maung), his mother Krain Nyung, M.K. Maung's wife Chin Kwai Hpru (Dolly), Aung Mra Ching with her daughter, and M.K. Maung's eldest son Hla Han Maung.

5 Among the assembled officials are the Forest Officer, the SDO Rangamati, the Superintendent of Police and the Headmaster of the Government High School.

## 19. Portraits

1 Although he published a few photographs in the first edition of his *A Fly on the Wheel*, he did not include any of his photographs of the Chittagong Hill Tracts.

2 From the left: Ching Kwai Hpru ('Dolly'), her son Hla Han Maung, and her mother-in-law Krain Nyung.

3 In 1972, M.N. Larma and J.B. Larma were among the founders of the Parbotyo Chottogram Jono Songhoti Somiti (PCJSS—United People's Party of the Chittagong Hill Tracts). Its armed cadre, Santi Bahini (Peace Troops), was formed in 1973. M.N. Larma was chairman of the PCJSS till his violent death in 1983, after which J.B. (Shantu) Larma took over as leader.

4 Dalton, who first published this illustration (from a photograph, probably by dr Simpson), was puzzled even by the ethnic identity of this person, whom he supposed to be a Barua, or Buddhist Bengali:

> 'A Mug. I know nothing of this miserable-looking creature. He does not at all correspond with the description of a Mug given at page 112. He is probably one of the hybrids from Chittagong so called, who serve us as cooks, and very good cooks they make' (Dalton, 1872).

Watson and Kaye also reproduced the photograph, but suggested that the man might be a Marma, who they assumed to be living in Arakan:

> 'Mugh Arracan—The Mughs are a highly Bengalised class of Rakoings, who call themselves Myami or Great Myams. They inhabit Arracan, where they form an industrious, active, and useful class of people, not without soldierly qualities. They are useful also as police; and in the Burmese war a levy of them, under the title of the Mugh levy, commanded and disciplined by English officers, did good service, distinguishing themselves in the defence of the frontier; and the force is still, we believe, in existence, serving in the Assam districts. We can, however, discover no details of their habits and customs among the official records' (Watson and Kaye, 1875).

5 'A Pankho youngman in festive dress' (Sattar, 1971); 'A Chakma youngman in a festive dress' (Sattar, 1975); 'Pankho youth in a festive dress' (Sattar, 1978).

## 20. Conclusion

1 For a general treatment of this theme, see Baud and Van Schendel, 1997.

2 This is, of course, most striking in the versions of history produced in many publications by the Jono Songhoti Somiti and the Bangladesh Government/Armed Forces, repectively, in the period since 1975. Another instructive example is the *Report* by the Chittagong Hill Tracts Commission (1990) and *Comments* (1991), an anonymous 94-page rebuttal of that report, believed to have been authored by the Bangladesh Army. The *Comments* dismiss the evidence in the *Report* as 'based on hearsay,' 'deviation from facts,' and an 'unfounded version of refugees.' Interestingly, the authors of the *Comments* themselves made no attempt to improve on the *Report* by basing their own version of history on available historical source material.

**Plate 416**. *'Gopi, daughter of Mong-Kro, Khumi.' (Lewin, about 1867)*

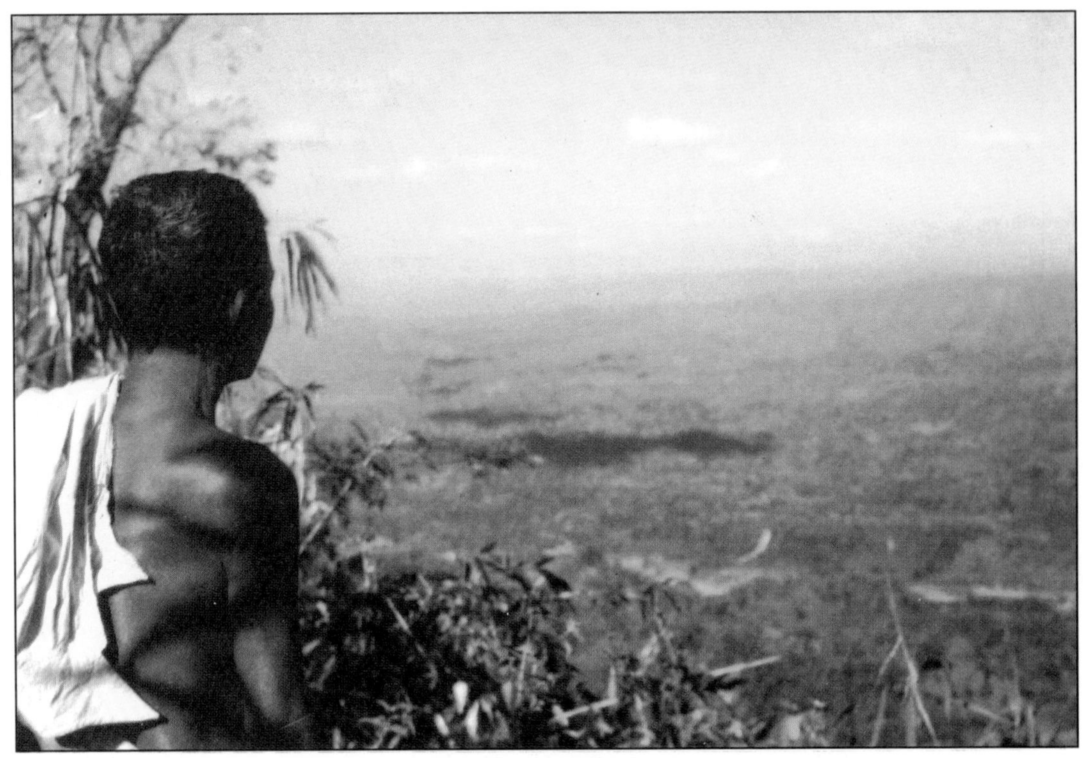

***Plate 417***. *A view from the hills. (Sopher, 1961)*

# *Glossary*

| | |
|---|---|
| *achkan* | long coat |
| *boro porong* | great exodus |
| *chaprassi* | office orderly |
| *darbar* | public ceremony of Indian prince or colonial official |
| *dewan* | office holder under a raja in the Chittagong Hill Tracts |
| *dhoti* | Bengali (Hindu) man's loincloth |
| *gaung-baung* | Burmese head-dress |
| *gayal* | semi-domesticated bull (bos frontalis) |
| *gengkhuli* | Chakma ballad singer |
| *jhum* | shifting cultivation, hill agriculture; hill field |
| *Jumma* | indigenous inhabitant of the Chittagong Hill Tracts |
| *karbari* | village leader |
| *khadi* | Chakma breast cloth |
| *khash mahal* | government estate |
| *khedda* | elephant-capturing operation |
| *khyong* | Buddhist village temple |
| *kukri* | curved knife |
| *kyoungtha* | groups living in the hill valleys ('children of the river') |
| *lungi* | Bengali sarong for men |
| *lungyi* | Burmese sarong |
| *mantra* | devotional incantation |
| *mauza* | administrative unit ('revenue village') |
| *mithan* | see: gayal |
| *mod, modh* | alcoholic drink, rice spirit |
| *muli* | type of bamboo |
| *Pali* | language of Buddhist ritual |
| *peon* | office orderly |
| *pinon* | Chakma woman's skirt |
| *puan* | Lushai woman's skirt |
| *punya* | auspicious day |
| *raja* | chief, king |
| *rajbari* | palace, chief's mansion |
| *roaza, roaja* | office holder under a raja in the Chittagong Hill Tracts |
| *sari* | Bengali woman's garment |
| *shishu* | a type of tree |
| *sraddh* | death ceremony |
| *talukdar* | office holder under a raja in the Chittagong Hill Tracts |
| *tiffin* | light meal |
| *toungtha* | groups living on the ridges of hills ('children of the hill') |
| *üa* | hill field |
| *wan-klai* | Mru woman's skirt |
| *zamindar* | landlord/tax-collector in (colonial) Bengal |

***Plate 418***. *Lake Kaptai. (Anderson, 1968-70)*

# *Credits*

The names of the photographers, when known, are in *italics*.

In the main text of this book, captions in inverted commas are the original captions found with the photographs.

**Frontispice**

*T.H. Lewin*, about 1867

## 1. Photographic Obsessions

1 Riebeck, Die Hügelstämme, 1885

2-3 Focal Encyclopedia, 1956

4-6 Riebeck, Die Hügelstämme, 1885

7-8 *Karl Seifert*, 1963 (Belitz collection)

9 *Claus-Dieter Brauns*, 1971

## 3. Creating a Colonial Aristocracy

10-12 *T.H. Lewin*, about 1867

13 Watson and Kaye, The People of India, 1875

14 Lewin collection, 1873; cf. Whitehead, Thangliena, 1992

15-18 Riebeck, Die Hügelstämme, 1885

19 *T.H. Lewin*, about 1867

## 4. How to be a Raja

20 Ghosh, Chakma Jati, 1909

21-24 Chakma Raja collection

25 Hutchinson, An Account, 1906

26-27 Mong Raja collection

28-29 Chakma Raja collection

30-31 Bohmong Raja collection

32 Chakma Raja collection

## 5. The Public Display of Power

33 *Willem Bientjes*, 1962

34 Chakma Raja collection

35 *Willem Bientjes*, 1962

36 Bohmong Raja collection

37 *Alan Taylor*, 1964

38 *C.C. Lindsey*, 1964

39 *David Sopher*, 1961

40-43 *Astrid Anderson*, 1968-70

44 *Enid Skirrow*, 1964

45-49 *Astrid Anderson*, 1968-70

## 6. The Colonial Overlords

50-55 Riebeck, Die Hügelstämme, 1885

56 Hutchinson, An Account, 1906

57-59 Water colours by T.H. Lewin (Lewin collection)

60-61 Riebeck, Die Hügelstämme, 1885

62 Baptist Missionary Society

63-64 Christie, Morning Drum, 1983 (BACSA collection)

65 Bottoms/Maslen collection, 1935

66 *Muriel Starke*, 1960 (Smith collection)

67-68 Lewin collection; cf. MacDonald, India–Sunshine, 1988

## 7. Pakistan and the Chiefs

69 *Franc and Jean Bowie Shor* (Jean and Franc Shor, 'East Pakistan Drives Back,' 1955)

70 Bernot, 'In the Chittagong Hill Tracts,' 1953

71-72 Bohmong Raja collection

73 *Lorenz G. Löffler*, 1956

74 *Astrid Anderson*, 1968-70

75 Rajput, The Tribes, 1965

76 *David Sopher*, 1961

77 *Lily Smith*, 1962

78 *H.E. Kauffmann*, 1955

79 *Erwin Sigl*, 1965-69

80 *Hans Meier*, 1961

81 Pakistani Khobor, 1959

82 Pak-Somachar, 1967

83-86 Pak-Somachar, 1965

87 Bohmong Raja collection

## 8. Innocence and Charm

88-89 *Claus-Dieter Brauns*, 1970
90 *Alan Taylor*, 1968
91 *Claus-Dieter Brauns*, 1969
92-95 *Karl Seifert*, 1963
96 Lewin collection, 1865
97 Water colour by T.H. Lewin, 1866 (Lewin collection)
98 Riebeck, Die Hügelstämme, 1885
99-100 *Claus-Dieter Brauns*, 1970
101 Konietzko collection, 1927
102 *J.F. Laurence*, 1961-63
103 *A. Mong Akhyai*, 1990s (Belitz collection)
104 *Karl Seifert*, 1963

## 9. Bodies and Costumes

105 Tate Gallery, London
106-107 Riebeck, Die Hügelstämme, 1885
108 Dalton, Descriptive Ethnology, 1872
109 Riebeck, Die Hügelstämme, 1885
110 Hutchinson, An Account, 1906
111-112 Konietzko collection, 1927
113-115 *J.P. Mills*, 1926
116 *Sigismond Diettrich*, 1960
117 *Karl Seifert*, 1963 (Belitz collection)
118 *Dick Recter*, 1965
119 *George Band*, 1968
120 *Claus-Dieter Brauns*, 1974
121-126 *Harry Belitz*, 1976
127-129 *Karl Seifert*, 1963 (Belitz collection)
130 *Alan Taylor*, 1968
131 Rajput, 'A Trek,' 1962
132 *Erwin Sigl*, 1965-69
133 *Erwin Sigl*, 1969
134 *Almut Mey*, 1968
135-136 *A. Mong Akhyai*, 1996 (Belitz collection)

## 10. Images of Nature and Destruction

137-140 *Håkan Wahlquist*, 1977
141 *Karl Seifert*, 1963
142 *Lorenz G. Löffler*, 1957
143 *Wolfgang Mey*, 1990
144-146 *Claus-Dieter Brauns*, 1971
147-148 *Håkan Wahlquist*, 1977
149 *Astrid Anderson*, 1977
150 *Wolfgang Mey*, 1990
151 Noon, 'Elephant Catching,' 1953
152 Konietzko collection, 1927
153 *Håkan Wahlquist*, 1976
154-155 *Willem Bientjes*, 1963
156 *Willem Bientjes*, 1961
157 *George Band*, 1970
158 *Astrid Anderson*, 1968-70
159 *Wolfgang Mey*, 1990
160-162 Meier collection, 1955-61
163 *Keith Sandercock*, 1964-65
164 *J.W. Welsh*, 1963
165 *Keith Sandercock*, 1964-65
166-167 *Harry Belitz*, 1990
168 *Dick Recter*, 1965
169-170 *Astrid Anderson*, 1968-70
171 *Willem Bientjes*, 1963
172 *Keith Sandercock*, 1964-65
173-174 *Eric Hosking*, 1966 (Mountfort and Hosking, The Vanishing Jungle, 1969)
175 *Willem Bientjes*, 1961
176 *Hugh Brammer*, 1965

## 11. Religions of the Hills

177-178 Riebeck, Die Hügelstämme, 1885
179-180 *Almut Mey*, 1968
181-184 *Claus-Dieter Brauns*, 1970
185 *David Sopher*, 1961
186 *Almut Mey*, 1968
187 *J.P. Mills*, 1926
188 *David Sopher*, 1961
189 *Keith Sandercock*, 1964
190 *Almut Mey*, 1970
191-192 *Astrid Anderson*, 1968-70
193 *Almut Mey*, 1970
194 *C.C. Lindsey*, 1964
195 *George Band*, 1969
196 Konietzko collection, 1927
197 *Karl Seifert*, 1963 (Belitz collection)
198 Riebeck, Die Hügelstämme, 1885
199 *T.H. Lewin*, 1867
200 *Peter Barblan*, 1959-61
201 Pak-Somachar, 1967

## 12. Spreading the Gospel

202 Snehomoyi, n.d.
203 Missionary Herald, 1912, 237
204 Baptist Missionary Society
205 *Enid Skirrow*, 1964

206 *Enid Skirrow*, 1963
207 *Lily Smith*, 1960
208 Prabhu Jishu Khrista, 1913.
209 Baptist Missionary Society
210 *Jill Bottoms*, 1930s (Bottoms/Maslen collection)
211 *Donald Bottoms*, 1959
212 *Lily Smith*, 1962
213 Baptist Missionary Society
214 *Alan Taylor*, 1954
215 *Enid Skirrow*, 1963
216 *Alan Taylor*, 1954
217 *Christine Manson*, 1953 (Arton collection)
218 *Enid Skirrow*, 1967
219 *Christine Manson*, 1958 (Smith collection)
220 *Muriel Starke*, 1940s (Arton collection)
221 *Christine Manson*, about 1940 (Arton collection)
222 *Muriel Starke*, 1941 (Arton collection)
223 M.K. Maung collection
224 *Almut Mey*, 1968
225 *Enid Skirrow*, 1960s

## 13. A Hospital at Chandraghona

226-229 Baptist Missionary Society
230 Bottoms/Maslen collection, 1936
231-233 Baptist Missionary Society
234 *Jill Bottoms*, 1930s (Bottoms/Maslen collection)
235 *Donald Bottoms*, 1959
236 Baptist Missionary Society, about 1910
237 *Jill Bottoms*, 1947 (Bottoms/Maslen collection)
238 *Alan Taylor*, 1957
239 *Alan Taylor*, 1962
240 *K.R.S. Captain*, 1958 (Skirrow collection)
241 Baptist Missionary Society
242 *Enid Skirrow*, about 1956
243 Taylor collection, 1957

## 14. Developing the Hills

244 Pakistan's Industries, 1953
245 *Alan Taylor*, 1953
246 *Jill Bottoms*, 1953 (Bottoms/Maslen collection)
247 *Jill Bottoms*, 1950s (Bottoms/Maslen collection)
248 *Donald Bottoms*, 1959
249-256 Meier collection, 1955-61
257 Karnaphuli Rayon & Chemicals Ltd. brochure, 1966
258-263 *Peter Barblan*, 1959-61
264 *Keith Sandercock*, 1964-65
265 *Willem Bientjes*, 1963
266 *Willem Bientjes*, 1962
267 *Dick Recter*, 1965
268 *Erwin Sigl*, 1965-69
269 *Dick Recter*, 1965
270 *Erwin Sigl*, 1965-69
271 *Peter Barblan*, 1959-61
272 *Dick Recter*, 1965
273 *David Sopher*, 1962
274-275 *J.F. Laurence*, about 1963
276 *C.C. Lindsey*, 1964
277 *Dick Recter*, 1965
278 Recter collection, 1965
279-280 *Dick Recter*, 1965
281 *Willem Bientjes*, 1963
282-283 *Dick Recter*, 1965
284 Perspectives, 1967
285 Rashid, 'Chittagong Hill Tracts,' 1969.
286 Van Tellingen collection
287 *Karl Seifert*, 1963 (Belitz collection)
288 *Håkan Wahlquist*, 1977

## 15. Getting Around

289 *Muriel Starke*, 1940s (Smith collection)
290 *Lily Smith*, 1940s
291 Baptist Missionary Society, 1908
292 *Christine Manson*, 1941 (Arton collection)
293-296 Baptist Missionary Society
297 *J.F. Laurence*, about 1963
298 *Willem Bientjes*, 1963
299 *C.C. Lindsey*, 1964
300-301 *Alan Taylor*, 1957
302 *George Band*, 1970
303 *C.C. Lindsey*, 1964
304 *W.J. Welsh*, 1963
305 *Astrid Anderson*, 1968-70

306 *Peter Barblan*, 1959-61
307 *David Sopher*, 1959
308 *Alan Taylor*, 1962
309-310 *C.C. Lindsey*, 1964
311-313 *Håkan Wahlquist*, 1977
314 Baptist Missionary Society
315 *Muriel Starke* (Baptist Missionary Society)
316 *J.F. Laurence*, about 1962
317 *W.J. Welsh*, 1963
318 *Keith Sandercock*, 1964-65
319 *C.C. Lindsey*, 1964
320 *Keith Sandercock*, 1964-65
321 *Håkan Wahlquist*, 1977

## 16. The Thrill of Freedom

322 Lübker collection, 1957-58
323 *Gerhard Lübker*, 1957-58
324-326 *Karl Seifert*, 1963 (Belitz collection)
327-328 *Claus-Dieter Brauns*, 1970
329 *Claus-Dieter Brauns*, 1969
330-333 *Karl Seifert*, 1963 (Belitz collection)
334 *Claus-Dieter Brauns*, 1970
335-337 *Karl Seifert*, 1963 (Belitz collection)
338 *Willem Bientjes*, 1961
339 *Alan Taylor*, 1968 (Band collection)
340 *Alan Taylor*, 1968

## 17. Lifestyles

341 Bottoms/Maslen collection, 1939
342 Meier collection, about 1957
343 Bottoms/Maslen collection, about 1950
344 *Jill Bottoms*, 1937 (Bottoms/Maslen collection)
345 *Lily Smith*, 1949
346 *Michael Flowers*, 1962
347-348 *Jürgen Seyfried*, 1960s
349 *H.W. van Tellingen*, 1969
350-351 *Hans Meier*, 1955-61
352-354 Chakma Raja collection
355 Chakma Raja collection
356 Dipak and Gautam Chakma collection, 1929
357 Talukdar collection, about 1940
358 Chakma Raja collection, about 1965
359 Saradendu S. Chakma collection, 1960s
360-361 *J.P. Mills*, 1926
362-363 M.S. Choudhury/Mee Shwe Hpru collection
364 Chakma Raja collection, 1964
365 M.K. Maung/Ching Kwai Hpru collection, 1973
366 Chakma Raja collection, 1953
367 *Michael Flowers*, 1962 (Skirrow collection)
368 *Dick Recter*, 1965
369-372 Chakma Raja collection
373 *Michael Flowers*, 1960s
374-375 Meier collection, 1955-61
376 *Donald Stevens*, early 1950s
377-378 Chakma Raja collection, 1957
379 *Erwin Sigl*, 1965-69

## 18. Encounters

380 *Keith Sandercock*, 1964-65
381 *Dick Recter*, 1965
382 *George Band*, 1968
383 Krishna Khisa (Karbari) collection, 1940s
384 *Edna Skirrow*, 1967
385 *Karl Seifert*, 1963 (Belitz collection)

## 19. Portraits

386-387 *T.H. Lewin*, 1867
388 *T.H. Lewin*, about 1866
389-390 *T.H. Lewin*, 1867
391 *Raja Tridiv Roy*, 1953
392 *M.K. Maung*, 1963
393 *Devashish Dewan*, 1976
394 *Devashish Dewan*, 1977
395 Saradendu S. Chakma collection, 1960s
396 *Nirmalendu Tripura*, 1968 (M.S. Choudhury/Mee Shwe Hpru collection)
397 M.K. Maung/Ching Kwai Hpru collection, 1968
398 Pankajini Larma collection, 1953
399 Sailendra N. Dewan collection, 1952
400 *W.J.L. Wenger*, 1937 (Leslie Wenger collection)
401 Leslie Wenger collection, 1971
402 Baptist Missionary Society, 1907
403 *Alan Taylor*, 1954

404 *Edna Skirrow*, 1958
405 *Christine Manson*, 1936 (Arton collection)
406 *Christine Manson*, 1948 (Arton collection)
407 *Benjamin Simpson* (Dalton, Descriptive Ethnology, 1872)
408 *Peter Barblan*, 1959-61
409 *Franc and Jean Bowie Shor* (Jean and Franc Shor, 'East Pakistan Drives Back,' 1955)
410 *Karl Seifert*, 1963 (Belitz collection)
411 *Claus-Dieter Brauns*, 1969
412 Rajput, 'Among the Murungs,' 1963
413 Rajput, The Tribes, 1965
414 Rajput, 'A Trek,' 1962
415 *Erwin Sigl*, 1969
416 *T.H. Lewin*, about 1867
417 *David Sopher*, 1961
418 *Astrid Anderson*, 1968-70
419 *Keith Sandercock*, 1964-65
420 *Peter Barblan*, 1959-61

N.B. Despite our best efforts at finding the copyright holder for each photograph, in a few cases we did not succeed in contacting him/her. We invite any non-contacted copyright holder to get in touch with the publisher to settle any claims.

***Plate 419***. *'Tripura girls.' (Sandercock, 1964-65)*

# References


Ahmad, Aftab,
*Banglar Muktishongram Shirajuddaula Theke Shekh Mujib* (Dhaka: Mrs. M. Aftab, 1996).

Ahmad, Nafis,
*An Economic Geography of East Pakistan* (London: Oxford University Press, 1958).

Ahmed, Noazesh, and Nazrul Islam,
*Bangladesh* (Dacca: Eastern Regal Industries, 1976).

Ali, Mohsin,
*'Colourful Kaptai,' Focus on Pakistan,* 1:1 (February 1971), 12-15.

Allen, Charles,
*Raj: A Scrapbook of British India, 1877-1947* (Harmondsworth: Penguin Books, 1979).

Allen, Charles, and Sharada Dwivedi,
*Lives of the Indian Princes* (London: Century Publishing, 1984).

Aris, Michael,
*The Raven Crown: The Origins of Buddhist Monarchy in Bhutan* (London: Serindia Press, 1994).

*Bangla Name Desh* (Calcutta: Ananda Publishers, 1972 (reprint 1992)).

*Bangladesh—Chittagong Hill Tracts, Kaptai & Rangamati* (Dacca: Bangladesh Parjatan Corporation, 1974).

*Bangladesh District Gazetteers: Chittagong Hill Tracts.'* See: Ishaq, 1971.

*Bangladesh Tourist Handbook* (Dhaka: Bangladesh Parjatan Corporation, n.d.).

Barros, João de,
*Ásia. Dos feitos que os Portugueses fizeram no descobrimento e conquista dos mares e terras do Oriente* (Lisboa: ed. Hernani, 1945-46), 4 Vols.

Baud, Michiel, and Willem van Schendel,
*'Towards a Comparative History of Borderlands,' Journal of World History,* 8:2 (September 1997), 211-242.

Beames, John,
*Memoirs of a Bengal Civilian: The Lively Narrative of a Victorian District Officer* (London/New York: Eland/Hippocrene, 1984 [1961]).

Beaton, Cecil,
*Indian Album* (London: Batsford, 1945-46).

Bengal, Government of, Revenue Department,
*Selections from the Correspondence on the Revenue Administration of the Chittagong Hill Tracts, 1862-1927* (Calcutta: Bengal Government Press, 1929).

Bernot, Lucien,
*'In the Chittagong Hill Tracts,' Pakistan Quarterly,* 3:2 (1953), 17-19, 61.

Bernot, Denise, and Lucien Bernot,
*Les Khyang des collines de Chittagong (Pakistan oriental): Matériaux pour l'étude linguistique des Chin* (Paris: Librairie Plon, 1958).

Bernot, Lucien,
*Les paysans arakanais du Pakistan du Pakistan oriental: l'histoire, le monde végétal et l'organisation sociale des refugiés Marma (Mog)* (The Hague: Mouton, 1967), 2 vols. (= Bernot, 1967a)

Bernot, Lucien,
*Les Cak: Contribution à l'étude ethnographique d'une population de langue loi* (Paris: Editions du Centre National de la Recherche Scientifique, 1967). (= Bernot, 1967b)

Bhaumik, Subir, Meghna Guhathakurta and Sabyasachi Basu Ray Chaudhury (eds.),
*Living on the Edge: Essays on the Chittagong Hill Tracts* (Calcutta: South Asia Forum for Human Rights/Calcutta Research Group, 1997).

Bølstad, Trygve, and Eirik Jansen,
*Sailing Against the Wind: Boats and Boatmen of Bangladesh* (Dhaka: University Press Limited, 1992).

Brauns, Claus-Dieter, and Lorenz G. Löffler,
*Mru: Bergbewohner im Grenzgebiet von Bangladesh* (Basel/ Stuttgart: Birkhäuser, 1986). Revised English translation: *Mru: Hill People on the Border of Bangladesh* (Basel/Boston/Berlin: Birkhäuser, 1990)

Chakma, Siddhartho,
*Proshongo: Parbotyo Chottogram* (Calcutta: Nath Brothers, 1392 B.E. [1985-86]).

Chakma, Harikishore, Tapash Chakma, Preyasi Dewan and Mahfuz Ullah,
*Bara Parang: The Tale of the Developmental Refugees of the Chittagong Hill Tracts* (Dhaka: Centre for Sustainable Development, 1995).

Chandan, Hasan Saifuddin,
*The People at Kamalapur Railway Station* (Biel: Photoforum Pasquart, 1994).

Chittagong Hill Tracts Commission,
*Life is Not Ours: Land and Human Rights in the Chittagong Hill Tracts, Bangladesh* (Copenhagen/Amsterdam: International Work Group on Indigenous Affairs (IWGIA)/ Organising Committee Chittagong Hill Tracts Campaign, 1991). Update 1 (1992); Update 2 (1994); Update 3 (1997).

*Chittagong Hill Tracts Soil and Land Use Survey 1964-66* (Vancouver: Forestal Forestry and Engineering International Limited, 1966), 9 Vols.

Chowdhury, S.H.,
'An Investigation of the Karnaphuli Paper Mill Effluents and Its Detrimental Effects on Fish and Other Aquatic Life of the River,' *Agriculture Pakistan,* 8:2 (June 1957), 138-153.

Christie, John,
*Morning Drum* (London: British Association for Cemeteries in South Asia, 1983).

Christie Papers, D 718/1, Oriental and Indian Office Collections, British Library, London.

*Comments on the Report of the Chittagong Hill Tracts Commission, May 1991* (n.p., 1991).

Dalton, Edward T.,
*Descriptive Ethnology of Bengal* (Calcutta: Office of the Superintendent of Government Printing, 1872).

Desmond, Ray,
*Victorian India in Focus: A selection of early photographs from the collection in the India Office Library and Records* (London: Her Majesty's Stationery Office, 1982).

*Dhaka 1971 - An Album of Liberation War* (Dhaka: Bangla Academy, 1988).

Diettrich, Sigismond deR.,
'Reconnaissance Trip to Gothiranpara: A Tippera Village, Chittagong Hill Tract, East Pakistan,' *The Oriental Geographer,* 4:2 (July 1960), 135-142.

Edwards, Elizabeth (ed.),
*Anthropology and Photography, 1860-1920* (New Haven and London: Yale University Press & The Royal Anthropological Institute, 1992).

*Focal, The—Encyclopedia of Photography* (London and New York: Focal Press, 1956).

Falconer, John,
'Photography in Nineteenth-Century India,' in: C.A. Bayly (gen. ed), *The Raj: India and the British 1600-1947* (London: National Portrait Gallery, 1990), 264-277.

Forestal Report.
See: *Chittagong Hill Tracts Soil and Land Use Survey 1964-66.*

Ghosh, Satish Chandra,
*Chakma Jati: Jatiyo Chitro O Itibritto* (Calcutta: Bongiyo Sahityo Porishot Gronthaboli, Vol. 24, 1316 B.S. [1909]).

Gutman, Judith Mara,
*Through Indian Eyes: 19th and Early 20th Century Photography from India* (New York: Oxford University Press & International Center of Photography, 1982).

Hobson, Geraldine,
*A Descriptive Catalogue of the J.P. Mills Photographic Collection in the Library of the School of Oriental and African Studies* (n.p. [London], 1996).

Hossain, Anwar,
*Dhaka Portrait (1967-1992)* (Dhaka: AB Publishers, 1992).

Husain, Kazi Zaker,
'Expedition to Chittagong Hill-Tracts (Bunderban Subdivision), 1965,' *Journal of the Asiatic Society of Pakistan,* 12:1 (1967), 122-170.

Hutchinson, R.H. Sneyd,
*An Account of the Chittagong Hill Tracts* (Calcutta: Bengal Secretariat Book Depôt, 1906).

Hutchinson, R.H. Sneyd,
*Eastern Bengal and Assam District Gazetteers: Chittagong Hill Tracts* (Allahabad: Pioneer Press, 1909).

Ishaq, Muhammad (gen. ed.),
*Bangladesh District Gazetteers: Chittagong Hill Tracts* (Dacca: Bangladesh Government Press, 1971).

Jacobs, Julian, et al.,
*The Nagas: Hill Peoples of Northeast India - Society, Culture and the Colonial Encounter* (London: Thames and Hudson, 1990).

Johnson, B.L.C., and Nafis Ahmad,
'The Karnafuli Project,' *Oriental Geographer,* 1:2 (1957), 59-64.

Jones, Rev. P.H.,
'Days in the Hill Tracts, By a Missionary Looking Back: III - Work Among the Children,' *Missionary Herald* (1936), 79-81.

Jones, Rev. P.H.,
'Days in the Hill Tracts, By a Missionary Looking Back: IV - Daily Life in Chandraghona,' *Missionary Herald* (1936), 141-143.

Jones, Rev. P.H.,
'Days in the Hill Tracts, By a Missionary Looking Back: V - Some Problems of Pioneering,' *Missionary Herald* (1936), 166-168.

Jones, Rev. P.H.,
'Days in the Hill Tracts, By a Missionary Looking Back: VIII - Evangelistic Work in Jungle Villages,' *Missionary Herald* (1936), 243-246.

Kauffmann, H.E.,
'Tagebücher, Deutsche Chittagong Hill Tracts Expedition' (2 volumes, 1955-56). Unpublished diaries in German.

Kermani, W.A.,
'Chittagong Hill Tracts,' *Pakistan Review,* 2:1 (1953), 32-34, 48.

Kisch Papers. Unpublished letters of Henry M. Kisch, ICS, when Commissioner at Chittagong, 1875; British Library, London (Oriental and India Office Collections, MSS Eur. B 155).

Kramer, Fritz W.,
'The Influence of the Classical Tradition on Anthropology and Exoticism,' in: Michael Harbsmeier and Mogens Trolle Larsen (eds.), *The Humanities Between Art and Science: Intellectual Developments 1880-1914* (Copenhagen: Akademisk Forlag, 1989), 203-224.

Lechenperg, Harald,
'Traumreise Asien,' *ADAC-Motorwelt* (1962), 1244-1248.

Lewin, T.H.,
*The Hill Tracts of Chittagong and the Dwellers Therein, with Comparative Vocabularies of the Hill Dialects* (Calcutta: Bengal Printing Company, Ltd., 1869).

Lewin, T.H.,
*Hill Proverbs of the Inhabitants of the Chittagong Hill Tracts* (Calcutta, 1873).

Lewin, T.H.,
*A Fly on the Wheel, or How I Helped to Govern India* (London: Constable, 1912).

Lewin letters. Unpublished letters by T.H. Lewin, Lewin Collection, London.

Lorrain, Reginald A.,
*5 Years in Unknown Jungles For God and Empire - Being an Account of the Founding of the Lakher Pioneer Mission, its Work amongst (with Manners, Customs, Religious Rites and Ceremonies of) a wild Head-hunting Race of Savage Hillmen in Further India, previously unknown to the Civilized World* (Guwahati/Delhi: Spectrum Publications, 1988 [1912]).

MacDonald, Betsy,
*India - Sunshine and Shadows* (London: British Association for Cemeteries in South Asia, 1988).

MacRae, John,
'Account of the Kookies or Lunctas,' *Asiatick Researches,* 8:5 (1801), 183-198.

Manson, Chrissie, and Muriel Starke,
'Ultachori: A Second Letter from Pioneers,' *Missionary Herald* (1935), 145-147.

*Master-Plan for the Chittagong Hill Tracts Development Project* (Dacca: East Pakistan Agricultural Development Corporation, n.d. [1967]).

Meier, Hans,
'Chandraghona 1955-1961: Begegnungen - Erlebnisse - Höhepunkte aus der Mitte meines Lebens' (unpublished typescript, 1996).

Mey, Wolfgang,
'"Ein gutes und freies Bergvolk": die Konietzko-Sammlung aus den Chittagong Hill Tracts (Bangladesh),' in: Eberhard Berg, Jutta Lauth and Andreas Wimmer (eds.), *Ethnologie im Widerstreit: Kontroversen über Macht, Geschäft, Geschlecht in fremden Kulturen - Festschrift für Lorenz G. Löffler* (Munich: Trickster Verlag, 1991), 427-441. (= Mey, 1991a)

Mey, Wolfgang,
*Vielleicht sind diese Dinge die einzige Spur, die wir hinterlassen: Die bedrohte Zukunft der Bergvölker in Bangladesh* (Hamburg: Verlag am Galgenberg, 1991). (= Mey, 1991b)

Mountfort, Guy,
'Saving the Wildlife of Pakistan,' *Pakistan Quarterly,* 14:4 (Spring 1967), 38-43.

Mountfort, Guy, and Eric Hosking,
*The Vanishing Jungle: The Story of the World Wildlife Fund Expeditions to Pakistan* (London: Collins, 1969).

Muhammed, Yunus (ed.),
*Ayalbam: Gono Andolon/Album: Mass Movement 1982-90* (Chittagong: Tolpaar, 1993).

Noon, Viquarunnisa,
'Elephant Catching in East Pakistan,' *Pakistan Review,* 7:1 (1953), 24-29.

'On the Bank of the Karnafulli A Paper Mill Comes Up,' *Pakistan Quarterly,* 11 (1952), 66-67.

Pakistan, Government of, Department of Tourism, *Pakistan: Chittagong* (Karachi: Ferozsons, 1968).

*Pakistan Moves Forward - Paper Industry* (Karachi: Pakistan Publications, 1956).

Pinney, Christopher,
*Camera Indica: The Social Life of Indian Photographs* (London: Reaktion Books, 1997).

*Prabhu Jishu Khrista: Tar Jibanar Kada* (Chandraghona: W.J.L. Wenger, n.d. [1913]).

Price, Mary,
*The Photograph: A Strange, Confined Space* (Stanford, Cal.: Stanford University Press, 1994).

Rajput, A.B.,
'A Trek in the Hills of Chittagong,' *Pakistan Quarterly,* 10:4 (Spring 1962), 26-33, 70.

Rajput, A.B.,
'Among the Murungs in Bandarban Forest,' *Pakistan Quarterly,* 11:3 (1963), 42-49.

Rajput, A.B.,
*The Tribes of Chittagong Hill Tracts* (Karachi/Dacca: Pakistan Publications, 1965).

Rashid, Haroon-er-,
'Chittagong Hill Tracts,' *Pakistan Quarterly,* 16:1-4 (Spring 1969), 67-73.

Rawlins, John,
'On the Manners, Religion, and Laws of the Cúcì's, or Mountaineers of Tipra—Communicated in Persian,' *Asiatick Researches,* 2:12 (1790), 187-193.

Riebeck, Emil,
*Die Hügelstämme von Chittagong: Ergebnisse einer Reise im Jahre 1882* (Berlin: A. Asher & Co., 1885).

Roy, (Raja) Tridiv,
*They Simply Belong* (Rawalpindi: National Publishing House, 1972).

Roy, (Raja) Tridiv,
*Untitled Memoirs* (typescript, n.d.[1991]).

Sattar, Abdus,
*In the Sylvan Shadows* (Dacca: Saquib Brothers, 1971).

Sattar, Abdus,
*Tribal Culture in Bangladesh* (Dacca: Muktadhara, 1975).

Sattar, Abdus,
*The Sowing of Seeds - The Sociology of Primitive Sex* (Dacca: Adeylebros, 1978).

Shafer, Robert,
'Classification of the Sino-Tibetan Languages,' *Word,* 11:1 (1955), 94-111.

Shapiro, Michael C., and Harold F. Schiffman,
*Language and Society in South Asia* (Dordrecht/Cinnaminson: Foris Publications, 1983).

Shor, Jean and Franc,
'East Pakistan Drives Back the Jungle: A Land of Elephant Roundups, Bengal Tigers, and a Bamboo Economy Takes Big Strides Toward Becoming a Modern Nation,' *National Geographic Magazine* (March 1955), 398-426.

Spielmann, Hans-Jürgen,
*Die Bawm-Zo: Eine Chin-Gruppe in den Chittagong Hill Tracts (Ostpakistan)* (Ph.D. thesis, Ruprecht-Karl-University, Heidelberg, 1966).

Teichmann, G.O.,
*Early Days in the Chittagong Hill Tracts* (Dhaka: Bangladesh Baptist Sangha, 1984).

Theye, Thomas,
'Ethnographische Photographie im 19. Jahrhundert: Eine Einführung,' *Zeitschrift für Kulturaustausch,* 40:4 (1990), 386-405.

Van Schendel, Willem (ed.),
*Francis Buchanan in Southeast Bengal (1798): His Journey to Chittagong, the Chittagong Hill Tracts, Noakhali and Comilla* (Dhaka: University Press Limited, 1992).

Van Schendel, Willem,
'The Invention of the "Jummas": State Formation and Ethnicity in Southeastern Bangladesh,' in: R.H. Barnes, Andrew Gray and Benedict Kingsbury (eds.), *Indigenous Peoples of Asia* (Ann Arbor, Mich.: Association for Asian Studies, 1995), 121-144.

Warren, Jon, and Barry Ison,
*Tanti* (Dhaka: IDEAS, n.d.)

Watson, J. Forbes, and John William Kaye (eds.),
*The People of India: A Series of Photographic Illustrations of the Races and Tribes of Hindustan..., Volume 8* (London: India Museum, 1875).

'"We want the land and not the people": Genocide in the Chittagong Hill Tracts,' *Survival International Review,* 43 (1983), 7-25.

Whitehead, John,
*Thangliena: A Life of T.H. Lewin Among Wild Tribes on India's North-East Frontier* (Gartmore: Kiscadale, 1992).

Worswick, Clark (ed.),
*Princely India: Photographs by Raja Deen Dayal 1884-1910* (New York: Pennwick Publishing/Alfred A. Knopf, 1980).

Worswick, Clark, and Ainslie Embree (eds.),
*The Last Empire: Photography in British India, 1855-1911* (London: Gordon Fraser, 1976).

*Ye Are My Witnesses: The Work of the Baptist Missionary Society in India During 150 Years, 1792-1942* (Calcutta: Baptist Mission Press, 1942).

# Index